The A. W. Mellon Lectures in the Fine Arts have been delivered annually since 1952 at the National Gallery of Art, Washington, DC, with the goal of bringing "the people of the United States the results of the best contemporary thought and scholarship bearing upon the subject of the Fine Arts." As publication was always an essential part of the vision for the Mellon Lectures, a relationship was established between the National Gallery and the Bollingen Foundation for a series of books based on the talks. The first book in the series was published in 1953, and since 1967 all lectures have been published by Princeton University Press as part of the Bollingen Series. Now, for the first time, all the books in the series are available in one or more formats, including paperback and e-book, making many volumes that have long been out of print accessible to future generations of readers.

This edition is supported by a gift in memory of Charles Scribner, Jr., former trustee and president of Princeton University Press. The Press is grateful to the Scribner family for their formative and enduring support, and for their commitment to preserving the A. W. Mellon Lectures in the Fine Arts for posterity.

Images in this edition may have been altered in size and color from their appearance in the original print editions to make this book available in accessible formats.

THE A. W. MELLON LECTURES IN THE FINE ARTS

DELIVERED AT THE NATIONAL GALLERY OF ART,

WASHINGTON, D.C.

1952. CREATIVE INTUITION IN ART AND POETRY,
by Jacques Maritain

1953. THE NUDE: A STUDY IN IDEAL FORM,
by Kenneth Clark

1954. THE ART OF SCULPTURE, *by* Herbert Read

1955. PAINTING AND REALITY, *by* Etienne Gilson

1956. ART AND ILLUSION: A STUDY IN THE
PSYCHOLOGY OF PICTORIAL REPRE-
SENTATION, *by* E. H. Gombrich

1957. CONSTANCY AND CHANGE IN EARLY ART
AND ARCHITECTURE, *by* S. Giedion

1958. NICOLAS POUSSIN, *by* Anthony Blunt

1959. ON DIVERS ARTS, *by* Naum Gabo

1960. HORACE WALPOLE, *by* Wilmarth Sheldon Lewis

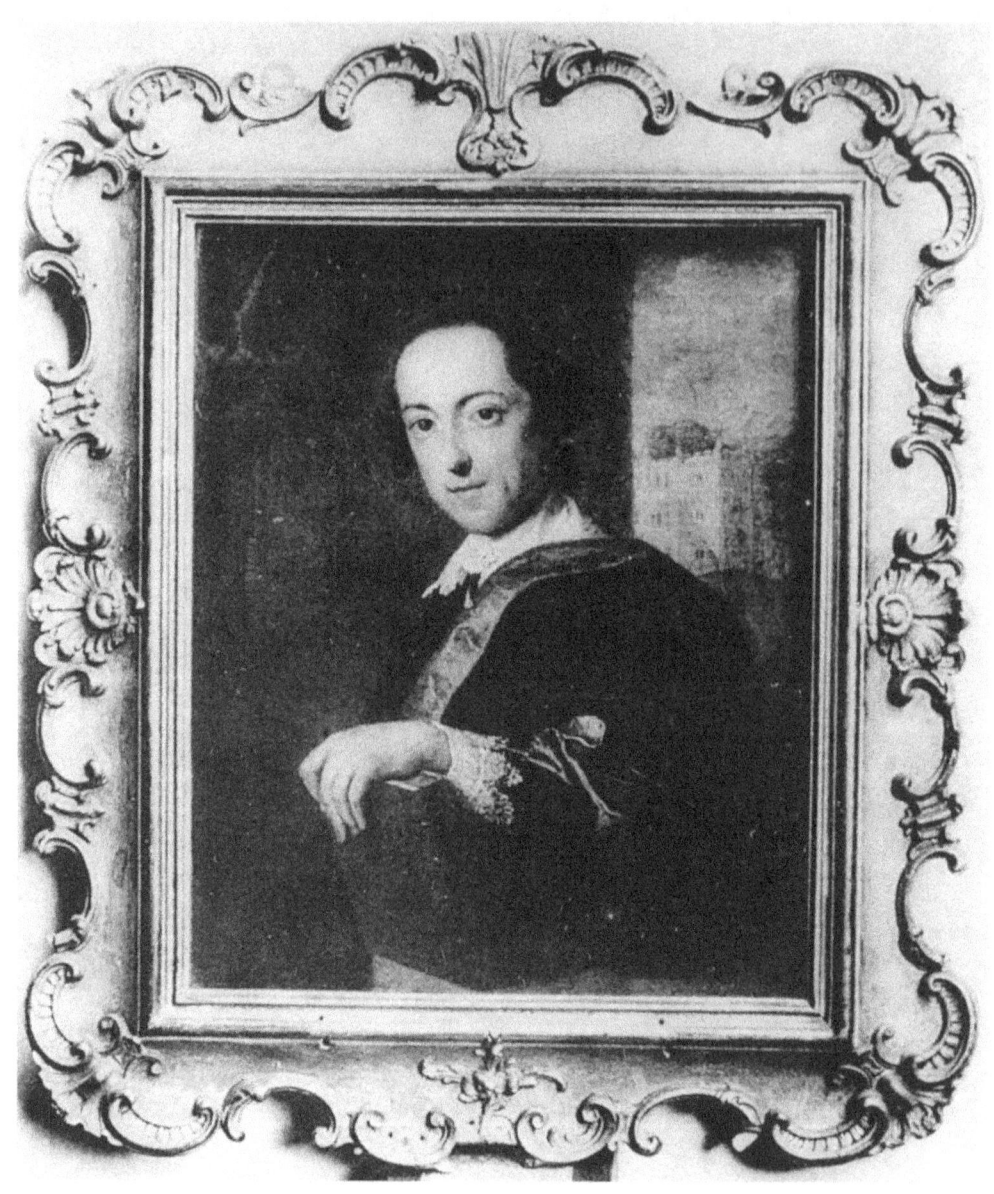

HORACE WALPOLE, *by J. G. Eccardt,* 1754

WILMARTH SHELDON LEWIS

HORACE WALPOLE

THE A. W. MELLON LECTURES
IN THE FINE ARTS
1960
NATIONAL GALLERY OF ART
WASHINGTON

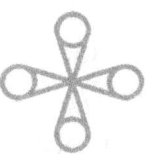

BOLLINGEN SERIES XXXV · 9

Princeton University Press

PUBLISHED FOR BOLLINGEN FOUNDATION, NEW YORK, N.Y.

THIS IS THE NINTH VOLUME
OF THE A. W. MELLON LECTURES IN THE FINE ARTS,
WHICH ARE DELIVERED ANNUALLY
AT THE NATIONAL GALLERY OF ART, WASHINGTON.
THE VOLUMES OF LECTURES CONSTITUTE NUMBER XXXV
IN BOLLINGEN SERIES, SPONSORED BY AND PUBLISHED FOR
BOLLINGEN FOUNDATION

LIMITED EDITION FOR PRIVATE DISTRIBUTION

New paperback printing 2023
ISBN (paper) 978-0-691-25206-3
ISBN (ebook) 978-0-691-25207-0

DESIGNED BY CARL PURINGTON ROLLINS

TO

ANNIE BURR AUCHINCLOSS LEWIS

1902–1959

PREFACE

A LECTURER whose remarks are going to be published is faced with two audiences, the one that hears him and the one that reads him. Since he hopes and trusts that the second will be the larger and more permanent of the two, he is tempted to write for the eye rather than for the ear. His readers, especially his fellow specialists and the reviewers whose good opinion he wants, loom larger in his mind than the friendly people who come to hear him (even though they come bearing pads and pencils). When his first audience goes home, he hopes that they have taken with them something of what he said, together with an agreeable impression of himself. Still, the fact is that they have dispersed.

A second course for the lecturer is to put his carefully prepared paper to one side and "talk" to his first audience, a solution that can be as unsatisfactory as a relentless reading. A third course is to remove all traces of the lecture hall and to lengthen the book with additional chapters; a fourth is the one that I have chosen to follow, which is to try to write a lecture that will interest both those who hear it and those who read it. Far from trying to decontaminate his printed text by removing every evidence that the book's existence is owing to a lectureship, I think the author should remind his readers occasionally that what they are reading is a lecture written for a particular audience. In any event, the text printed here is virtually the same as the one I read in our National Gallery in February and March 1960, the A. W. Mellon Lectures for that year.

When most of us go to a lecture, we are braced for an hour and are grateful when the trial is shortened. How much may it be shortened? Ten minutes, certainly, but there are those who feel that in a greater curtailment the lecturer has let them off too lightly. Therefore I have kept these lectures to about fifty minutes, resisting the temptation to exceed the limit imposed by the auditorium and to take another year or so adding to the book. This self-control has forced me to spend a good deal of time (three years) in choosing and arranging my material, in saying what I had to say as briefly as I could, and in writing with both audiences in mind. The limitations of a lecture can, I think, be turned to advantage if the lecturer will take them seriously. At any rate, I have lain upon my Procrustean bed without flinching, and I don't expect to rise and write a longer book on Horace Walpole.

As suggested in my first lecture, I have thought a great deal about what aspect of him I should take for my subject. Over thirty years ago I started off bravely to write his biography. As I wrote it I asked myself, Why should I try to say what he himself has said so much better? I began quoting more and more from him until I had a mere scrapbook of the facts of his life and amusing passages from his letters. Fortunately, I gave it up. Then, in the thirties, Mr. Ketton-Cremer came twice to Farmington for several months and wrote the biography that makes, I think, another full account of Walpole's life unnecessary. Accordingly, I have concentrated here on the man as I see him after thirty-five years of collecting, editing, and study. What was he like? What is the explanation of the contradictions and complexities of his character, behavior, and achievement? Why have so many found him baffling?

I hope that this book will answer these questions. I have been mindful of the expedient Plutarch says ancient cartographers resorted to when they crowded into the margins of their maps some such remarks as " 'All beyond is nothing but dry and desert sands, inhabited only by wild creatures; or dark unpassable bogs, or Scythian cold, or frozen sea' . . . beyond which 'is nothing but monstrous and tragical fictions. There the poets, and there the inventors of fables dwell.' " Expeditions to these fabulous regions are full of peril, but the audience to which

Preface

the Mellon Lecturer is introduced is a most congenial company in which to make such an attempt.

There remains for me only the pleasant duty of thanking those who have read these lectures or have heard me read them privately and who have helped me by their suggestions and criticism: Mrs. Francis W. Cole, Mrs. Blair Flandrau, Mr. Robert Halsband, Mr. Ketton-Cremer, Dr. J. H. Mannheim, Sir Lewis Namier, Dr. J. H. Plumb, Mr. A. L. Rowse, Mr. Romney Sedgwick; the friends in New Haven to whom I read them first, Mr. and Mrs. Herman W. Liebert, Mr. and Mrs. Andrew C. Ritchie, Mr. and Mrs. Carl P. Rollins (who also designed the book), Miss Isabel and Mr. Thornton Wilder. Among the Walpolians at Yale and Farmington I am particularly grateful to Messrs. Allen Hazen, George Lam, Robert Smith, Warren Smith, and Dayle Wallace, Miss Mabel Martin and Miss Julia McCarthy.

Finally, there is my indebtedness to my wife. To her great knowledge of Walpole and his time she brought judgment, impeccable taste, critical perception, and patience. Not long before she died I came across hundreds of slips on a Walpolian subject that she had made so many years ago that both of us had forgotten about them. Throughout our library are similar studies that will leave scholars in her debt to the end of time. She read four of these lectures before she died in May 1959. They have been rewritten as a result of her advice. No husband can have owed more to his wife than I owe to her, and no dedication of a book was ever more fitting than the one that I have made to her here.

W. S. L.

Farmington, Connecticut, May 1960

CONTENTS

LIST OF ILLUSTRATIONS

Unless otherwise noted, the originals of these illustrations are in the possession of W. S. Lewis, Farmington, Conn. Grateful acknowledgment for reproduction of the others is made to the Marquess and Marchioness of Cholmondeley; City Art Gallery, Bristol, England; Harvard College Library; the Earl of Lonsdale; the Minneapolis Institute of Arts; and the Earl Waldegrave for permission to reproduce the pictures or manuscripts in their possession.

xv

List of Illustrations

List of Illustrations

following page

Mann's musicales. Mann is the second figure from the right. The tall figure in the center is Lord Beauchamp, afterwards 2d Marquess of Hertford, Walpole's cousin, then on his travels with Lord Berkeley, who is on his right. Patch has painted himself on the extreme left, entering with a basket in which is a set of the *Vocabolario della Crusca*. Patch included in his conversation pieces topical references and satire, which, for the most part, are missed by us.

Painted in Venice for Sir Robert as a companion to the pastels done by Rosalba of Robert and Edward Walpole when they were in Venice on their Grand Tours some fifteen and eleven years earlier. It is now at Houghton and is reproduced here for the first time by kind permission of its present owners, the Marquess and Marchioness of Cholmondeley.

Painted at Florence for Walpole. Conway said it was extremely like, but Walpole wrote Mann, 23 March 1752, "Mr. Chute cannot bear it; says it wants your countenance and goodness; that it looks bonny and Irish. I am between both." It was sold in the Strawberry Hill sale, 21st day, lot 42, with a portrait of Mann's twin brother, Galfridus, for 6 guineas, and was resold at Sotheby's 1 February 1950 (Hastings sale), lot 71. Walpole has written on the back, "Horace Mann, Resident at Florence, by Astley, 1751." It was engraved by William Greatbatch for Cunningham's edition of the *Letters* (1857), I, 71.

Reproduced by kind permission of the Harvard College Library, from the Percival Merritt Collection.

The original was sent to Walpole by Mme du Deffand, who writes at length about it in her letter to him of 26 January 1768. The picture was sold in the Strawberry Hill sale, 21st day, lot 111, to a dealer. Its present whereabouts

This is a copy by Berwick. Tradition ascribes the original
to both Gainsborough and Reynolds. The original was
painted for Faneuil Hall, Boston, at the request of the people of Boston in a town meeting (Justin Winsor, *Memorial
History of Boston* [1881], III, 19; Samuel J. Drake, *History and Antiquities of Boston* [1856], pp. 703–5. Two
years later, in 1767, Conway sent the picture, with apolo-
gies for the delay that was no doubt extended by the painting of this copy. The original was lost during the Revolution.
The copy passed from Conway to his daughter, Mrs. Damer,
and from her to members of her mother's family, the Camp-
bell-Johnstons, from one of whom it was acquired by W. S.
Lewis. Conway (who later became a Field Marshal) is here
shown as the soldier-statesman. At the time, he was secretary
of state for the Southern Department, which included the
Colonies. He is indicating with his right hand the manuscript of the Free Port Bill that opened the West Indian
trade to Boston merchants and paved the way for the
Repeal of the Stamp Act. The head and shoulders were

List of Illustrations

engraved for Peter Cunningham's edition of Walpole's
letters in 1857; the rest is shown here for the first time.

27. HENRY FOX 56

Bentley's design for the *Memoirs* and the portrait of Fox
by an unknown artist, allegedly Reynolds. The design,
with the head of Fox in place, was engraved by Thom-
son for the *Memoirs of the Last Ten Years of the Reign
of George the Second* (1822), II, 1. Walpole's explanation of Fox's plate is: "Shield of his arms and of Lenox,
whose daughter he married. On one side a view of Holland House. In a corner a pen and gauntlets, to imply
the Test and Contest, papers written for and against him.
By Mr. Bentley." Walpole's intimate and frequently unsatisfactory relations with Fox may be followed in the
Yale Walpole, Vol. 30.

28. WALPOLE, BY BENTLEY, ca. 1755 56

The drawing for the frontispiece to the *Memoirs of . . .
George the Second*. Walpole's explanation of it is: "The
Author, leaning on a globe of the world, between Hera-
clitus and Democritus, presents his book to the latter. In
the landscape is a view of the Author's villa at Strawberry-
Hill, near Twickenham, where the *Memoires* were chiefly
written. At bottom is the date of the year, with emblems,
and the Author's arms and motto. [*Added at a later date*:]
The ivy over the mantle, that is lifted up and discovers a
mask and caduceus, imply that time and history reveal
what has been concealed." The editor of the *Memoirs* cut
off the objects below the mantle. Walpole's explanation
was printed in full, including the reference to the part
of the drawing that had been cut off. The date, 1751,
refers to the date when the *Memoirs* were begun, not to
the date of the drawing, which must have been after 1754,
since the Library, which was completed in that year, is
shown in the view of Strawberry Hill in the background.

29. A PAGE FROM THE "FOUL" COPY OF THE
MEMOIRS 56

Reproduced by kind permission of the Earl Waldegrave.

30. NOTES FOR THE *MEMOIRS* 64

Reading from left to right these scraps have notes for
Walpole's *Last Journals* for July 1775, 17 December

List of Illustrations

Walpole has written on the back of this drawing: "View from the Hall at Strawberry Hill, by John Carter, 1788." The Little Cloister is seen through the door and so is the blue and white China tub on which the pensive Selima reclined and in which she was drowned. Walpole wrote in the *Description:* "You first enter a small gloomy hall paved with hexagon tiles, and lighted by two narrow windows of painted glass, representing St. John and St. Francis. This hall is united with the staircase, and both are hung with Gothic paper, painted by one Tudor, from the screen of Prince Arthur's tomb in the Cathedral of Worcester. The balustrade was designed by Mr. Bentley; at every corner is an antelope (one of Lord Orford's supporters) holding a shield."

The *Description* reads, p. 47: "The Gallery. Fifty-six feet long, seventeen high, and thirteen wide without the five recesses. The ceiling is taken from one of the side aisles of Henry 7th's Chapel. In the windows, by Peckitt, are all the quarterings of the family. The great door is copied from the north door of Saint Alban's, and the two smaller are parts of the same design. The side with recesses, which are finished with a gold net-work over looking-glass, is taken from the tomb of Archbishop Bourchier at Canterbury. The chimney-piece was designed by Mr. John Chute and Mr. Thomas Pitt of Boconnoch. The room is hung with crimson damask: the chairs, settees, and long stools are of the same, mounted on black and gold frames. The carpet made at Moorfields. . . . Vespasian, in basaltes; a noble bust, bought out of the collection of Cardinal Ottoboni" appears on the right.

This room and the Library above it were built in 1754. It was thirty feet long, twenty wide, twelve high, and was hung with paper in imitation of stucco. The chimney-piece was designed by Bentley. Above it on the left is the Astley of Horace Mann (see above, no. 19); next to it is Reynolds' conversation piece of Selwyn, "Gilly" Williams, and Edgcumbe (see above, no. 14), and the Astley of Galfridus Mann (now at Farmington). On the opposite wall is Reynolds' portrait of the Ladies Waldegrave (now in the National Gallery of Scotland). The Gothic chairs (now at Farmington) were designed by Walpole and Bentley. From Bull's copy of the 1784 *Description.*

Description, p. 55: "It is a square with a semicircular recess in the middle of each side, painted stone-color with gilt ornaments, and with windows and niches, the latter taken from those on the sides of the north door of the great church at Saint Alban's; the roof, which is taken from the chapter-house at York, is terminated by a star of yellow glass that throws a golden gloom all over the room, and with the painted windows gives it the solemn air of a rich chapel." The cabinet shown in the middle was designed by Walpole. It is now in the Victoria and Albert Museum.

The inscription is in Walpole's hand; from his collection of Bentley's "Designs."

The pool is "Po-Yang," in which Walpole kept goldfish.

The drawing is in Walpole's extra-illustrated copy of the *Description.* "The great North Gate" opened on the Oratory (shown on the left). Above it is the Holbein Chamber. The oriel windows are in the Great Bedchamber, beyond which projects the Tribune.

The drawing is in Walpole's extra-illustrated copy of the *Description.* The inscription, "The Cottage, drawn by J. C. Barrow, 1791," is in his hand. The figure is Kirgate. The cottage had two rooms, a tea-room and a library. It was designed by Chute. The rivulet with the two cascades ran through the right-hand corner of this garden.

List of Illustrations

Horace Walpole

List of Illustrations

HORACE WALPOLE

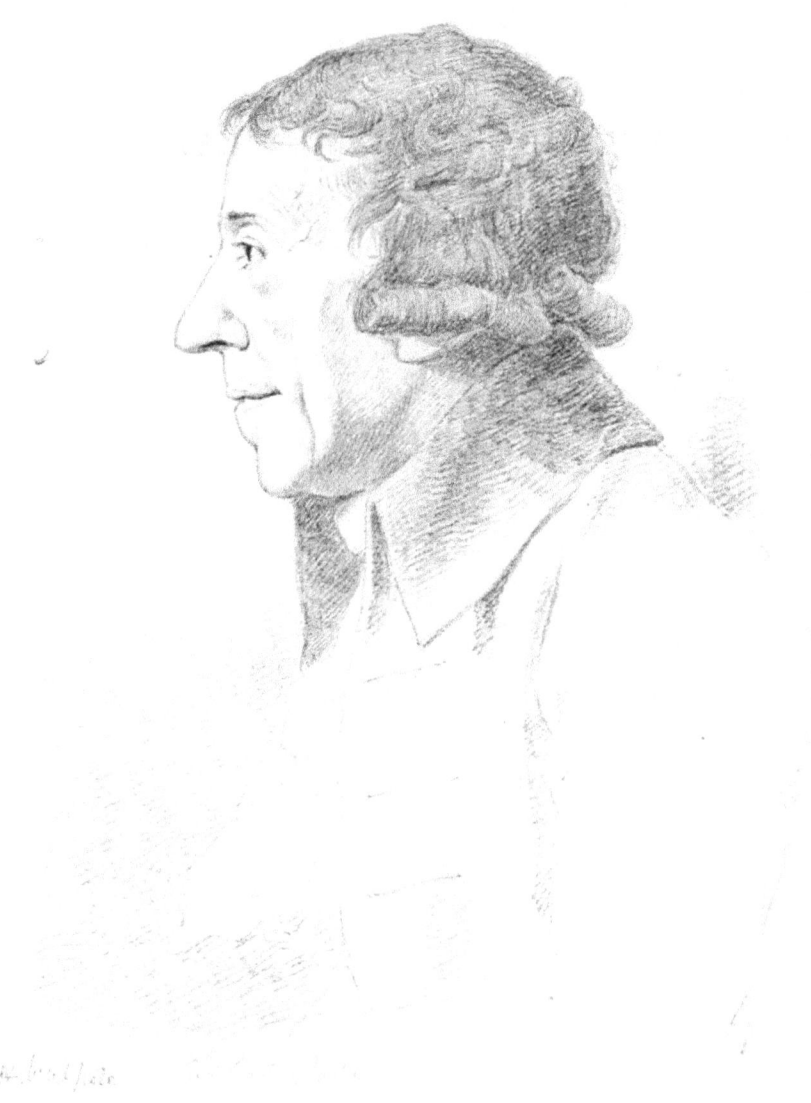

1. HORACE WALPOLE, 4th EARL OF ORFORD, *by George Dance the Younger,* 1793

I

FAMILY

WHEN one talks about Horace Walpole it is well to make it clear at the start who he was not. He was not the eighteenth-century prime minister; that was his father, Sir Robert Walpole. He was not the novelist who died a few years ago; that was his remote cousin, Sir Hugh. Horace Walpole is the man who brought the art of letterwriting to the highest point it has reached in our language. He is also the pioneer historian of the fine arts in England, a major figure in the revival of Gothic architecture and in the history of the Gothic novel. He is a chief source for the study of mid-eighteenth-century politics in England. We learn more about his time from him than from any other person.

I have had a hard time choosing a subject for these lectures from among the many subjects that he offers. Should it be Walpole the historian of his age or the arbiter of taste, the literary artist or the antiquary? Should it be Walpole as one of the germinating forces of the eighteenth century whose long shadow reaches us today? Six lectures could be given on each of these subjects, but the one I have chosen is more interesting to me than any of them. It is the man himself.

We begin with his family; next week we go on to his friends; the third lecture deals with his political career, such as it was, and his *Memoirs;* the fourth, with his house, Strawberry Hill; the fifth, with his works, other than his *Memoirs* and letters; the last lecture will be on his letters and will conclude with a summary of what I have come to believe about him during the past thirty-six years. This is the outline of our course, and the route by which I hope to reach the man himself.

He was an extremely complicated man, full of inconsistencies and contradictions that have amused many, angered some, and puzzled others. Lytton Strachey said that we read on and on in him until we come to feel that we know him as well as a living friend—"one of those enigmatical friends about whom one is perpetually in doubt as to whether, in spite of everything, one *does* know them at all."[1] According to Lord David Cecil, "Countless writers have discussed him, but at the end all have confessed themselves baffled."[2] It is my hope that when we have Walpole's weaknesses and strength in perspective and his life work is seen in the light of the obstacles that he had to overcome to carry it out, he will be less baffling.

There are obvious reasons why he has baffled his readers. One is the vast extent of his writing—his four thousand-odd letters that have been preserved, his *Memoirs* and works, his histories, fiction, plays, verse, essays, political pieces, art catalogues, and notebooks—together with three thousand letters to him, a grand total of several million words. Few people have taken the time to read all this, nor have they studied his library and the contents of Strawberry Hill, as well as the building itself. To understand him one must explore his relations with his parents and family, and one should know as much about his time as it is possible for us to know six or seven generations later, not only its principal actors and events, but its tastes and tacit assumptions and the shifting background of his long life: if we look at Horace Walpole solely through our present-day lenses we shall get him out of focus. Instead of making a sympathetic study of him, readers in the past have tended to seize upon part of the whole man and have judged the whole by that part, like the blind philosophers and the elephant in the fable, but with this difference: the philosophers approached the elephant dispassionately. Objectivity is difficult with Horace Walpole: he was an emotional man and he has an emotional effect upon his readers. When they have had

[1] *Characters and Commentaries* (New York, 1933), p. 250.
[2] *Two Quiet Lives* (New York [1948]), p. 122.

Family

only one aspect of him in their grasp their pronouncements upon him have been grotesque.

He was an enigma in his own day. Although he was a Member of Parliament for many years and always had close relations and friends in highest office, he did little to advance his own interests. Instead of having the sort of house that everybody else had, he built a sham castle. Usually careful about money, he went on sprees of collecting furniture, pictures, prints, coins, china, and bric-a-brac. When he was young he was a good deal of a dandy, but he spoke out against the African slave trade years before Wilberforce was born and he wished to alleviate the lot of the poor and afflicted at home instead of shrugging his shoulders as sensible men did. He called himself an infidel,[3] and vigorously supported the Established Church against atheists, Roman Catholics, and Methodists. No one had more friends or was more tireless in his attentions to them, and no one could be more bitter about friendship. As a young man he took equal pleasure in the tea tables of dowagers and the card tables at White's Club. Apparently anything but robust, he lived to his eightieth year, bearing great physical pain and discomfort half his life with cheerful fortitude. When he was charged outrageously and ironically with driving Chatterton to suicide he stood up to the ordeal with coolness and dignity, which is another apparent contradiction, since he was hypersensitive to ridicule and abuse. He sought both privacy and fame and achieved both: he lived by himself and became, it was said, as much a curiosity to all foreigners as the tombs in Westminster Abbey and the lions in the Tower.[4]

He was a controversial figure after his death. Wordsworth, Coleridge, Keats, and Hazlitt, who knew nothing of his altruism, attacked him on the score of Chatterton. Walter Scott and Byron, on the other hand, praised him to the skies as a writer. His surviving friends received a jolt when the first of his *Memoirs* appeared in 1818. They recol-

---

[3] *Walpoliana* [ed. John Pinkerton (1799)], I, 74. (Unless otherwise specified, London is the place of publication for all works cited.)

[4] George James "Gilly" Williams to Selwyn, 13 Nov. 1764 (*George Selwyn and His Contemporaries,* ed. J. H. Jesse [1843], I, 322).

3

lected "good-natured Mr. Walpole," who was tireless in his attention to his friends and who would sit up all night with a sick dog and open a window for a moth rather than kill it; yet his *Memoirs* are filled with portraits of his contemporaries that were written with the intention of destroying their characters. The *Memoirs* caused John Wilson Croker, who admired Walpole's letters, to conclude that Walpole had poisoned history at its source and that therefore he was "as bad a man as ever lived."[5] Macaulay followed Hazlitt's line[6] that Walpole was a heartless fribble. His mind, Macaulay said, "was a bundle of inconsistent whims and affectations. His features were covered by mask within mask"; he was merely "a gentleman-usher at heart,"[7] yet Macaulay conceded that no one who has written so much is so seldom tiresome.

Speaking up for Walpole was the person best qualified to do so, Miss Mary Berry, who with her father and sister had lived in a cottage at Strawberry Hill in Walpole's old age. She said that Macaulay's "hasty and general opinion" was "entirely and offensively unlike the original" and that "the warmth of Walpole's feelings and his capacity for sincere affection continued unenfeebled by age." As to Macaulay's much quoted remark that Walpole "sneered at everybody," she pointed out that "sneering was not his way of showing dislike. He had very strong prejudices, sometimes adopted on very insufficient grounds, and he therefore often made great mistakes in the appreciation of character; but when influenced by such impressions, he always expressed his opinions directly, and often too violently. The affections of his heart were bestowed on few," she also conceded, "but they were singularly warm, pure, and constant; characterized not by the ardor of passion, but by the constant preoccupation of real affection."[8]

Macaulay's caricature survives, Miss Berry's portrait has been forgotten, but Walpole has not lacked still later friends. Thackeray

---

[5] *The Croker Papers,* ed. Louis J. Jennings (1884), I, 270.

[6] In the *Edinburgh Review,* Dec. 1818, an unsigned review of Walpole's letters to Montagu, which has been overlooked since by critics.

[7] *Edinburgh Review,* Oct. 1833; *Critical and Historical Essays* (1907), I, 331–46.

[8] Walpole's *Letters* (1840), VI, ix–xvi.

was sentimental about him;[9] Carlyle called him "a small steady light," and "an irrefragable authority."[10] Austin Dobson, Saintsbury, Lytton Strachey, Virginia Woolf, Mr. Ketton-Cremer, and others have written of him with warmth and enjoyment, yet hostility to him persists. Critics are still confused by Horace Walpole.

Virginia Woolf said that the most complicated life "falls into shape directly we have found the connecting word. . . . Is it love or ambition, commerce, religion, or sport? . . . Once found there is no biography without its form, no figure without its force."[11] I trust that the "connecting word" in Walpole's life will emerge as we proceed.

So far as the outward man goes, if he should appear now at the door and come up to the platform, what impression would he make on us? Not a very good one, I'm afraid. He was never at ease with strangers, and here he would be in the presence of the audience that he had in mind all his life, posterity. We should be struck by the prominence and brightness of his eyes and the pallor of his long face and tapering fingers. He was short even by eighteenth-century standards and much too thin. We should find him over-mannered, but however little we may know about the niceties of eighteenth-century clothes, we should sense that his were in the best of taste, unobtrusive (after his early "very fine" period), but smart. If he came as an old man he would be looking remarkably like Disraeli, or rather, like George Arliss as Disraeli. His gait would be brisk and darting in early life, limping and awkward from the gout later. And what would he sound like? Not like an Old Etonian of today. Students of eighteenth-century speech believe that his accent was closer to a Down East Yankee's, but we shall have to wait for the invention of the time machine to be sure. Whatever it was, the eighteenth century found his tones "extremely pleasant, and . . . highly gentlemanly."[12] A military neighbor in later life had to go to *Paradise Lost* for the effect on his ear of Walpole's speech: he said that it was "like a shoot-

---

[9] In *The Four Georges* (1860), p. 85.
[10] *History of Frederick II* (New York, 1865), V, 52.
[11] *Granite and Rainbow* (1958), p. 205.
[12] Laetitia Matilda Hawkins, *Anecdotes . . . and Memoirs* (1822), I, 106.

ing star or like Uriel, gliding on a sunbeam,"[13] an effect that seems almost too dazzling. Some did find him too witty. "He talked as he wrote," a younger friend said, "and one left him, at least I did, fatigued, though charmed with his enlivening sallies."[14] When he left off writing a letter and continued in dictation there is no break in style.

In his first portrait[15] he is standing above a monumental flight of steps and is indicating with his left hand a sundial on which Cupid has placed his arrow just before the number X. That is, he is nearing his tenth birthday and the year is 1727, the year he went to Eton. No doubt Lady Walpole had this portrait painted in compensation for her loss. Horace is superbly dressed in silk and gold braid and lace. His right hand rests elegantly on his hip with the ease and grace of his gesture towards the sundial. He is a credit to his dancing-master. His fair hair is parted in the middle and is combed to above his ears, at which point curls, big and little, burst out and fall to his shoulders. He is looking directly at us with his bright dark eyes and pale long face. His smile is somewhat disconcerting. He is inviting conversation, but are we, perhaps, not quite up to it?

The terrace on which he is standing in the portrait was probably the one at Orford House in Chelsea, which his father moved into when he became paymaster of the forces and where he remained after he was prime minister. At Orford House, Horace had the run of a garden with exotic shrubs, an orangery, an octagonal summerhouse, his mother's famous shell-grotto, and a "vollery," filled with singing birds—goldfinches, linnets, and parakeets.[16] He had fewer playmates than most children, but many dogs and cats.

Splendor was new to the Walpoles. They were of old Norfolk stock,

---

[13] General the Hon. John Fitzwilliam, in a manuscript note bound into a copy of *An Essay on Modern Gardening* (Strawberry Hill, 1785) that Walpole gave him; now at Farmington.

[14] John Nichols, *Literary Anecdotes* (1814), VIII, 525. The friend was George Hardinge, Byron's "Jefferies Hardsman."

[15] Probably by Philip Mercier. Its present owner is the Earl of Lonsdale.

[16] J. H. Plumb, *Sir Robert Walpole, the Making of a Statesman* (1956), p. 206.

Family

which Horace was later at pains to link up with other ancient Norfolk families, but wealth they had lacked. A notebook of Sir Robert's father shows that he spent less in a whole session of Parliament than Horace laid out on fans and bibelots for princesses in Florence. As for the other side of his family, Horace pointed out that his mother's father had been in trade, but that he had been "an honest sensible Whig," and Horace said he was very proud of him.[17] One of his mother's relations produced a chart that showed how they descended side by side with the kings of England from Cadwallader, last king of the Britons, and that was reassuring.

Sir Robert and his wife made the most of their new riches, and Horace had his full share of them. Bills for his toys came to £39 11s. 9d. I hesitate to say what that represents today, but perhaps $1,000 is not excessive. Two of his tailor's bills in 1725 and 1726 (when he was seven and eight) came to £71[18] or the present equivalent of over $1,500. His mother lavished money on him as well as on herself.

According to Lady Mary Wortley Montagu, Lady Walpole was "an empty, coquettish, affected woman, anything rather than correct in her own conduct, or spotless in her fame."[19] The portraits of her show a languorous ex-beauty with a settled grudge against the world. She concentrated her affections on her youngest son. Late in life he explained her "extreme partiality" for him by her grief over losing his two much older sisters, and her fear of losing him. He was used to hearing people say that he could not possibly live.[20] The "supposed necessary care of me," he wrote as an old man, "so engrossed the attention of my mother, that compassion and tenderness soon became extreme fondness."[21] He does not tell us that her extreme fondness for him was also

---

[17] Walpole to the Rev. William Mason, 13 April 1782.
[18] As appears in the Robert Walpole papers at Houghton (kindly communicated to me by Dr. Plumb).
[19] *Letters,* ed. W. Moy Thomas (1861), I, 69.
[20] "Reminiscences," *Works* (1798), IV, 275.
[21] Ibid.

no doubt increased by her hatred of his father, of whom she had been jealous—with every justification—from the early days of their marriage.

One hundred and twenty years after Horace's birth it was said that he was not the son of Sir Robert. The skeptics asked, How could the red-faced, virile Robert Walpole have such a pale, epicene son? Horace, they pointed out, was more like the Herveys—"Men, women, and Herveys," Lady Mary Wortley Montagu said—and what about that affair his mother had had with Carr, Lord Hervey? If the Walpoles had any doubts about Horace's paternity they were very charitable about it. He was given the name of Sir Robert's younger brother, who also stood as one of his godfathers; his godmother was Lady Townshend, Sir Robert's sister; Lord Townshend paid for his christening.[22]

Did he ever hear this gossip about his birth? So far as we know he did not. There are contemporary references to his mother's alleged infidelities, none that I have seen to his not being Sir Robert's son.[23] Had it been rumored at the time he would probably have figured in an opposition lampoon and certainly in private letters, but there seems to be no contemporary hint of anything of the kind. Had any reached him, I do not think that he would have made his mother and himself ridiculous

---

[22] *The Yale Edition of Horace Walpole's Correspondence,* ed. W. S. Lewis (New Haven, Conn., 1937–), 13. 3, n. 1.

[23] Lord Hervey in his *Memoirs* states that Sir Robert Walpole did not believe that George, later third Earl of Orford, was his grandson. Hervey adds that the world gave the boy to Sir George Oxenden, but that "from the extreme aversion" that his mother showed to "this poor little animal from the very hour of its birth" the judicious believed that the child really was her husband's (whom she detested). Mr. Romney Sedgwick notes in his edition of the *Memoirs,* "This is clearly the origin of the much later story that Sir Robert Walpole's youngest son Horace was really the son of Lord Hervey's elder brother" (*Lord Hervey's Memoirs* [1952], p. 267 n.). He has also pointed out: "If a similar misfortune had been generally supposed to have befallen Sir Robert, it is most improbable that both Hervey and Egmont would have failed to comment on the coincidence, and quite incredible that Hervey, when earlier in his memoirs he mentions an attempt of Sir Robert to seduce Lady Hervey, would have refrained from pointing out that the Herveys had got in first" ("Horace Walpole," in *From Anne to Victoria,* ed. Bonamy Dobrée [1937], p. 270).

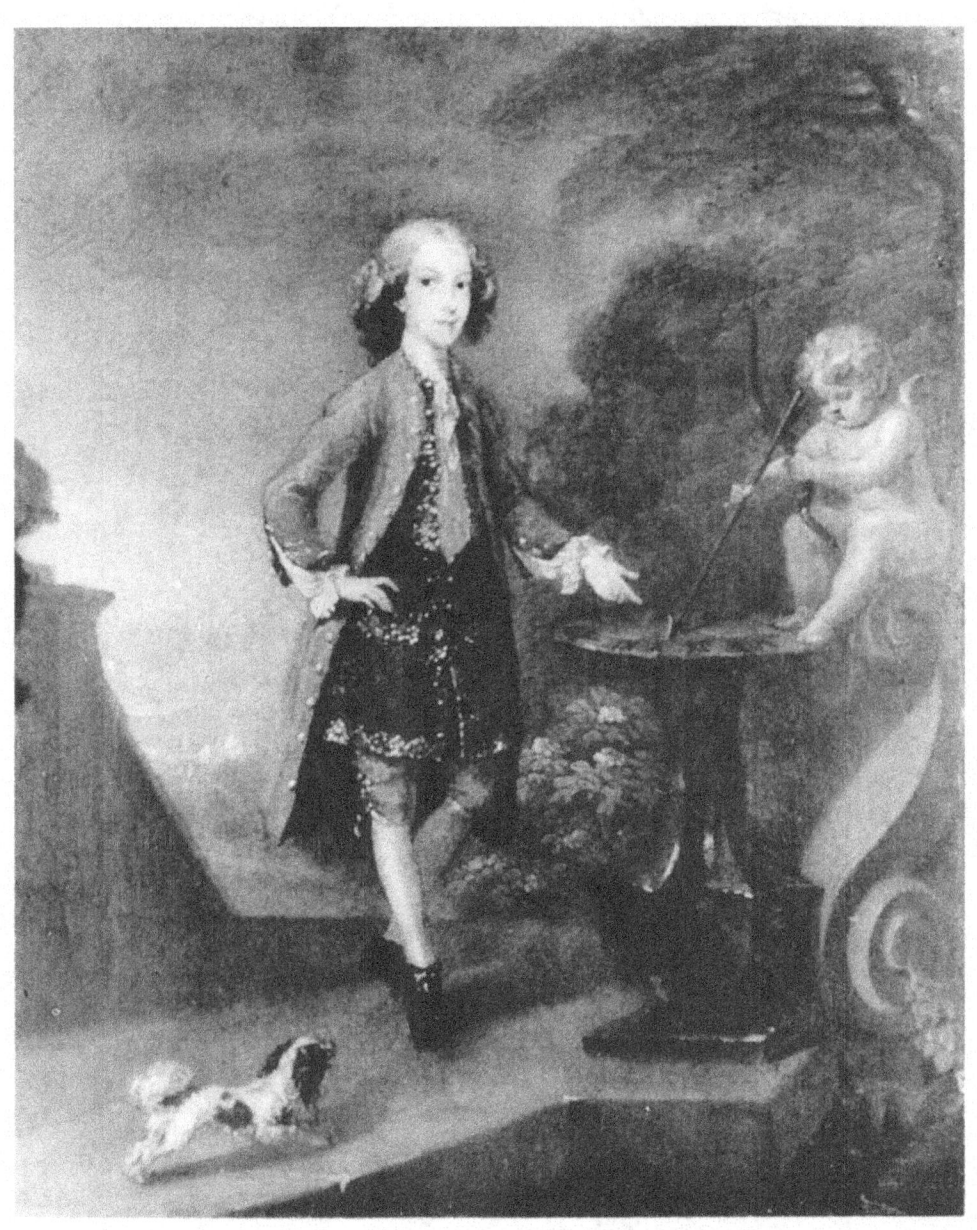

2. HORACE, AGED 10, *by Philip Mercier*, 1727

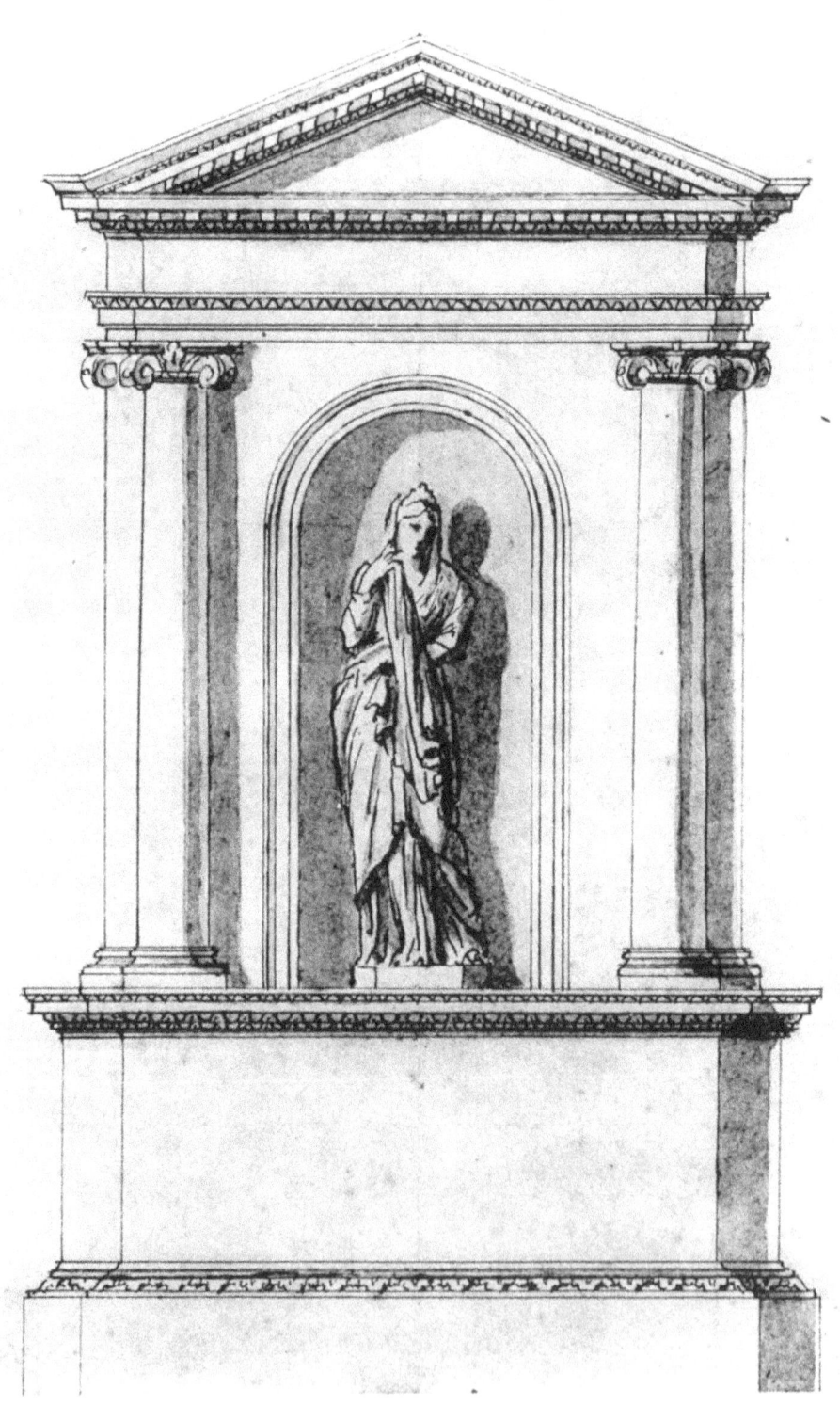

3. Lady Walpole's Cenotaph

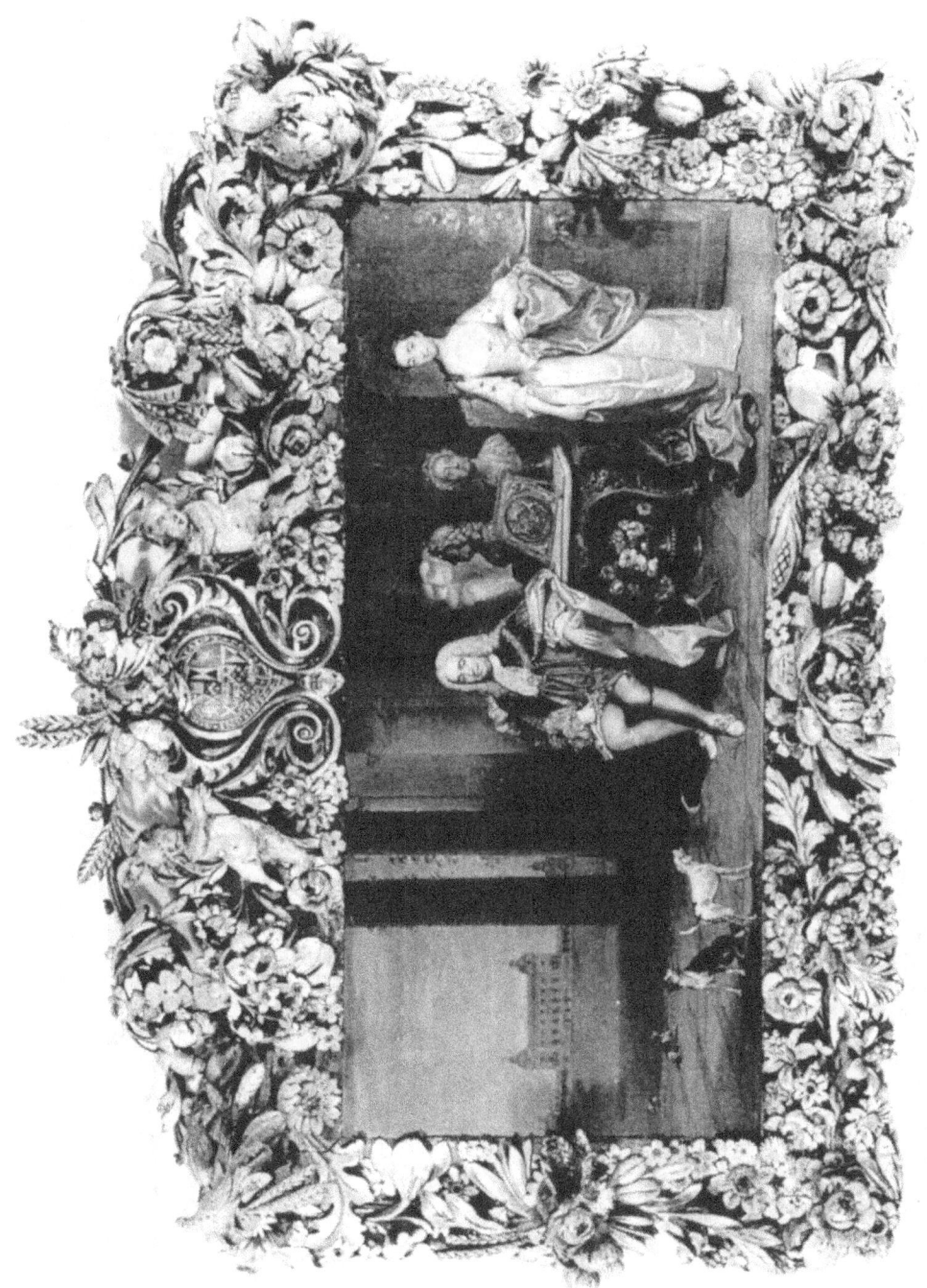

4. Sir Robert and Lady Walpole, *by J. G. Eccardt and John Wootton, ca. 1746*

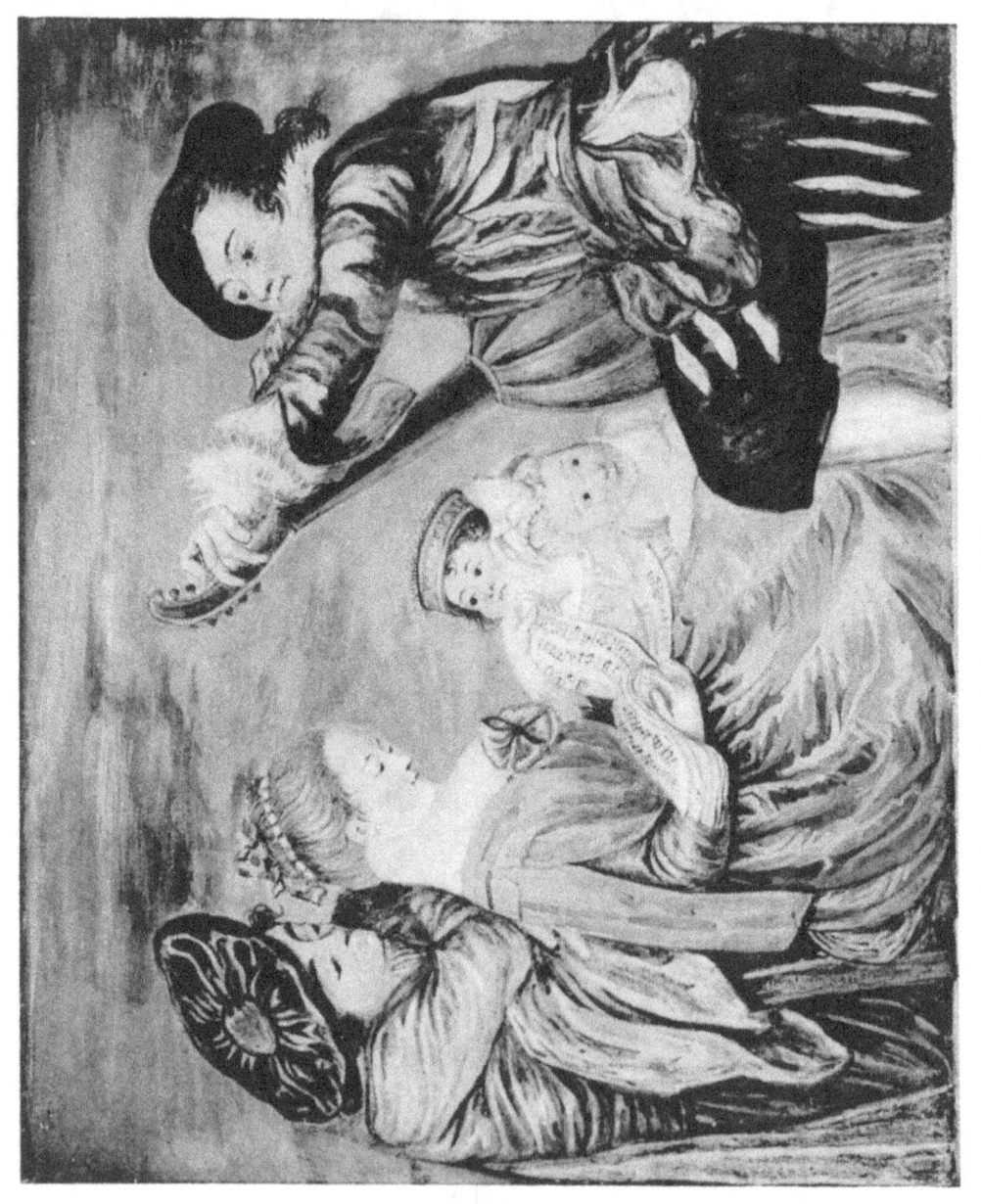

5. Watteau's "Music Party," by Walpole, 1736

Family

by putting up a cenotaph to her in Westminster Abbey with the inscription that he wrote for it and the figure that he chose to represent her. This is the inscription:

To the Memory

of

Catherine Lady Walpole,

Eldest Daughter of John Shorter, Esq. of Bybrook, in Kent,

and

First Wife of Sir Robert Walpole, afterwards Earl of Orford,

Horace,

Her youngest Son,

Consecrates this Monument.

She had beauty and wit

Without vice or vanity,

And cultivated the arts

Without affectation.

She was devout,

Though without bigotry to any sect;

And was without prejudice to any party,

Though the Wife of a Minister,

Whose power she esteemed,[24]

But when She could employ it to benefit the miserable,

Or to reward the meritorious.

She loved a private life,

Though born to shine in public;

And was an ornament to Courts,

Untainted by them.

She died August 20, 1737.[25]

The figure that he chose to represent her was Modesty.

Although the marriage of Sir Robert and Lady Walpole was a failure, they continued to share, with long intervals of separation, the same

---

[24] In what appears to be Walpole's first draft of this epitaph, written at Florence in 1740, he wrote "despised." There are other minor changes.

[25] The original manuscript is now in the Liverpool Public Library.

houses at Chelsea and in Downing Street, and later at Richmond and Houghton. Horace seems to have been brought up entirely by his mother and the women about her. His brothers and sisters were so much older that he was like an only child. Robert, the eldest brother, was married to a woman whom he and his family detested; Edward was not married, but owing to the complaisance of a milliner's apprentice he was not without children. Both brothers tried to injure Horace with his parents. He later became devoted to Mary, Sir Robert's illegitimate daughter, but at this time she lived with her mother, Maria Skerrett.

One can imagine pale, high-strung, very observant little Horace watching his engaging, ruthless, and adroit father from a distance, admiring his power and resenting his indifference to himself. The bustle of public business followed Robert Walpole wherever he went. Politicians and clerics swarmed through his houses: placemen after richer places, bishops after richer bishoprics, a stimulating spectacle for the son who was to become the ablest reporter of his time. Sir Robert said, "Every man has his price,"[26] and he got full value for what he paid. Noise and cynicism filled the air. Sir Robert "laughed the heart's laugh" and talked bawdy to the women. Independence and self-indulgence were the rule of the family. Its motto was "Fari quae sentiat," "Say what you think," a sentiment that they all lived up to, along with "Do what you please." Self-indulgence and insecurity were gifts to Horace from his parents and he preserved them as long as he lived.

He was much happier at Eton than at home. Next week I shall tell you something about his life there. Cambridge meant less to him. Being a Fellow Commoner at King's he could come and go as he pleased, and much of the time he spent with his mamma in London. They copied Watteau and Parmigianino together in water colors, no doubt laughing and chattering a great deal. He also catalogued his father's four hundred and thirty pictures in his various houses, listing them with their dimensions, room by room,[27] and occasionally adding a comment, such as

---

[26] Walpole states this in his *Memoirs of George III* (1894), I, 283, but later forgot it (Pinkerton, *Walpoliana* [1799], I, 88; "Book of Materials," 1759, p. 44).

[27] This catalogue is now in the Pierpont Morgan Library.

that on Murillo's *Adoration of the Shepherds,* "All the light in the picture comes from the Child." Throughout the catalogue are additions in Sir Robert's hand,[28] which suggest that Horace had achieved a closer relationship to his father and a growing independence of his mother; yet when Lady Walpole died, in his twentieth year, his grief was so protracted that his friends became alarmed for his health. His closest friend at Cambridge, Thomas Gray, feared that Horace's religious faith might be unable to support him in the loss of "the best of mothers," and Conyers Middleton, the older man who was the chief influence on him there, begged him to "show that command of himself in grief that he exerted so successfully against pleasure." Only one of his letters of the next two years has been recovered. He had returned to Cambridge, he wrote, "out of a house which I could not bear."[29] His mother was no longer there and Sir Robert was about to marry Maria Skerrett, his mistress, who was good-natured and understanding, but who had naturally been hated by her predecessor. The new Lady Walpole died shortly in childbirth.

Sir Robert died in 1745, in Horace's twenty-eighth year. He suffered dreadfully from the stone and even more from the treatment of it, a violent new lixivium. Horace was with him constantly during his last illness. Among the manuscripts at Farmington is a scrap that shows a Boswellian desire to record what a man actually said:

" 'Dear Horace, this lixivium has blown me up. It has tore me to pieces. The affair is over with me; that it may be short, Dr. Ranby, is all I desire. Give me more opium, knock me down. I expect nothing but to have ease. Dear Horace, if one must die, 'tis hard to die in pain.

" 'Why do ye all stand round me! Are ye all waiting there because this is the last night?'

"[He] insisted," Horace continued, "on Ranby's telling him if he should die before morning: Ranby gave him no hopes: he then talked in private with Ranby; then a quarter of an hour just before three with

---

[28] I am indebted to Dr. Plumb for calling these to my attention.
[29] Walpole to Charles Lyttelton, 18 Sept. 1737.

11

Horace Walpole

Lord Walpole. Afterwards again with Ranby. To Ranby, "'Tis impossible not to be a little disturbed at going out of the world, but you see I am not afraid.' "

Sir Robert left Horace his house in Arlington Street, £5,000 in cash, and an additional place in the Customs. Horace's income reached £8,000 in 1784,[30] which I am told represents perhaps $200,000 today, and which Horace was the first to point out was a very generous provision for a younger son. He became a violent champion of his father, heaping abuse upon Sir Robert's enemies, extolling his virtues, and making his faults attractive, yet we shall see as we go along that beneath this outward loyalty lay quite opposite emotions.

Fifty years after Sir Robert died, Horace, then in his eightieth year, wrote to Lady Ossory the last of his four hundred and fifty letters to her. In it he spoke of "about fourscore nephews and nieces of various ages, who are each brought to me about once a year, to stare at me as the Methusalem of the family."[31] They came to see him not only because he was the titular head of it—he had succeeded his nephew as Earl of Orford—but because he was very good with young people. These nephews and nieces and great- and great-great-nephews and nieces were the children and descendants of his brother Edward, his sister Lady Malpas, and his half-sister Lady Mary Churchill, a total of nearer fifty than eighty, but the eighteenth century was not accurate about family relationships, and younger Walpole and Conway cousins also came. For much of his life he was the man to whom his family turned for advice and help. It had not always been so, as his brother Edward and his uncle Horace Walpole of Wolterton would have been the first to say fifty years earlier.

At that time Edward had sent Horace a furious letter in which he complained of Horace's contemptuous and arrogant treatment and much besides. Horace answered at once quoting Edward's charges one by one.

---

[30] It receded in that year when on the death of his brother Edward he lost his place in the Customs worth £1,400.
[31] 9 Jan. 1797.

Family

Here is an extract: Edward: "You have assumed to yourself a pre-eminence, from an imaginary disparity between us in point of abilities and character." Horace: "Who told you so? not your eyes, but your jealousy. I'll tell you, brother, the only superiority I ever pretended over you, was in my temper." After answering each charge Horace went on to get their past history straight. "In my mother's lifetime, you accused me of fomenting her anger against you. The instant she died, did I not bring you all my letters to her which she had kept, in never a one of which was your name mentioned, but to persuade her to continue that love to you, *which your behavior has always labored to extinguish in the hearts of all your relations.*" Having poured out his rage and hatred, Horace put his letter to one side, and in two days wrote Edward[32] more in sorrow than in anger, a display of self-control that must have made Edward hate him more than ever. Six years later Horace proved that he was a good brother when Edward was the victim of a gang that charged him with sodomitical assault. Horace came up to London and helped to convict the conspirators, who were heavily fined, made to stand in the pillory, and imprisoned at hard labor.[33] As time went on he became fond of Edward, even going so far as to collect his drawings, which he directed should be preserved in his family,[34] and when Mason in his life of Gray called Horace Sir Robert's favorite son, he made Mason delete it in order not to wound an "innocent, meritorious brother."[35]

He was neither temperate nor judicious in his quarrels with his Uncle Horace. The worst one took place when they joined forces to rescue the fortunes of their nephew and great-nephew, Lord Orford, whose father's and grandfather's extravagance had left him deep in debt. An obvious solution presented itself in a sixteen-year-old Miss Nicoll, an heiress "of above £150,000." Her inclinations and Lord Orford's, who

---

[32] 17 May 1745.

[33] *The Whole Proceedings on the Wicked Conspiracy Carried on against the Hon. Edward Walpole, Esq., by John Cather, Adam Nixon, Daniel Alexander, Patrick Cane alias Kane, and Others* (1751).

[34] The drawings are now bound with Walpole's master copy of his *Description of Strawberry Hill* (1774), at Farmington.

[35] Walpole to Mason, 2 March 1773.

was then twenty-one, were not consulted, and the affair was a fiasco, owing in part to the conduct of the two Horaces. Young Horace found
Old Horace and his wife ill-dressed, penurious, and unwashed, and said
so openly and often; the elder man regarded the younger as a treacherous
little freak. Soon each was suspecting the other of double-dealing in
letters ringing with abuse. While these exchanges were taking place
Lord Orford rejected Miss Nicoll for a good woman named Patty Turk,
with whom he lived openly the rest of his life. Miss Nicoll ended up a
marchioness.[36] Five years later Horace had another great row with his
uncle about the family trust, and this time he seems to have been in the
right.[37] From then on he cut his uncle whenever they met. The "Wars of
the Walpoles," as he called them, came to an end when his uncle died,
and in due course he formed affectionate friendships with several of his
Wolterton cousins whose children went to Strawberry Hill to see him in
his old age.

Why did he hate Old Horace? I think that he made Horace senior
a scapegoat for the latent hostility that he continued to have for his
father, and that made him resent authority as long as he lived. Young
Horace also disliked sharing the same name, not only with his uncle, but
with his uncle's eldest son and grandson. All his life when he found his
own name in print he would add, "Youngest son of Sir Robert Walpole,
afterwards Earl of Orford": he did not want to be confused with anyone
else, least of all with an old man whom he regarded as a swindling buf-
foon. Uncle and nephew were able to join forces in the Nicoll affair because of their common interest, but when that undertaking went wrong
young Horace's hatred leapt out. He later admitted that he had behaved

[36] The younger Horace wrote a "Narrative of the Proceedings on the Intended Marriage between Lord Orford and Miss Nicholl." It fills twenty-one pages in the Yale
Walpole; supplementary letters and memoranda fill nineteen more (14. 193–233),
and recently still other letters relating to it have come to light. Horace had copies
made of his "Narrative," which he circulated. He wanted posterity to see it and
must have believed that we should applaud what he had done.

[37] He also wrote an account of this affair, which he kept for us to see, but again
prudently withheld publication.

with too much peevishness,[38] and years later still, that he had been "an untractable nephew."[39] At other times when he spoke of his "follies and weaknesses" it was with a certain pride. He enjoyed his tendency to "warmth," by which he meant excited partisanship, and he spoke of "my natural ferocity and wildness."[40] He once quoted Dryden,

> *from a little elf,*
> *I've had a high opinion of myself,*
> *Though sickly, slender, and not large of limb.*[41]

The emotional uncertainties of his childhood left him subject to gusts of fear and aggressiveness as long as he lived.

From middle age on, his conduct to his family was exemplary. The head of it, his nephew Orford, became more and more of a problem. Patty Turk did what she could for him, but Orford's extravagance reduced still further his impoverished estate. He kept a racing stable and was an ardent falconer. Mr. Ketton-Cremer has brought together the record of his exploits, which included driving four red deer in a phaeton, a race for £500 of five turkeys against five geese from Norwich to London, and a trip through the Cambridgeshire fens in a fleet of nine boats. This last must have put a strain on his relations with the inhabitants through whose country the flotilla passed, because when its progress was impeded by a bridge the crew, under orders of Admiral Orford and Vice-Admiral Turk, dismantled the bridge and, apparently, did not put it back.[42] Orford's eccentricity proceeded to insanity. When he had his first attack the conscientious members of the family asked his uncle Horace to try to straighten out his involved affairs. Although Horace protested his ignorance of business and his ill health, he dropped everything and did

---

[38] Yale Walpole, 14. 207.
[39] Walpole to Mann, 13 July 1773.
[40] Walpole to John Chute, 20 Aug. 1743.
[41] Walpole to Montagu, 1 Aug. 1745.
[42] R. W. Ketton-Cremer, *A Norfolk Gallery* (1948), p. 179.

the best he could "to stop," as he said, "the torrent, which in another year would have swept away even the ruins." Orford was surrounded by what his uncle called "a rookery of harpies." Walpole repaired buildings, secured proper leases and rentals for the farms, and saved nearly £1,200 a year by discharging unnecessary servants and selling horses and dogs.[43] One of his Wolterton cousins expressed the family's obligation for his "administration of a mass so complicated with error, neglect, and imposition." Walpole was pleased to discover this unsuspected talent in himself. Then Orford recovered, brought back his dishonest retainers and dogs and horses, and spent what his uncle had saved as rapidly as possible. During the next eighteen years this exhausting farce was repeated several times. Walpole wrote, "When the law says he is mad, I will take care of him; when it says he is in his senses, I shall not dispute it."[44] The last time Orford relapsed he mercifully died, and his uncle Horace became, so he said, "the poorest earl in England."

He was also foster father to his brother Edward's children, as his brother was the first to say.[45] When they were ill he took them to Strawberry Hill and looked after them until they were well, because Edward's house was filthy as well as casually run. There were three girls and a boy. The boy, who was badly treated by his father, drank himself to death early, but the three girls made great marriages. They continued to turn to their uncle Horace for help and advice when they were grown and brought their children to Strawberry Hill for him to enjoy.

The middle sister, Maria, a great beauty, was his favorite. He tells how on discovering that Lord Waldegrave liked her, he "drew him to make his declaration and proposal of marriage, in two days less than a month."[46] By Lord Waldegrave she had three daughters (the Ladies Waldegrave of Reynolds' picture), one of whom she named Horatia. Following in the footsteps of their mother, they also made great marriages.

---

[43] These details are in a letter from Walpole to Thomas Walpole, 4 Sept. 1773, in the possession of Mr. David Holland, who kindly communicated them to me.
[44] Walpole to Mann, 27 March 1778.
[45] *Last Journals* (1910), I, 93.
[46] "Short Notes" of his life, Yale Walpole, 13. 31.

Dr Horace This lixivium has blown
me up. 2. It has tore me to pieces.
The Affair is over with me; that it
may be short Dr Ranby, is all I desire.
Give me more Opium; knock me down.
I expect nothing but to have ease.
Dr Horace if one must die, tis hard
to die in pain.
Why do ye all stand round me! are
ye all waiting here, because this
is the last night.
Insisted on Ranby's telling him if he
shd die before morning: Ranby gave
him no hopes: he then talk'd in private
with Ranby; then a quarter of an hour
just before three wth D Walpole. after
wards again wth Ranby. To Ranby, Tis
Impossible not to be a little disturbd at
going out of the world, but you see I am
not afraid.

6. SIR ROBERT'S LAST WORDS

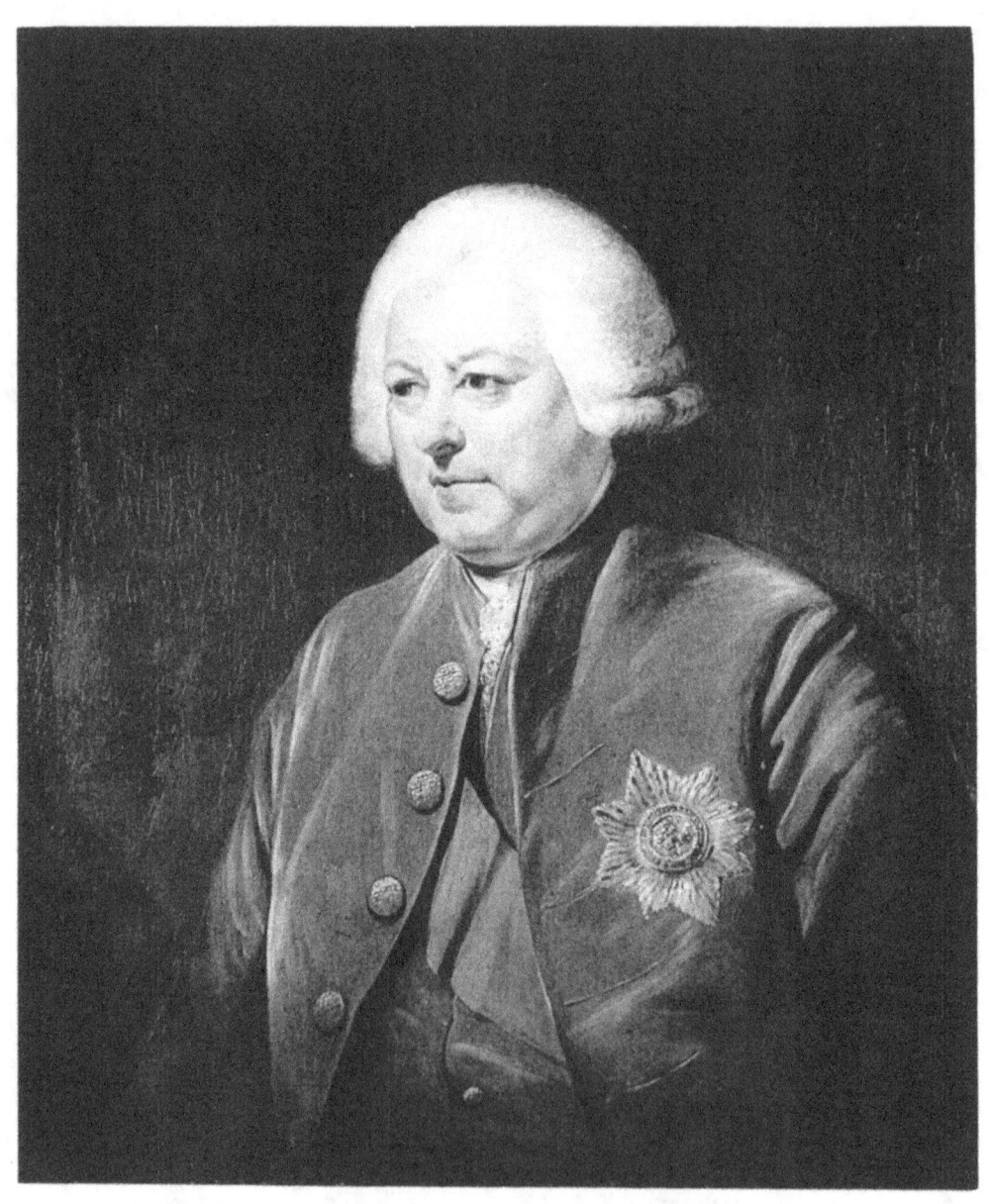

7. SIR EDWARD WALPOLE, *by Edward Edwards,* ca. 1780

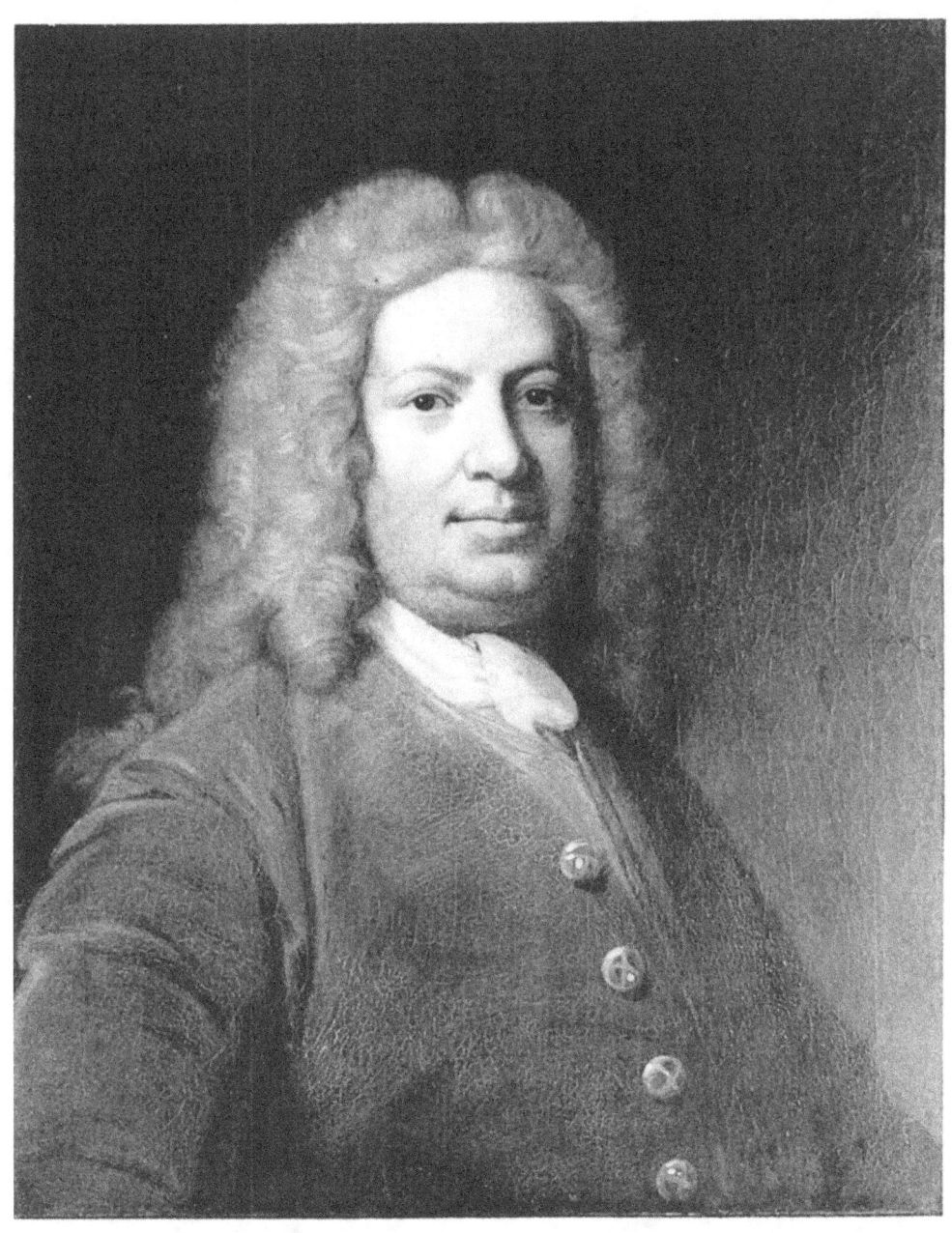

8. "OLD" HORACE WALPOLE, *by J. B. Van Loo,* ca. 1728

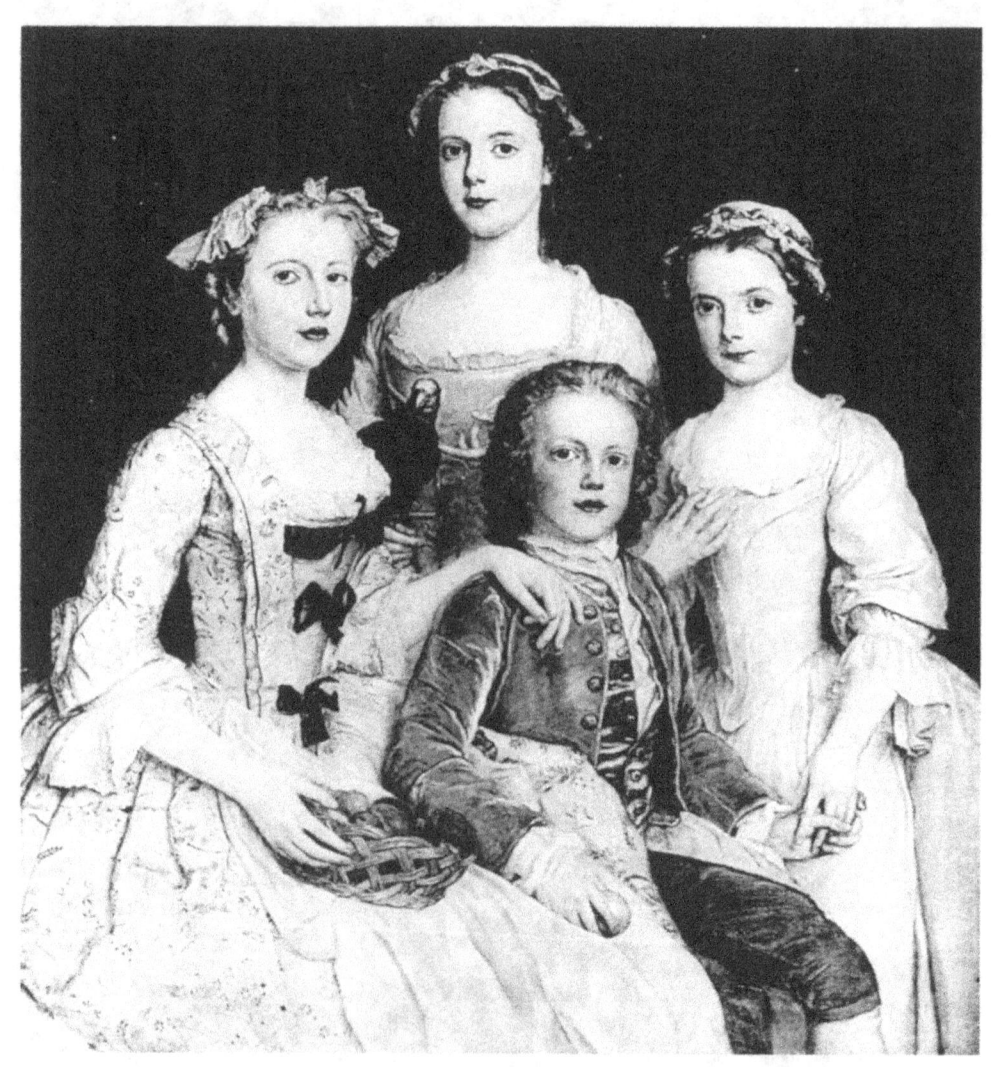

9. SIR EDWARD WALPOLE'S CHILDREN, *by Stephen Slaughter,* ca. 1747

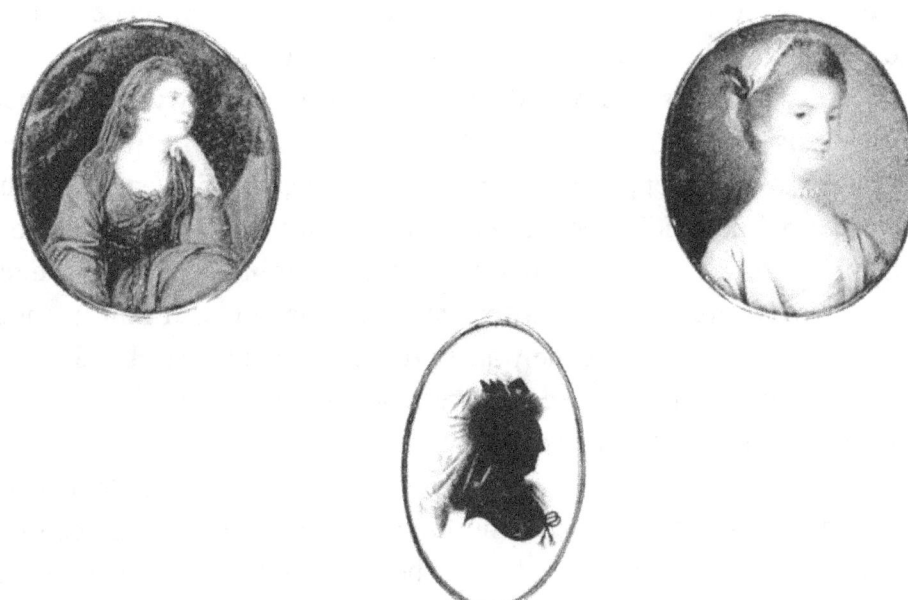

10. MARIA WALPOLE, COUNTESS WALDEGRAVE,
AFTERWARDS DUCHESS OF GLOUCESTER

Family

A few years after Waldegrave's death Maria married George III's brother, the Duke of Gloucester, against the King's wishes and the advice of her Uncle Horace, who foresaw the unhappiness ahead for her. Her attentions to her uncle Horace were not disinterested: a letter has recently come to light in which she confided to an aunt that she wished he would leave her a bequest of £10,000 and Strawberry Hill to her family.[47] Both wishes were granted in twenty years.

Walpole's half-sister, Lady Mary Churchill, is a shadowy figure, since the hundreds of letters that he wrote to her have disappeared.[48] After their father had had her given the style and precedence of an earl's daughter she was publicly ridiculed and humiliated. This treatment made Horace her friend and champion. They walked together in the park at Houghton; she played the harpsichord to him, and laughed with him at their neighbors. Rumor said that she was a great heiress, and her brother believed that she might have become the Duchess of Devonshire or Lady Fitzwilliam. Instead, she married Colonel Charles Churchill, who was also an illegitimate. Horace thought it a foolish match, but stood godfather to the first of their seven children; one of the boys was named for him. We can gather something of what the Churchills meant to him from his account of how he appointed George and Horace Churchill his aides-de-camp when he put on a sword and received the Queen and eight princesses at Strawberry Hill in his very old age, so that if he should tumble down they would be able to get him up again. After one of their sisters married a grandson of Old Horace the "Wars of the Walpoles" seemed far away.

A second natural daughter of Sir Robert's by a different mistress was seven years younger than Horace. Sir Robert left her £100 a year and bought a rich living that he presented to a clergyman with the understanding, so Horace said,[49] that he should marry the daughter when she came of age. The young man took the living, but Sir Robert dying

---

[47] Maria, Duchess of Gloucester, to her cousin, Mrs. Clements, 11 Jan. 1777. The letter is at Farmington.

[48] W. S. Lewis, *Collector's Progress* (New York, 1951), pp. 185–86.

[49] Yale Walpole, 2. 371–73. See also Walpole to Mann, 11 Dec. 1752.

soon after, he declined to complete the plan, marrying instead a fortune and going on to become Bishop of Chester and of Ely. Mrs. Catherine Daye, as the forsaken lady called herself, disappeared until a few years before her death when Horace discovered her living in great poverty with her mother. He brought her to Strawberry Hill, where she spent half of each year the rest of her life and where she died.[50] That she did not add to the Strawberry Hill dinner parties is indicated by a visitor there, who described her as being of a "squab, short, gummy appearance,"[51] but perhaps when more fashionable company was present she preferred to have a tray upstairs.

Although Mrs. Daye completes the roster of Horace's immediate family, mention should be made of two gentlewomen in reduced circumstances, intimate friends of his mother's, who enveloped him in the warm affection of motherly aunts. He returned their love with the ardor of a high-strung little boy. One of them, Miss Leneve, later lived with him. There was nothing "squab" or "gummy" about her; she was witty and understanding. A trait that Walpole shared with Dr. Johnson was his readiness to take into his house the poor and afflicted.

Walpole's Conway cousins, the children of his mother's sister, stand in a special place, particularly Francis Lord Conway, afterwards Earl and Marquess of Hertford, his wife and children, and above all, Henry Conway, who became a secretary of state and a field marshal, his wife, Lady Ailesbury, and their only child, Anne Seymour Conway, Mrs. Damer. Only thirty-nine of Walpole's letters to Hertford have been recovered, but in the British Museum are more than two hundred letters to Walpole from him and his wife and eldest son. When they are published the place of the Hertfords in Walpole's life will be clearer than it has been.

Henry Conway was his closest friend as well as favorite relation. To Walpole he was as perfect as a man could be: a brave and skillful soldier, an incorruptible statesman, a model husband, father, brother,

---

[50] He set up a trust fund of £3,500 for the benefit of her two half-sisters.
[51] William Cole, Yale Walpole, 2. 371.

and friend. When Conway wanted to marry Lady Caroline Fitzroy, but could not for lack of money, Walpole, although he disapproved of the match, offered him half his income. "I am sensible," he wrote, "of having more follies and weaknesses, and fewer real good qualities than most men. . . . I always want to begin acting like a man, and a sensible one, which I think I might be if I would. Can I begin better than by taking care of my fortune for one I love? . . . If I ever felt much for anyone (which I know may be questioned), it was certainly for my mother. I look on you as my nearest relation by her, and I think I can never do enough to show my gratitude and affection for her."[52] Conway declined Walpole's offer and before long married Lady Ailesbury, with whom he lived happily ever after. Walpole adopted her as a sister and their only child, Anne Conway, as a daughter. His affection extended to Lady Ailesbury's daughter by her first marriage, the Duchess of Richmond, to her husband, and their family. History has written off Conway as "a better soldier than he was a general, a better general than a statesman,"[53] but new villages were named for him in Massachusetts and New Hampshire and the people of Boston requested his portrait for Faneuil Hall, when, as secretary of state, he pushed through the repeal of the Stamp Act. All his life he was interested in the theater and the arts that solaced his old age. One does not often find so very congenial a friend among one's close relations.[54]

When Anne Conway was little, Walpole would take her to Strawberry Hill while her parents were out of the country, and there he would amuse her when she was well and care for her when she was ill. She grew up to be a redoubtable woman. Her husband, John Damer, committed suicide. Thereafter she was preoccupied with her sculpture and affairs with other women. Towards the end of Walpole's life she turned

---

[52] Walpole to Henry Seymour Conway, 20 July 1744. The original of this letter is missing. I have taken the liberty of substituting "anyone" for "anything" in the penultimate sentence.

[53] *Dictionary of National Biography, s.v.* Henry Conway.

[54] Walpole's tireless dedication to his welfare received one severe check, as we shall see later, but Conway remained closer to him than any other man.

against him for some reason or other, but we have a pleasant glimpse of her and him earlier. On the night of her return from an extended trip abroad she went first to her parents' house hoping to find them or "dear Mr. Walpole alone, sitting by the fire, as I often have [found him] waiting their arrival." Nobody was at home, and so she went on to her uncle Lord Frederick Campbell's where they all were. "At past ten Mrs. Damer was announced!" Walpole reported. "Her parents ran down into the hall and I scrambled down some of the stairs."[55] Mrs. Damer saw him at the top of the stairs. "He seemed," she wrote Mary Berry, "and is as well as ever; *I* perceive no difference, not thinner, less lively, or less all that you left him, or all that you can wish."[56] When Conway died, Walpole made Mrs. Damer his residuary legatee and executrix. He also left her the life-tenancy of Strawberry Hill, £2,000 a year to maintain it, and £8,000 in cash. In addition, he insisted that she was one of the greatest sculptors that had ever lived. He made a list of her works, some forty of them, ranging in subject from an osprey in terra cotta "taken in a rage" to George III in stone, eight feet, three inches tall.[57] Her attitude towards Walpole at the end of his life may be judged by what she wrote to Mary Berry on his recovering from an illness: "I am sure, when I think of *what* his dinners are, and *how* he eats them, I wonder he and his cat are not sick together every day for their dessert."[58] In the end she destroyed all his letters to her. No other correspondence, I think, would have shown him in a better light.

He never regretted that he did not marry. Throughout his life he liked young women if they were pretty, well-read, and amusing, but he never seriously considered making one of them his wife. The arch references to the beautiful Mme Grifoni in his correspondence with Sir Horace Mann hint that she was his mistress while he was at Florence, a pos-

[55] Walpole to Mary Berry, 12 May 1791.
[56] Yale Walpole, 11. 265, n. 32.
[57] I am indebted for this precise dimension to Sir James Fergusson, Bt., and Mr. John Imrie, Keeper and Assistant Keeper of the Scottish Record Office and General Register, Edinburgh, where the statue now stands. The crown and scepter are of "gilt metal."
[58] Mrs. Damer to Mary Berry, 8 Oct. 1795, Yale Walpole, 12. 171.

sibility strengthened by one of his juvenile verses and the presence of her portrait in his bedroom at Strawberry Hill. Lord Edgcumbe thought that when his mistress left him she had passed into Walpole's keeping[59] and made him trustee for her successor because, he said, Walpole had "more feeling" and had given better advice about mistresses than the rest of his acquaintance. However, as Walpole wrote to Mann at the age of thirty-two, he lay alone.[60] Years later when Chatterton linked his name with Kitty Clive, the actress, in some verses, Walpole noted in his copy of them that he had given her a house near Strawberry Hill, and that "on this foundation she was represented as his mistress, though they were both between fifty and sixty."[61]

The present age wants to know what evidence there may be of homosexuality in the subjects of biography. The modern reader whose suspicions are easily aroused may misinterpret a few of Walpole's early letters and those of his friends, not realizing that eighteenth-century men expressed themselves and acted with what seems to us today unmanly abandon: close friends kissed each other on both cheeks when they met after an absence; they shed tears much more readily than we do today. A suspicious modern reader may believe that some of Walpole's youthful letters, especially those to Lord Lincoln and Conway, are all the proof of "overt behavior" that is needed; but a handful of letters written in extravagant high spirits in the manner of the time are not proof of it, and none has come to light. The verse written by a friend at Cambridge, who described him as "untossed by passion," is a description that fits him throughout his life if one means, as the writer did mean, sexual passion.

Although in his last years he was crippled by the gout that came more and more often, he pointed out cheerfully that he still had his sight, hearing, and teeth. He never "gave up." He made new friends as the old ones died one by one. Visitors continued to stream to Strawberry Hill. When the gout was very bad he was carried from room to room by two

---

[59] Edgcumbe to Walpole, 10 Aug. 1744.
[60] Walpole to Mann, 11 March 1750.
[61] Yale Walpole, 16. 345–46.

footmen who dumped him down on a sofa with his prints and books and newspapers. Around his neck was a whistle that he worked up to his lips when he wanted something and that he then blew with vigor.

The women of his family did not leave him by himself for long. Hovering about were Lady Mary Churchill and the Duchess of Gloucester, both jealous of Mrs. Damer, the Berrys, and each other. The recurring sessions with his lawyer must have made them uneasy, yet they had no cause for worry as it turned out. Mrs. Damer complained of his "grand fusses," but no doubt he rather enjoyed them, since they gave him a sense of power and importance. Until the very end, when he imagined that he had been abandoned by those he loved best, he busied himself with his birds and plants and prints and the notebooks in which he continued to enter the "scraps" that he hoped would inform and amuse us today.

II

FRIENDS

ONE day in 1759, Lady Sarah Lennox had her head dressed in a *toupet retapé* with powder, put on her blue feather pompons, her diamond cross, her *coque de perle* earrings, her black silk gown and petticoat, her blond ruffles, white shoes, and blue bugles, and so dressed walked down the steps of Richmond House into her chair and jogged away to St. James's Palace. There she was singled out by George II and the future George III, who was in love with her. She found him and his grandfather ridiculous and left as soon as she could for Lady Hervey's, where she would see Horace Walpole. "Mr. Walpole," she reported, "was charming. In short, I am quite in love with him, for I like no place where he is not, and he diverts me vastly."[1] Lady Sarah was fifteen at the time, Walpole forty-two. Twenty-six years later another beautiful young woman, Mary Hamilton, wrote to her fiancé how Mr. Walpole carried her to an evening party where Mrs. Garrick and Hannah More were present, and where they were all "mighty agreeable." Then, Miss Hamilton said, "At half past ten Mr. Walpole brought me home. Poor Miss More, she certainly will not sleep tonight; before we parted she looked as yellow as saffron, whilst I with an air of triumph treated her with the disdain of a favored rival! Do you not think Mr. Walpole is a happy man to have *two* such *paragons* of perfection in love with him!"[2]

---

[1] *Correspondence of Emily, Duchess of Leinster,* ed. Brian Fitzgerald (Dublin, 1953), II, 75–77.

[2] *Mary Hamilton,* ed. Elizabeth and Florence Anson (1925), pp. 272–73.

Horace Walpole

Walpole had an immense number of friends all his life. Some of them are widely remembered today: Gray, Mme du Deffand, Hannah More; others are familiar to the Common Reader who knows the eighteenth century: George Selwyn, Henry Conway, Henry Fox, William Mason, Lady Mary Coke, Mary Berry. Our knowledge of still others is owing largely to Walpole's letters: such people as George Montagu and Lady Ossory. It is easy to see why they were fond of him: he was entertaining, and he practiced what he called "the delicacies and attentions of friendship."[3] These might be sending a pair of English scissors to Paris or a watch to Florence, or printing complimentary verses to visitors at Strawberry Hill. He once said, "I have passed my life in studying the service of others and have heaped endless favors."[4] He liked finding houses for his friends to rent, matching their broken tea cups, and sending them presents.

His concern for the comfort and pleasure of others came from his heart and mind: he was not deeply moved physically by women or men. They had to be amusing, good listeners, well-read, well-mannered, and well-dressed. His daily acts of friendship were inspired as much by his longing for occasional companionship with congenial people as by innate goodness. Friendship was not the first concern of his life; he did not quite love his neighbor as himself; yet his self-love did not prevent his being a friend of exceptional intensity and constancy. Like most eighteenth-century Englishmen, he could pour out his feelings. When he heard from Lady Ossory of a serious illness in her family, he wrote to her that it was "One of those solemn moments in which nothing is left to us but resignation and silence. . . . Life seems to me as if we were dancing on a sunny plain on the edge of a gloomy forest where we pass in a moment from glare to gloom and darkness. . . . I know not what comfort to give you, Madam. There is none for real grief, but the two that were providentially given to us in spite of ourselves, Hope and Time."[5]

Walpole's gift for friendship became evident early. His success at

---

[3] Walpole to Mann, 13 April 1762.
[4] Ibid., 21 Jan. 1767.
[5] Walpole to Lady Ossory, 12 July 1778.

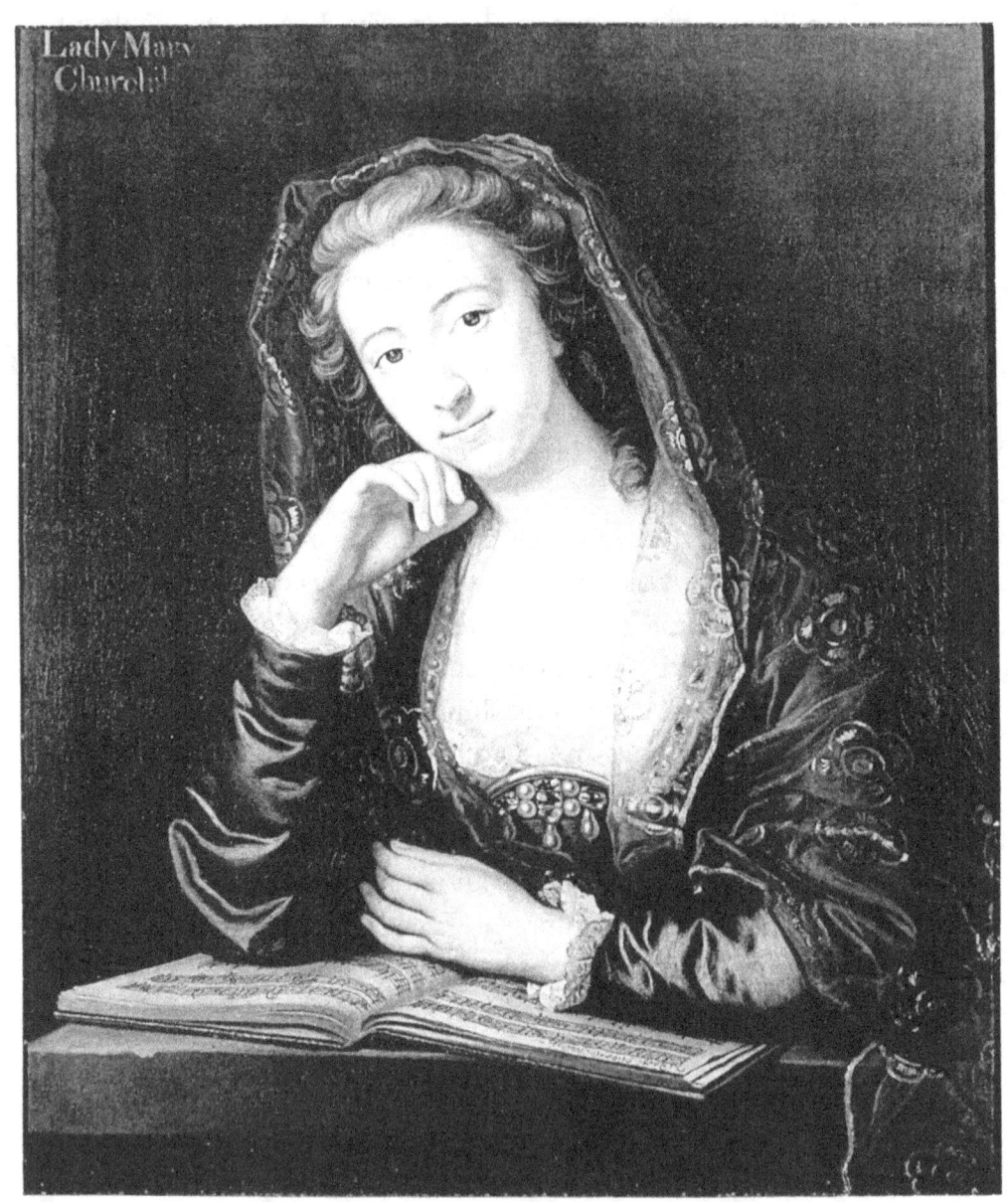

11. LADY MARY CHURCHILL, *by J. G. Eccardt,* ca. 1752

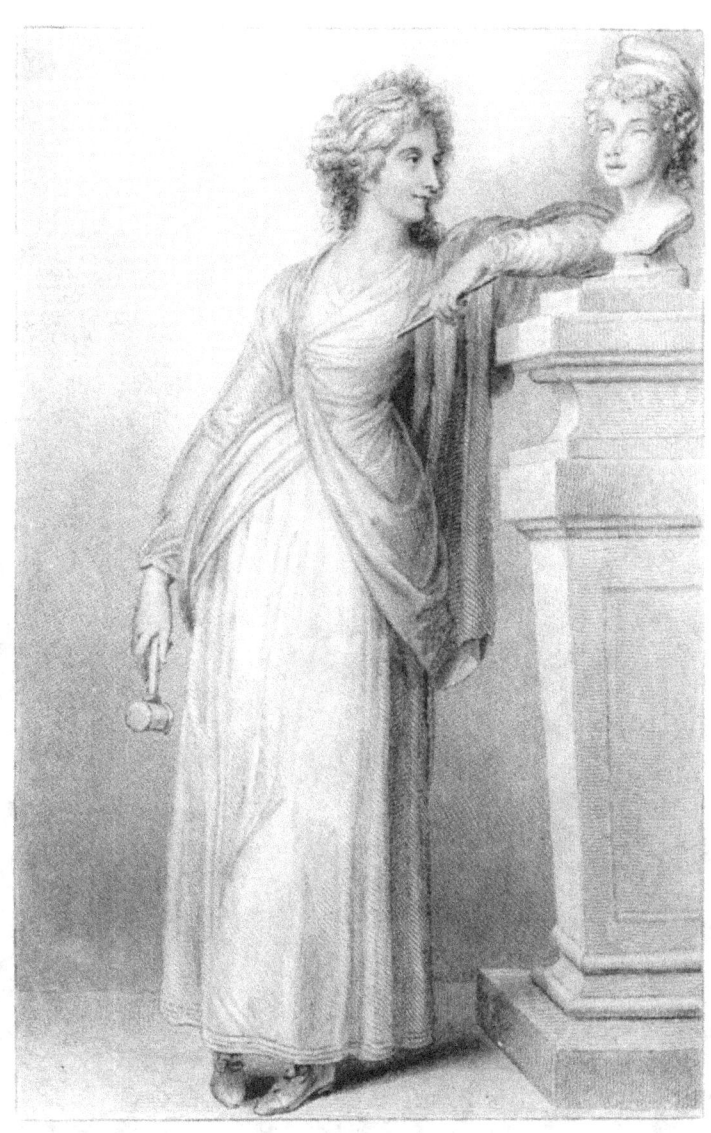

12. MRS. ANNE SEYMOUR CONWAY DAMER,
by Richard Cosway, ca. 1788

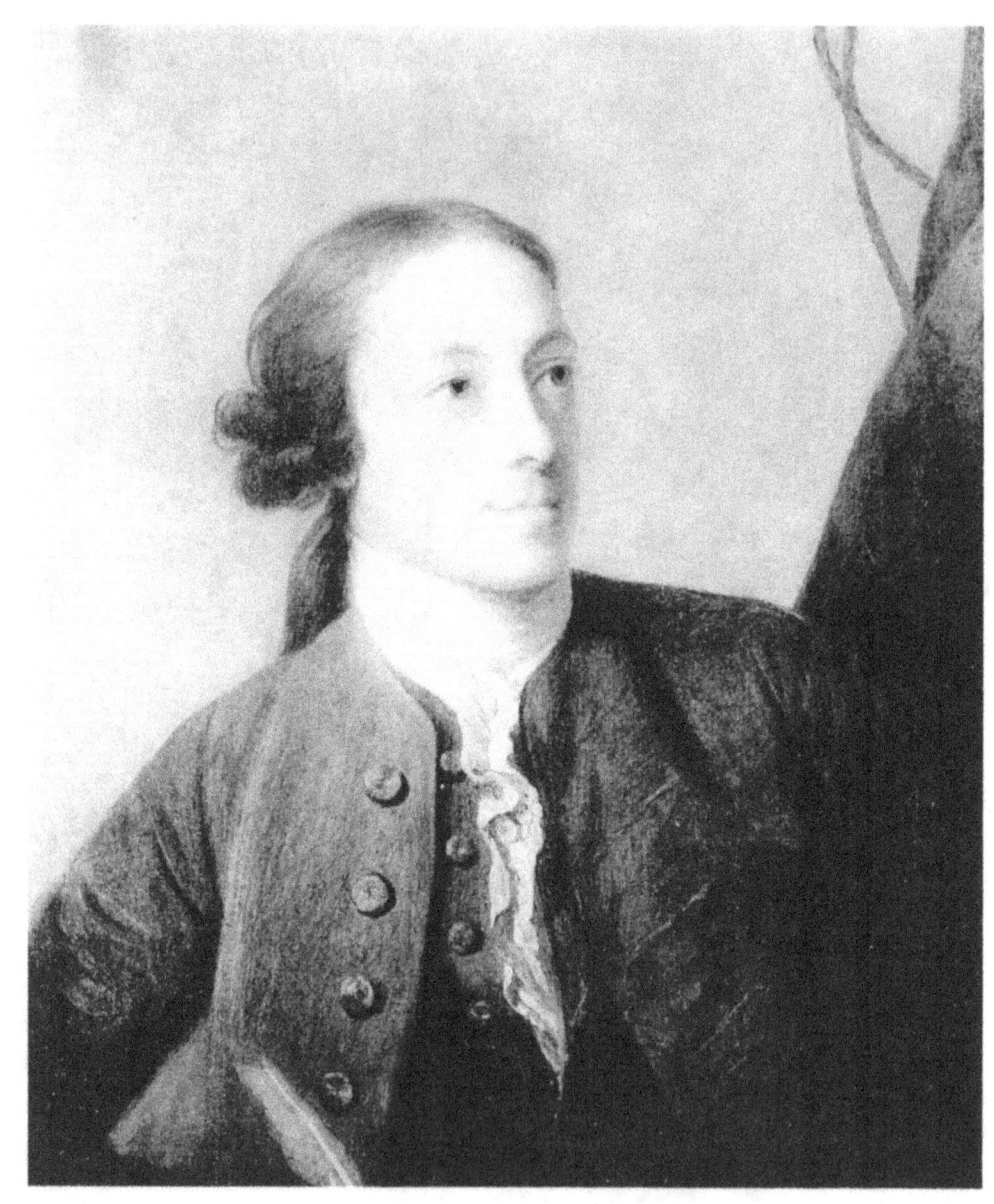

13. Horace Walpole, *by Allan Ramsay,* 1758

Friends

Eton was not because his father was prime minister, or because he was good at sports or bossing people about (which he was not), but because he loved the life there; not cricket, not fighting with bargemen, not clubbing a ram to death, but reading, building up his own library, making friends, and the place itself. While at home, he had been ignored by his father, disliked by his brothers, and spoiled by his mother; at Eton, he was treated as a human being, and his affections flowed out uninhibited.

Our knowledge of many of these early friends depends largely upon the survival of their correspondence with him. We do not have the letters that he exchanged with several of them, such as "Gilly" Williams. The loss of the "Gilly" Williams correspondence is particularly regrettable because Williams throws more light on Walpole (in his letters to Selwyn) than all the rest of Walpole's English friends put together. He was a member, with Selwyn and Dick Edgcumbe, of the "Out of Town Party" that spent Christmas and Easter at Strawberry Hill for many years. It was Williams who said, "I can figure no being happier than Horry. *Monstrari digito praetereuntium* ["to be pointed out by the finger of those passing by"] has been his whole aim. For this he has wrote, printed, and built."[6] Walpole's letters to Williams may yet emerge from a country house or be discovered in a public library. When, as, and if they turn up, we can be certain that they will be busy, affectionate, and amusing. We do have hundreds of such letters to other Eton contemporaries: Henry Conway, Lord Hertford, George Selwyn, George Montagu, and William Cole.

Selwyn was a droll character whose *bons mots* and practical jokes were laughed at in society for fifty years and whose eccentricities included a passion for going to executions and caring for the Duke of Queensberry's illegitimate daughter, whom he adopted. He seems to have kept everything that came to him through the post, including tradesmen's bills. It is possible that Walpole knew this and that it helped him to overlook Selwyn's maddening casualness, because letters that are kept may reach future historians.

---

[6] *George Selwyn and His Contemporaries,* ed. John Heneage Jesse (1843), I, 310.

Horace Walpole

George Montagu was another undependable bachelor. He buried himself in Northamptonshire, drank a great deal of port, and dozed away his life by the fire, his hands in "a decent, smallish, muff." When he ventured up to London, as often as not he missed his friend in spite of weeks of planning to meet. Walpole bore with him for thirty years and more until Montagu became so apathetic and humorsome that although he kept Walpole's letters in a box and talked of the treasure that they would be "a hundred years hence to a Mme Sévigné of the House of Montagu,"[7] he no longer answered them. The correspondence faded away, which is a pity, because Montagu's letters are occasionally surprisingly good, and he spurred Walpole on to excel them.

With Cole there was no question of letters going unanswered. He became a clergyman who enjoyed antiquarian research more than his parochial duties. His extracts from parish registers, particularly of Cambridgeshire, and his copies of deeds, charts of pedigrees, and heraldic drawings fill one hundred and fourteen folio notebooks, which he left to the British Museum. These he called his only delight, his wife and children. He also transcribed his correspondence with Walpole, not hesitating to touch up the copies of his own letters to make them appear more spirited and familiar than the letters that went through the post. When the first two volumes of *Anecdotes of Painting in England* appeared, he wrote Walpole an immensely long letter. He had found the book "a continual feast from one end to the other," adding, however —with the voice of the scholar speaking through eternity—"I met with two or three errata or false printings, which I hope you will excuse me for pointing out." He also volunteered "two or three trifling observations of another sort."[8] These continued for pages: notes on Lady Danvers's tomb at Stowe Nine Churches, on a brass at Gothurst of Lady Venetia Digby with a long inscription on the pediment that Cole would copy out, and much, much more besides. With this promising start the two friends went on writing to each other regularly until Cole died twenty years later. Walpole would tell him about his discoveries of early Wal-

---

[7] Montagu to Walpole, 3 Feb. 1760.
[8] Cole to Walpole, 16 May 1762.

polian baronies in fee and alliances that mounted to royalty itself, and he would savor Cole's envy of such proofs of ancestry, not knowing that privately Cole qualified his enthusiasm for them. "Mr. Walpole," Cole confided to his notebook, "is one of the best writers, an admirable poet, one of the most lively, ingenious, and witty persons of the age; but a great share of vanity, eagerness of adulation, as Mr. Gray observed to me, a violence and warmth in party matters, and lately even to enthusiasm, abates, and takes off from, many of his shining qualities."[9] That is, they occasionally strayed upon controversial ground (Cole was a High Church Tory), but Walpole kept his temper and led the way to safety, back to the fifteenth century and the gout to which Cole was also a martyr. "It is a misfortune," Cole told him, "to have so much sensibility in one's nature as you are endued with: sufficient are one's own distresses without the additional encumbrance of those of one's friends."[10] Among Walpole's dozens of antiquarian correspondents Cole was easily first.

More has been written about the little club that Walpole formed at Eton with Thomas Gray, Richard West, and Thomas Ashton than about any other eighteenth-century schoolboy association. They called themselves the Quadruple Alliance. To increase their intimacy they assumed secret names, Celadon, Orozmades, Favonius, Almanzor. West was the most beloved of the four and was believed to have the greatest promise as a poet, Gray was the most learned, Ashton the most self-seeking, Walpole the most volatile. Those who think of the eighteenth century as being rigidly classbound should note that Gray was the son of a scrivener, West the son of an Irish Lord Chancellor, and Ashton the son of a schoolmaster. The word "snob" was not yet invented in either of its senses, of "one who meanly or vulgarly admires and seeks to imitate or associate with, those of superior rank or wealth," or of one who being possessed of superior wealth, position, or brains, looks down on those less favored in these respects. The Quadruple Alliance accepted the prerogatives of wealth and rank. We sense in Ashton a

---

[9] Yale Walpole, 2. 372. Walpole was aware of his "eagerness of adulation": "Pride, which I have, likes homage" (to Mann, 21 Jan. 1767).
[10] Cole to Walpole, 28 July 1776.

pioneer of the snob's ancestor, the toad-eater,[11] but to call Walpole a snob for regarding Gray and Ashton as his social inferiors is to impose upon the eighteenth century an epithet that it would not have understood.

The four read the Latin classics, French novels, and fairy tales, and English authors from Spenser to Pope, with particular affection for the recent and contemporary men—Congreve, Vanbrugh, Garth, and Addison. When they finished the school exercises of turning Virgil and Statius into English and Dryden and Pope into Latin, they tossed off imitations from Propertius and Martial, Passerat and St. Gelais, or a tragedy about Pausanias. Eighteenth-century Etonians were "the mob of gentlemen who write with ease"—but the poetical flights of the Quadruple Alliance were more ambitious and sustained than those of their contemporaries and were based upon wider reading and romantic visions. "Wild wit, invention ever new," Gray was to write of this time, and for Walpole also thoughts of Eton continued "To breathe a second spring."

West, alone of the Quadruple Alliance, went to Oxford, where Walpole visited him and wrote such a panegyric on its charms that "all the great heads round the theatre shouted for joy."[12] West, who died at an early age, is remembered only for his correspondence with his three closest friends and Gray's sonnet to him, "In vain to me the smiling mornings shine." Gray and Ashton preceded Walpole to Cambridge, where he spent comparatively little time, preferring, as we have seen, to be with his mother in London. He seems to have met no undergraduates who were not Etonians, and such lectures as he attended—civil law, mathematics, anatomy—meant little or nothing to him. He did learn Italian—he had learned French at Eton—and that was to prove useful to him on the Grand Tour. King's College Chapel left a lasting impression on him, and so did the teaching of Conyers Middleton, the University Librarian, who was a controversial deist and an ardent collector of classical antiquities that he subsequently sold to Walpole. Early in his Cambridge career Walpole used to go with Ashton to pray with the prisoners

---

[11] Walpole's use of this meaning of the term is the earliest recorded in the *OED*.
[12] Richard West to Walpole, 1 June 1736.

Friends

in the jail, but Middleton stopped all that so effectively that Walpole's religious life withered away and never revived.

Gray could hardly wait for Walpole to get to Cambridge. "Be thou unto me," he wrote, "as Mohammed to Ajesha, as the bowers of Admoim to those whom the sun hath overtaken, or as the costly sherbets of Stamboul to the thirsty."[18] He was the obvious person for Walpole to take with him on the Grand Tour.

They set out in 1739 (neither bothering to take a degree) and were gone over two years. It took them eight and a half months to get from Paris to Florence, where they spent over a year with a long side trip to Rome and Naples. In Florence they stayed with Horace Mann, the English Resident, who was a distant Walpole cousin and whose family owed their prosperity to Sir Robert. Mann laid himself out to make his amusing young kinsman's stay as agreeable as possible, which was not difficult in the Italy of Panini, Guardi, and Canaletto.

Walpole and Gray quarreled, of course. How many friendships can survive two years of travel at any age? We don't know what caused the final blow-up, yet the wonder is not that they came home by separate routes, but that they endured each other as long as they did. The younger of the two was paying all the bills and making all the decisions. As the son of the most powerful man in England he received marked attentions wherever he went, and he returned them with gaiety and grace. In his wake came Gray, ill at ease, touchy, plain, and shy. He was more like a traveling tutor than a traveling companion. While Walpole was enjoying "all the beauties, all the jewels, and all the sugar-plums" of wherever they were, Gray was grimly visiting churches or sitting at home writing to his mother. I suspect that the lines in his "Eton Ode,"

And hard Unkindness' alter'd eye,
That mocks the tear it forc'd to flow,

is a scar left by Walpole, but Walpole on his side was not without complaint. They had not got to Calais before Gray was dissatisfied. "I was too

---

[18] Gray to Walpole, 6 Jan. 1735.

29

young," Walpole said years later, "too fond of my own diversions, nay, I do not doubt, too much intoxicated by indulgence, vanity, and the insolence of my situation, as a prime minister's son, not to have been inattentive and insensible to the feelings of one I thought below me; of one, I blush to say it, that I knew was obliged to me."[14] He insisted that he, as the survivor, should take the blame for their quarrel at Reggio.

The immediate result of it was that Walpole fell ill "of a kind of quinsy" and nearly died. Gray had gone on to Venice, and Walpole was left alone with his servants, who did nothing to help him. Had not Lord Lincoln and Joseph Spence happened by and got a doctor from Florence, Spence wrote, "one of the best-natured and most sensible young gentlemen that England affords would in all probability have been now under the cold earth."[15] Walpole came home with Lincoln and Spence, after arranging secretly for Gray to have money regularly so that he should not be stranded.

Much more has been made of this youthful quarrel than of the subsequent reconciliation, which took place in a few years. Gray described the reunion. "He came to meet me, kissed me on both sides with all the ease of one who receives an acquaintance just come out of the country, squatted me into a fauteuil, begun to talk of the Town and this and that and t'other, and continued with little interruption for three hours . . . but treated [me] with wondrous good breeding."[16] This went on for four days and opened the way to a new and sounder friendship that lasted unbroken until Gray's death. They visited each other at Cambridge and Strawberry Hill, where Gray delighted in the lilacs and nightingales and Gothicism. He helped Walpole with many of his antiquarian projects by advising and criticizing, transcribing manuscripts, and reading proof, which last chore he said Walpole knew that he could not do: Gray never became, Walpole admitted, "a flatterer to self-love." Wal-

---

[14] Walpole to Mason, 2 March 1773.

[15] Spence to his mother, 29 May 1741 (Yale Walpole, 13. 10, n. 62 ad fin.).

[16] Gray to Wharton, Nov. 1745 (*Correspondence of Thomas Gray*, ed. Paget Toynbee and Leonard Whibley [Oxford, 1935], I, 226).

Friends

pole, on his side, was responsible for the printing of nearly all of Gray's poems, which he acclaimed with the Walpolian drums and trumpets sounding fortissimo. It has been said, apropos of his erratic judgment of contemporaries, that his enthusiasm for Gray's poetry was owing to friendship rather than to critical insight, and I think that there is a grain of truth in the charge. Walpole really did believe that Gray's poetry was "superlative," but had Gray been a Tory or a member of Dr. Johnson's circle, we can be quite certain that instead of printing "The Bard" and "The Progress of Poesy" Walpole would have ridiculed them. People tended to be black or white with him, and Gray, as an old friend, was white, whatever may have happened in the inn at Reggio. Each criticized the other to friends, yet when Gray heard the false report that Walpole had had a stroke he was deeply stirred, and when Walpole heard of Gray's death he started up from his chair as if he had received a bodily blow.[17] Gray's portrait was one of the first that Walpole commissioned Eccardt to paint for Strawberry Hill. It hangs now in the National Portrait Gallery beside Eccardt's portrait of his traveling companion, and that is as it should be.

After Walpole's return home, Ashton lived with him for the next several years. He had gone into orders, his success as a preacher was immediate, a brilliant career in the Church seemed assured, but he began showing signs of independence of his friend and benefactor. Gray sensed trouble between them and counseled "a timely *éclaircissement,* a full and precise one without witnesses or mediators, and without reserving any one disagreeable circumstance for the mind to brood upon in silence."[18] We do not know whether this admirable course was followed, but we do know that Ashton's zeal for self-advancement led him three years later to attack Conyers Middleton, and that that was fatal so far as his host went. "I believe," Walpole wrote to Mann in his most imperious style, "you have often heard me mention a Mr. Ashton, a clergyman, who, in one word, has great preferments, and owes everything upon earth to me. I have long had reason to complain of his behavior; in short, my father is

[17] Walpole to Cole, 12 Aug. 1771, and to Conway, 11 Aug. 1771.
[18] Gray to Walpole [? 10 Nov. 1747].

31

dead, and I can make no bishops. He has at last quite thrown off the mask, and . . . against my will, has written against my friend Dr. Middleton. . . . I have forbid him my house."[19] A few months later we learn that Ashton had struck up an intimacy with Edward Walpole and was trying to foment a new quarrel between him and Horace.[20] The rest is silence, except for the mention thirteen years later that Ashton had had a stroke of apoplexy while preaching in the chapel at Eton. Then the silence enveloped him again, but his portrait was left hanging at Strawberry Hill in its master's bedroom, along with Middleton, Mme Grifoni, John Chute, and Patapan, "a Roman dog"—all early intimates.

The friendships that Walpole formed at Florence with Horace Mann and John Chute lasted as long as they lived. Mann was a good diplomat in spite of his old-womanish flutter. Although humanly eager for advancement and honors, he was courageous in his country's interest and firm on occasion. His entertainment of visiting Englishmen and foreigners left him with little money, but secured him a reputation for elegance and hospitality that was noted in many contemporary journals, including Casanova's. There is no sign of his inner uncertainties in the conversation pieces that Thomas Patch painted of the English colony at Florence. However many figures there may be in the picture or of what rank, Mann is conspicuous: small, wrinkled, amiable, presiding over the assemblage of visiting admirals, generals, and Grand Tourists who made his house their headquarters.

After Walpole left Florence he and Mann never met again, but they exchanged nearly eighteen hundred letters before Mann died forty-five years later. Although this longest and most famous of Walpole's correspondences soon turned into an informal history of the time, the amenities of friendship were not relaxed. Mann laid himself out for Walpole's friends who went to Florence and sent curious and expensive presents to Strawberry Hill; Walpole was tireless in praising Mann to his superiors in England and helped him to get a baronetcy, a promotion in diplomatic rank, and the red riband of the Bath, this last after years

[19] Walpole to Mann, 25 July 1750.
[20] Ibid., 22 Dec. 1750.

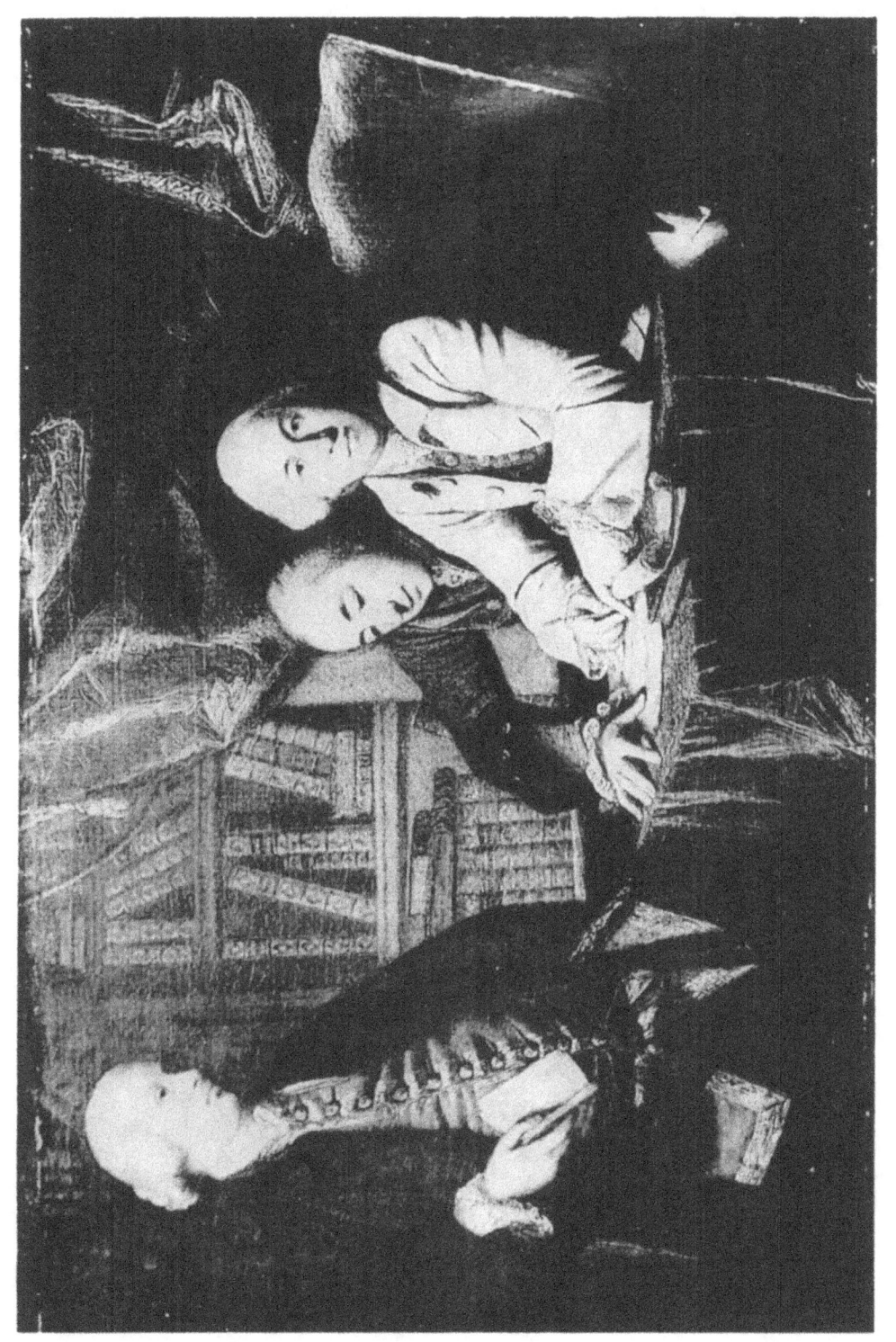

14. "THE OUT OF TOWN PARTY," *by Reynolds, 1761*

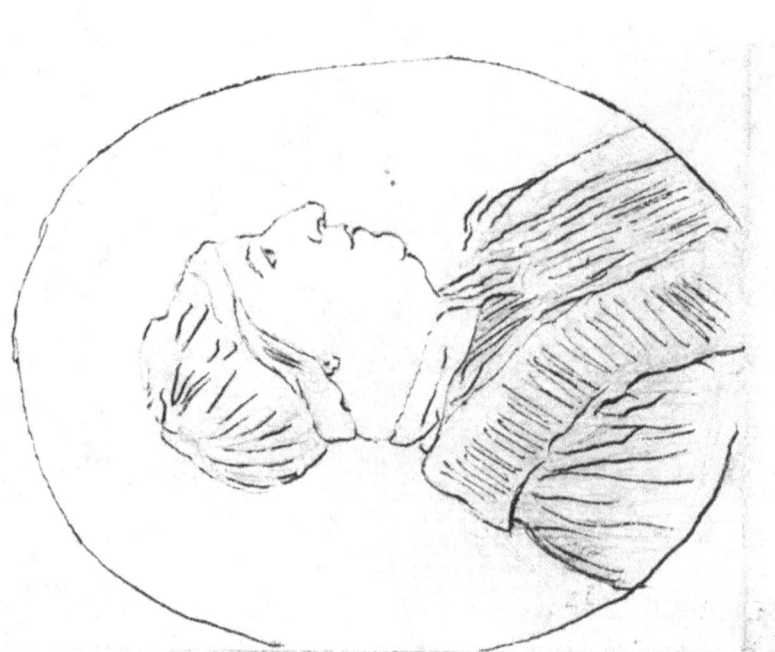

Wm Cole de Milton
juxta Cantab rigiam,
A: M: Vicarius de
Burnham juxta Win-
desoriam 1775

Johan Gooch Arm: Ædis
Christi apud Oxon Filius
Dñi Thomæ Gooch Baro-
netti, fecit 1771.

15. WILLIAM COLE

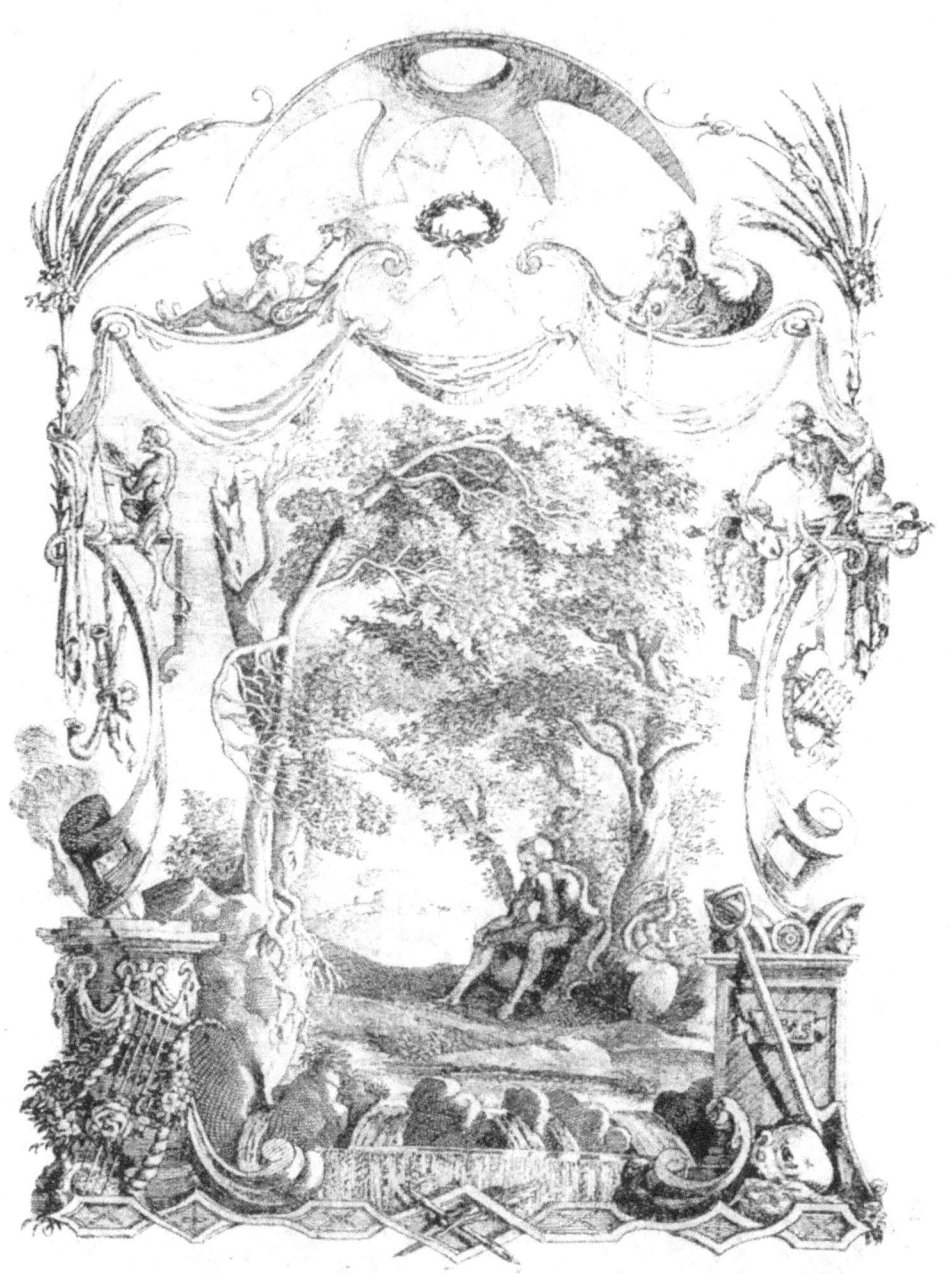

16. RICHARD BENTLEY'S FRONTISPIECE FOR GRAY'S POEMS, 1753

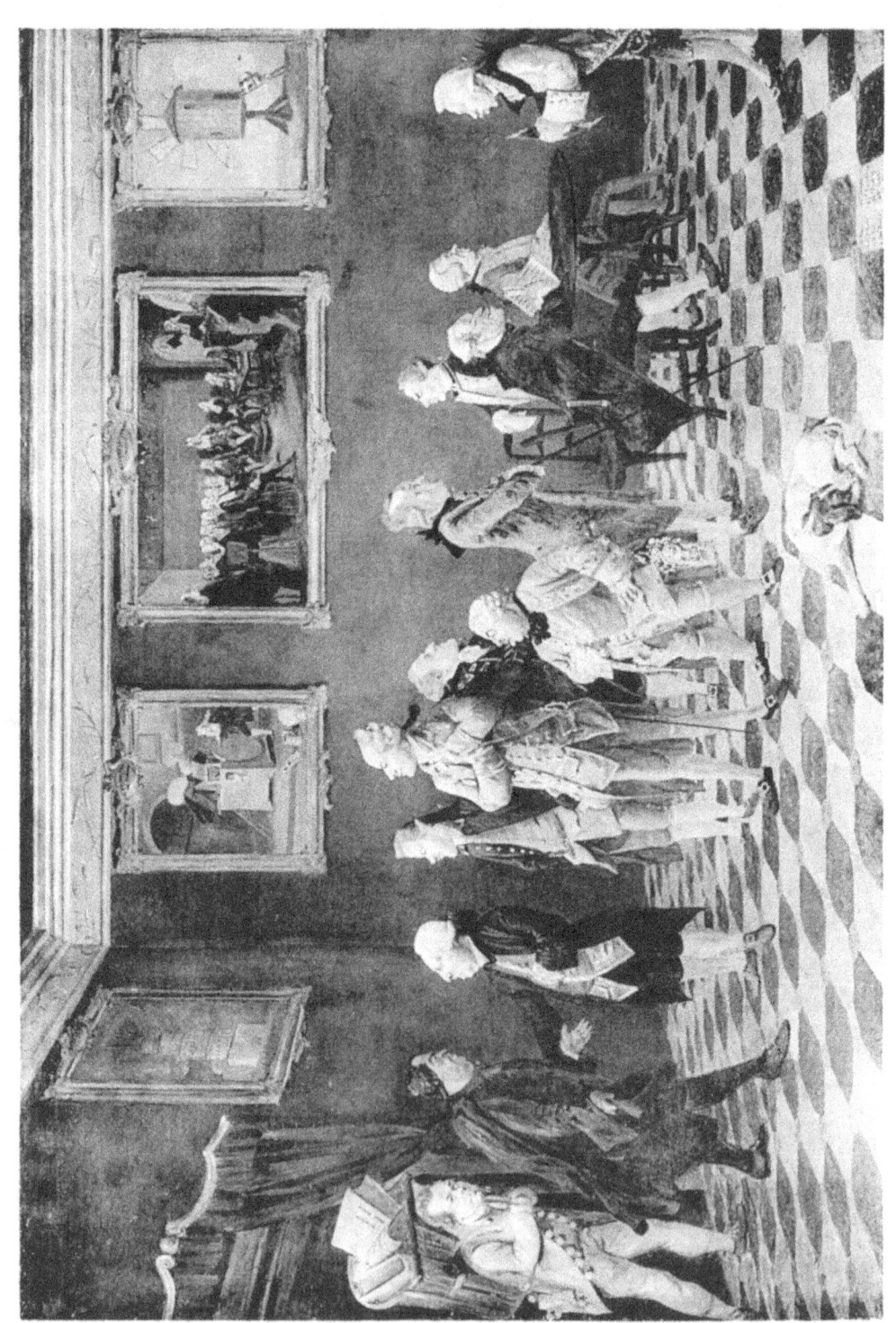

17. "A Rehearsal at Sir Horace Mann's," *by Thomas Patch, 1765*

of struggle and disappointment. Mann sent his portrait by Astley to Strawberry Hill; Walpole, on the other hand, returned only McArdell's print of his portrait by Reynolds.

When Walpole met Mann and Chute he was not yet on easy outward terms with his father and he unconsciously sought the guidance of congenial older men. Mann was eleven years older, Chute sixteen. Chute was a wit, a connoisseur, and a dabbler in medievalism. An unknown artist shows him wearing a wig with long curls over the ears and holding eye-glasses in an aggressively affected manner. He encouraged Walpole's aesthetic and antiquarian tastes, his tendency to be witty at the expense of others, and his independence. When Chute inherited The Vyne in Hampshire he was near enough to Twickenham to permit frequent visits back and forth, in spite of his violent attacks of gout; in fact, Walpole saw him more often than any man and turned to him in every difficulty. His designs for Strawberry Hill show that Walpole was not exaggerating when he called Chute his "oracle in taste" and "the genius that presided over poor Strawberry."[21] It was Chute who produced the sixteen-year-old Miss Nicoll with the intention of securing her fortune for Lord Orford. He started off that project well by abducting her from her guardians, but when things began going wrong he became hysterical and threatened her in a scene that she soberly recorded.[22] His final effort to retrieve the situation was to write and print some obscene verses that he sent anonymously to her and her guardians. It is not strange that Old Horace Walpole regarded Chute as young Horace's evil genius, but the younger man was not subservient to him, nor to anyone else: the moment that he was threatened by domination he rebelled. When he congratulated Chute on inheriting his house and fortune he added, "if I should grow to love you less, you will not be surprised—you know the partiality I have to the afflicted, the disgraced, and the oppressed, and must recollect how many titles to my esteem you will lose, when you are rich Chute of The Vyne, when you are courted by chancellors of the exchequer for your interest in Hampshire; by a thousand [nephews] for your estate, and

---

[21] Ibid., 27 May 1776.
[22] Yale Walpole, 14. 218–20.

by my Lady Brown for her daughter."[23] Still I do believe that Walpole carried his identification with Chute to the point of taking on his gout when his subconscious selected an illness that would enable him to avoid unpleasant duties, such as attendance at the House of Commons.[24]

The man who has been given more credit for the designing of Strawberry Hill is Richard Bentley, son of the great Master of Trinity. What gave him his special niche at Strawberry Hill was Walpole's belief that he "alone of all mankind could unite the grace of Grecian architecture and the irregular lightness and solemnity of Gothic."[25] He was, with Chute and Walpole, a member of what they called "The Committee" on the construction of the house and the chief draftsman of it, but he acted under his colleagues' direction. More than once his sketches were discarded for Chute's. What were his own invention were his rococo designs for an edition of Gray's poems, which Walpole paid for and which made Bentley a pioneer of English book illustration. Walpole put up with his laziness and imprudence for ten years in the hope of extracting from him the immortal work that he believed Bentley could produce. He pleaded, flattered, and scolded: "Is not it provoking," he asked, "that, with the best parts in the world, you should have so gentle a portion of common sense?"[26] Walpole paid him well for his work on two of the Strawberry Hill Press books, but it was no use: Bentley had to fly to Jersey to escape his creditors and his wife, whom Walpole called "Hecate" and "Mrs. Tisiphone." On his return Bentley wished to bring her to Strawberry Hill, and that was the end. He later told Cole that "whim, caprice, and pride were too predominant" in Walpole, but that he had "many amiable virtues and qualities."[27] These included Walpole's

---

[23] Walpole to Chute, 21 May 1754.

[24] After his first attack Walpole wrote, "I would fain have persuaded myself that it was a sprain; and then, that it was only the gout come to look for Mr. Chute at Strawberry Hill . . . I still know where to look for it whenever I have an occasion for a political illness" (Walpole to Bentley, 16 Nov. 1755).

[25] Walpole to Mann, 24 Oct. 1758.

[26] Walpole to Bentley, 20 Nov. 1754.

[27] John Nichols, *Illustrations of the Literary History of the Eighteenth Century,* VIII (1858), 573.

Friends

securing a sinecure for him in the Customs worth £100 a year, after their break.[28]

Among the generalizations that have been made about Walpole none is more untrue than that he quarreled with all his friends. He could be bitter about them when he felt that they had thrown him over. "Falsehood, interest, and ingratitude, the attendants of friendship, are familiar to me," he wrote from Paris in 1765,[29] whither he had escaped after the failure of his political allies, above all Conway, to offer him a post in the Rockingham government that he had helped to create. He told "Fish" Craufurd, who first met him then and who was captivated by him, as members of the younger generation so often were, that there must be no talk of friendship between them. "My heart," Walpole wrote, "is not like yours, young, good, warm, sincere, and impatient to bestow itself. Mine is worn with the baseness, treachery, and mercenariness I have met with. It is suspicious, doubtful, and cooled . . ."[30] But Mme du Deffand knew better. She ended her "portrait" of him: "You have friends, you are entirely devoted to them, their interests are yours, and all your talk and all your reasoning against friendship do not persuade that you are not the man in the world who is most capable of it."[31]

Few Englishmen were ever launched into French society with more éclat. He arrived with introductions from Lady Hervey, George Selwyn, and Miss Anne Pitt; the Duc de Nivernois and the Comte de Guerchy, both of whom had been ambassadors in London, smoothed his way; the Duke of Richmond, a family connection to whom he was devoted, was about to take Lord Hertford's place as ambassador in Paris. Walpole kept a journal of this and his four subsequent visits in which he put down the names of everyone who called on him, and upon whom he called, whom he met at dinner and supper, and where he met them. It must have taken a good deal of time after he got back to his rooms in the rue du Colombier to recall all those names and to write them down in his

[28] Walpole to Mann, 6 Feb. 1777.
[29] Ibid., 13 Nov. 1765.
[30] Walpole to John "Fish" Craufurd, 6 March 1766.
[31] Yale Walpole, 8. 73.

35

beautiful hand, but he was good at names, which was one reason why he was so popular. Even a severe attack of gout did not interrupt his career. Visitors crowded to his bedside: Nivernais, Guerchy, Baron d'Holbach, Mme Geoffrin, Hume, Wilkes, and many more. Paris was filthy; the *philosophes* were overbearing, tiresome, and underbred and talked irreligion even in the presence of servants (which Walpole said he would not have suffered in his own house, even on the Old Testament, if a single footman was present); the hours were topsy-turvy; the Parisians' "boasted knowledge of society" was reduced to discussing suppers and illnesses, the scatological details of which were fully described at the dinner table; yet even so, Paris was preferable to the House of Commons. In Paris he did not have to try to help anybody or improve anything; the *anglomanie* was at its height; the French were terrified of Pitt; the shops were intoxicating. He rolled about in a chariot decorated with Cupids, and looked, he said, like the grandfather of Adonis.

He reported his brilliant progress in letter after letter to England and was then tormented by the fear that he had been fatuous. He dreaded being ridiculous, but he had to excel in whatever he did and to have it recognized that he did excel. Malice and wit were essential to success in what Mme du Deffand called "une société infernale." He was richly endowed with both, which were sharpened by the bitter and cynical state of his mind at the time. Yet even while he submitted to the pitiless routine of the place and the construction of clever remarks in a language that at first he found difficult, his charity and good nature rose up to oppose what he was doing. "My greatest ambition," he wrote home, "is not to grow cross, which is a spiteful way of communicating the misfortunes of age and illness to other people."[32] This generous impulse did not prevent him from trying to reach a commanding place in the infernal society; and great as his initial popularity was, it became even greater when he wrote a pretended letter from the King of Prussia to Rousseau in which the King offered Rousseau asylum to be as unhappy as he pleased. Copies of the letter were handed about Paris; Walpole himself sent several back to

---

[32] Walpole to Miss Anne Pitt, 4 Nov. 1765.

Friends

England, where one finally got into the *St. James's Chronicle* and helped to destroy the friendship between Rousseau and Hume, his English benefactor. Paris restored Walpole's confidence.

He found the women far superior to the men. Their salons were the meeting place of society. In the beginning he went most frequently to Mme Geoffrin's, but soon moved to her great enemy, Mme du Deffand's, whom he first described as "an old blind débauchée of wit."[33] She was sixty-eight when they met, twenty years his senior, a member of his mother's generation and so especially attractive to him. Forty years earlier she had been a mistress of the Regent Orléans, and that gave her an added bloom, even though the connection had lasted only two weeks. To her Walpole was a radiant newcomer who exorcised more successfully than anyone else the devil ennui that possessed her. Before long they were meeting every day. His delight in her company and his pride in having made a Platonic conquest of the wittiest woman in Paris fused with his indignation at the "barbarity and injustice" of those who ate her suppers when they could not go to a more fashionable house, who laughed at her, abused her, and tried to convert her nominal friends into enemies. That is, she was a fellow sufferer from the inhumanity of man.

When he returned to England they began the correspondence that went on until she died fourteen years later, some eight hundred and fifty very long letters on each side. He got her to return his letters, and presumably directed Mary Berry, his literary executrix, to make extracts from them as footnotes to a posthumous edition of Mme du Deffand's letters to him, after which Miss Berry was to destroy his side of the correspondence. His reputation as a person has suffered in consequence of our not knowing more of what he actually wrote; only seven of his letters have survived.[34] Mme du Deffand was emotional and demanding; she clamored on about love and coldness and flung herself into luxurious analyses of him and of herself, all of which he found embarrassing, especially when he learned that their letters were being opened at the post

---

[33] Walpole to Conway, 6 Oct. 1765.
[34] They are now at Farmington. Miss Berry printed extracts from ninety-three others.

office. He begged her to stick to proper names. She was hurt, angrily defended herself, and obeyed for a while. Then she burst out again in a fresh flood of emotion, and the pattern was repeated. We have both sides of the conversation for one month only,[35] but in it the cycle is complete, and it shows how exaggerated her reaction was to his mild expostulations, and how mistaken it is on the basis of her letters alone to condemn him as an unfeeling scold. He made four special trips to see and entertain her and to bring her what comfort and pleasure he could. When her income was cut he offered to make up the loss from his own pocket. Following an afternoon and evening of visiting and being visited she would drive him about the streets until daybreak to lessen the horror of returning alone to her modest apartment, where sleeplessness, boredom, and bitterness awaited her. She wanted to leave him all she had, but he would accept only her manuscripts[36] and her dog Tonton, who was not housebroken and who bit people. For good measure, she also had a gold snuffbox made for him with Tonton's portrait in wax on the cover, and this became one of the most treasured objects at Strawberry Hill.

She died in 1780. The remaining seventeen years of his life saw no weakening of his capacity for friendship. He fortified himself against a lonely old age by continuing to practice the art of pleasing young and old. Venison and game, plants and goldfish were sent hither and yon, complimentary verses continued to be written, his anecdotes and mishaps still enlivened the evenings at dear Mrs. Vesey's in Clarges Street and a dozen houses at Twickenham and Richmond. Hannah More rose high in his affections. To her wit, ability to write, and wide reading she added a crusading humanitarianism that moved him deeply. She really did intend to do something about the slave trade and rural schools for girls. He scolded her for her Sabbatarianism, and he went out of his way to shock her by enlarging upon her charities in terms of Cybele's multiple "founts of benevolence" and the mythical Countess of Hainault

---

[35] January 1775.

[36] They are mostly at Farmington, except for her letters to him which are in the Bodleian, and drafts of Voltaire's correspondence with her, which are in the Bibliothèque Nationale.

suckling her three hundred and sixty-five children—expressions that Miss More inked out in the original letters and for which she substituted unoffending words and phrases. He admired Miss More as much as anyone he knew, and she showed her regard for him by adopting his style in her affectionate replies.

With the young, in addition to his outward good nature and vivacity, he had the advantage of being a sympathetic neutral in the wars of the generations: he had no children of his own; he favored the weaker side and was against authority. His quizzical detachment and wisdom mingled with his desire to please and made him unlike anyone else. He also had the attraction of being famous, a man who could make a new writer or painter and whose conversational brilliance was known throughout Europe. Walpole had brought his system of living to perfection, and this the young admired.

When he was at Strawberry Hill he continued to see as much of the dowager set as his gout would permit. And then Mary and Agnes Berry came to visit in the neighborhood. He was seventy when he met them; they were twenty-four and twenty-three. He called them "the best-informed and the most perfect creatures I ever saw at their age . . . entirely natural and unaffected, frank, and, being qualified to talk on any subject, nothing is so easy and agreeable as their conversation."[37] They were pretty and smart, "but without the excrescences and balconies with which modern hoydens overwhelm and barricade their persons." Their father, "a little merry man with a round face," had married a woman of no fortune for love and had in consequence been disinherited by a rich Scottish uncle, and this was an added point in their favor. Walpole called them both his "wives," although there was never any question that he preferred the quickness of Mary to the sweetness of Agnes. Within two years he had installed all three at Little Strawberry Hill, his cottage across the fields where Kitty Clive and her brother had lived for many years.

Long after Walpole died it was repeatedly said that he had offered

---

[37] Walpole to Lady Ossory, 11 Oct. 1788.

to marry Mary, and on her refusal, Agnes. Nothing, I should say, was less likely to have happened in spite of the gossip spread at the time and passed on to the nineteenth century.[38] How he felt about marrying he made clear in some verses that he had Mary Berry include in his posthumous *Works*.

EPITAPHIUM VIVI AUCTORIS, 1792
An estate and an earldom at seventy-four!
Had I sought them or wish'd them, 'twould add one fear more,
That of making a countess when almost fourscore.
But Fortune, who scatters her gifts out of season,
Though unkind to my limbs, has still left me my reason . . .

He had not lost his fear of ridicule or his common sense. His alarm when the Berrys went abroad during the French Revolution was extreme, and his distress over their rough Channel crossing and the accident to Mary's nose when she fell down a bank at Pisa was excessive; but marriage had never been in his scheme of life. Marriage asks that one receive as well as give: one must accept the love of one's partner and acknowledge the indebtedness that gift brings with it. In his earliest years he had protected himself against love by digging a moat that his friends might cross only when he let down the drawbridge and raised the portcullis, but they were not to move in and share his castle with him. The obligations and concessions of marriage were not for him, and he knew it.

Nor is it likely that Mary Berry wanted to be his wife: she was in love with General Charles O'Hara, the Governor of Gibraltar. O'Hara's

---

[38] Just after Walpole became Lord Orford in December 1791 a newspaper suggested that the Berrys' intimacy with Walpole was not disinterested. Harcourt (whose friendship with Walpole had cooled) wrote to Mason that Walpole in his rage had offered to marry either of them but that they wisely declined (Yale Walpole, 29. 365). Greville over forty years later discussed this report with Mary Berry, who told him that Walpole's niece, the Duchess of Gloucester, who was jealous of the newcomers, one day asked Walpole point blank if he intended to marry Miss Berry and that he replied, "That is as Miss Berry herself pleases" (Charles C. F. Greville, *A Journal of the Reign of Queen Victoria from 1837 to 1852* [1885], II, 202). I think that Walpole's outburst was petulance and that both he and Miss Berry knew that it was not to be taken seriously.

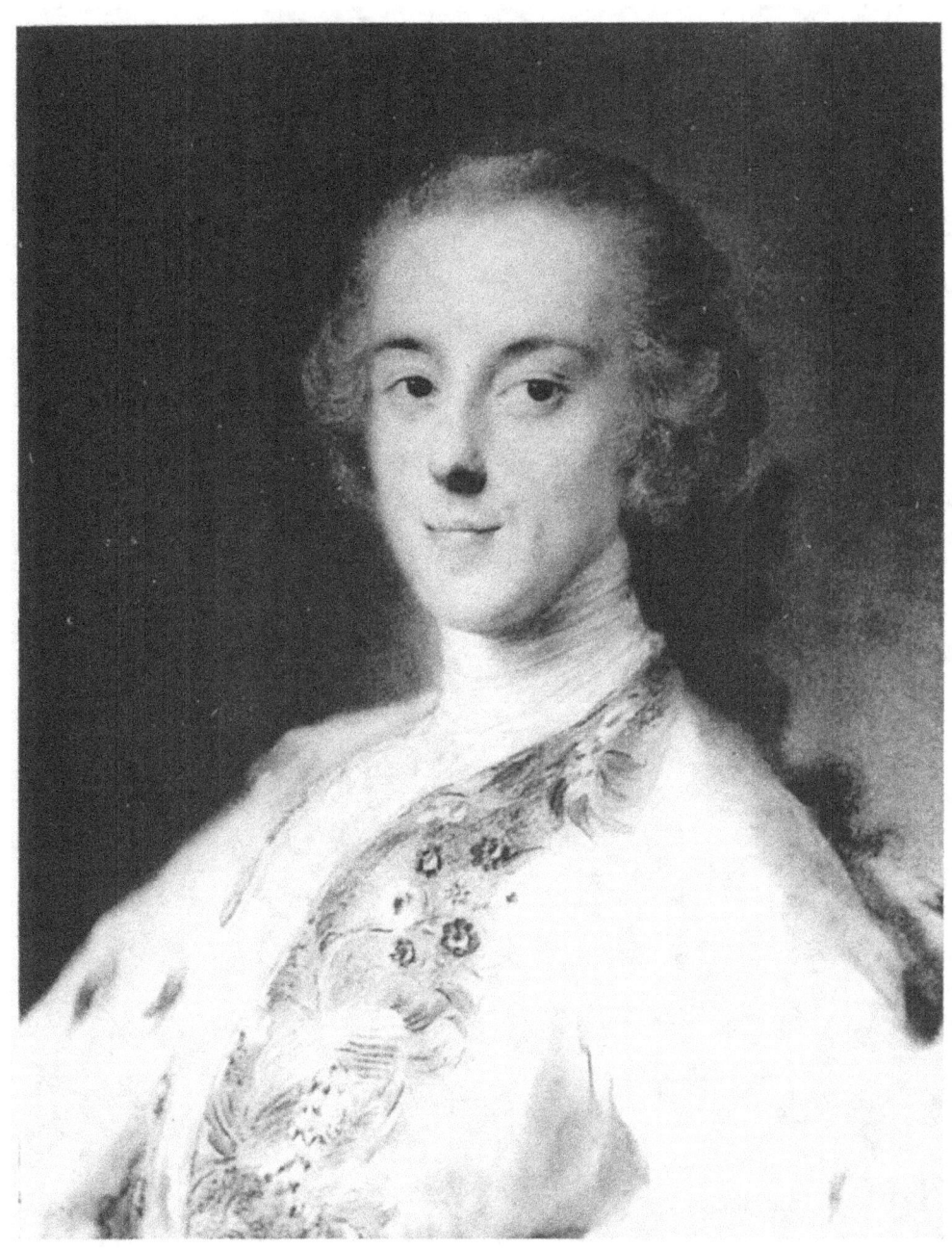

18. HORACE WALPOLE, *by Rosalba Carriera,* 1741

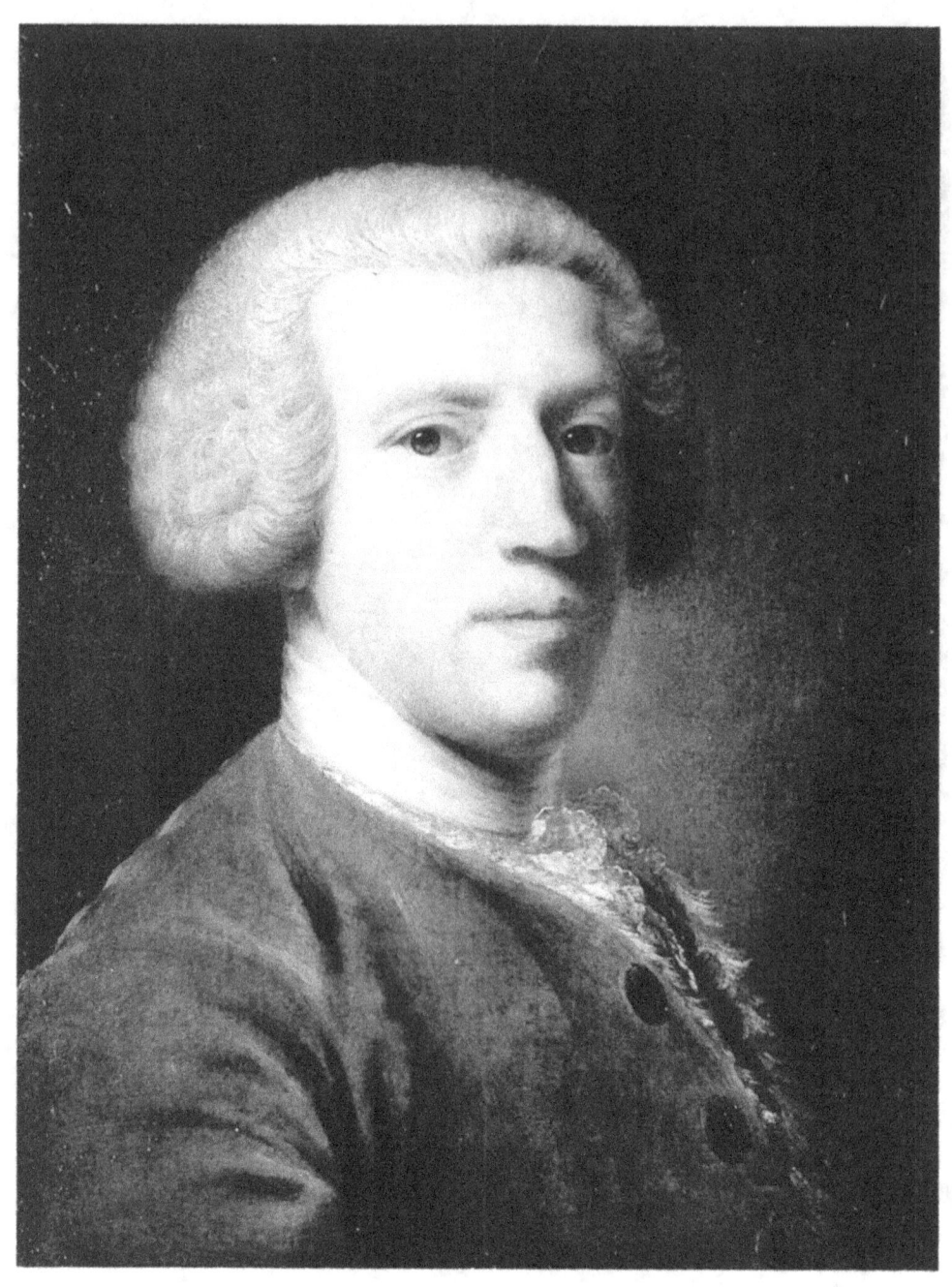

19. SIR HORACE MANN, BART., *by John Astley,* 1751

20. A PAGE FROM WALPOLE'S PARIS JOURNALS

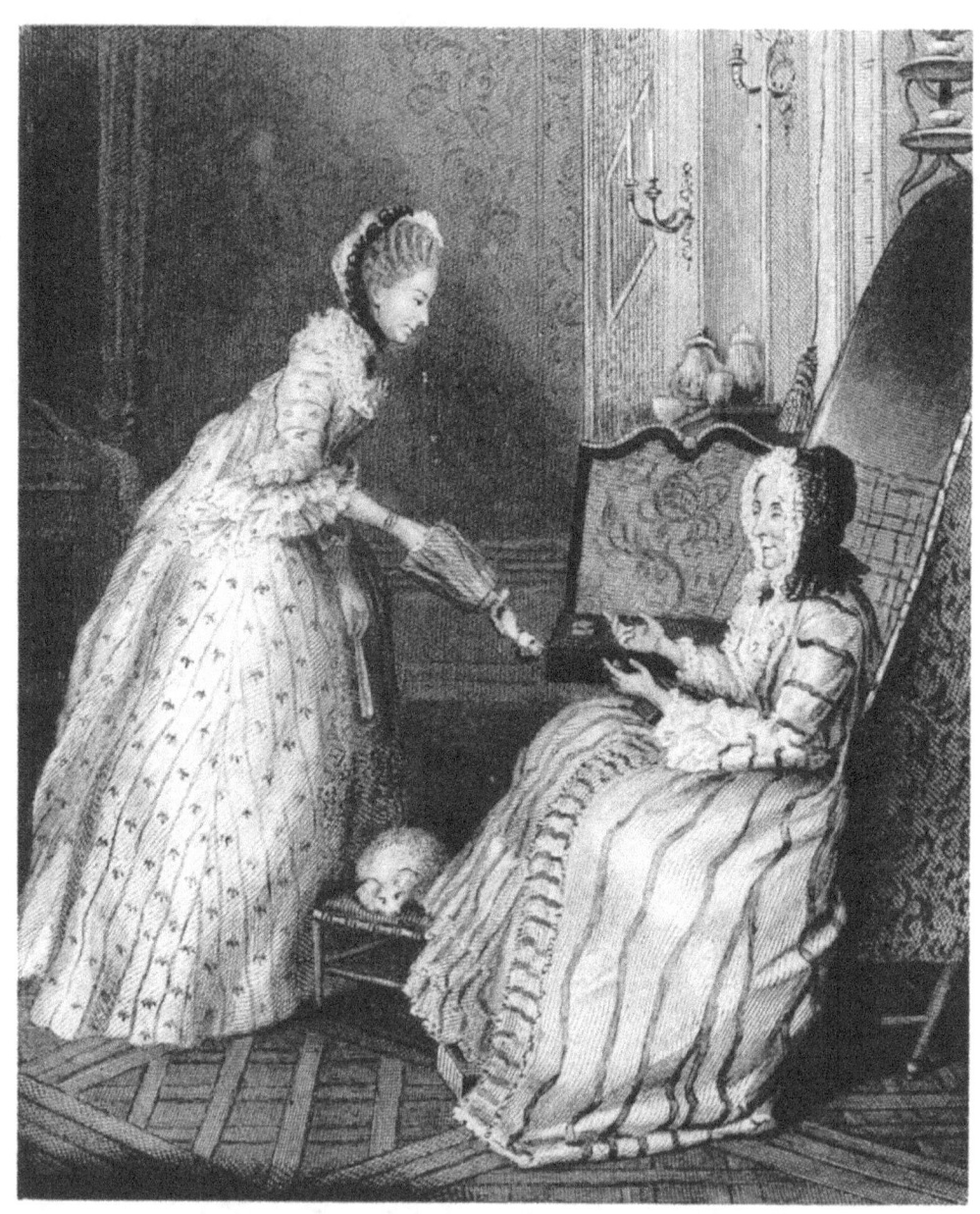

21. MME DU DEFFAND AND MME DU CHOISEUL, *by Carmontelle,* 1767

Friends

courtship was conducted so secretly that not even Agnes, only Mrs. Damer, knew of it. She warned Mary not to sacrifice her happiness to Walpole; should she do so "there would be no end to his encroaching fancies."[39] Miss Berry at length did tell him, whom she called her "second father," that she would soon be leaving him for a "still dearer friend,"[40] but when the time came for O'Hara's return to Gibraltar he went alone, and thereafter consoled himself with two unmarried ladies, each of whom, in generous rivalry, presented him with families. We do not know how Walpole took the news of the engagement, but a few months later when Mary spoke to him of "future absences," his "wildness," which he never wholly tamed, burst out. "Mortified as I have been," he wrote to her, "by finding so little return of a friendship that had been the principal occupation of my whole life . . . and decayed in spirits and in every agreeable light, I naturally dread being grown a burden to those whom I chiefly cultivate."[41] He died within six months, suffering, as I have said, from the delusion that he had been abandoned by those he loved best.

Mary Berry lived on alone with Agnes for fifty-five years, a museum piece from the eighteenth century. Walpole left the sisters the life use of Little Strawberry Hill (which they gave up after a few years) and £4,000 each. He told Mary which of his works he wanted published after his death.[42] She carried out his wishes carefully and, as we have seen, years later answered Macaulay's attack upon him with spirit and authority. Walpole's last close friend was constant to the end.

---

[39] Lewis Melville, *The Berry Papers* (1914), p. 159.

[40] *Journals and Correspondence of Miss Berry,* ed. Lady Theresa Lewis (1865), II, 320.

[41] Walpole to Mary Berry, 7 Sept. 1796.

[42] She and her father and sister were to divide the profits from the work.

III

POLITICS

ON the 24th of February, 1757, Horace Walpole gave a dinner at King's Lynn to celebrate his election to Parliament by that town. The dinner came to £183, which is perhaps the equivalent of $5,000 today. The chief item of expense was £57 8s. for wine, three hogsheads of it. The ale and beer came to over £5, and seven hams brought from London to almost as much. More than £26 went to the local butchers, grocers, and bakers. The men who carried the flags at the dinner had £13 16s.; the ringers of bells, three guineas; the drummers, one; and those who fired off the guns, half a guinea. The eight men who carried the chair of the new member had five shillings each.[1] Carrying the chair on this occasion was a symbolic gesture, since Walpole was not in it. He had not bothered to journey down to Lynn for the dinner, a slight that moved a Royal Chaplain to call him "a most delicate Italian fop."[2]

This was his fourth election to Parliament. The first was in 1741, while he was still on the Grand Tour. He was then chosen for a Cornish borough, Callington, controlled by his sister-in-law, Lady Walpole. His election was contested then and again in 1747, but the Walpole interest was strong enough to put him at the top of the poll without any effort on his part. In the next election, in 1754, he was returned for Castle Rising in Norfolk, a Walpole seat, without opposition: all twenty-six of its electors supported him.

---

[1] From the unpublished account at Farmington.
[2] *Memoirs of a Royal Chaplain, 1729–63,* ed. Albert Hartshorne (1905), p. 287.

Horace Walpole

He did present himself to the three hundred voters of King's Lynn when they re-elected him without opposition in 1761. At that time he received the freedom of the town. He had been voted it nineteen years earlier, but had not bothered to accept it, although Houghton was only a few miles away. "Think of me," he wrote, "the subject of a mob! . . . addressing them in the town hall, riding at the head of two thousand people through such a town as Lynn, dining with above two hundred of them, amid bumpers, huzzas, songs, and tobacco, and finishing with country dances at a ball and sixpenny whisk!" He went to hear misses play on the harpsichord, and to see an alderman's copies of Rubens and Carlo Maratti.[3] He even submitted to the ordeal of being chaired, but offended his ancient Aunt Hamond by sitting instead of standing as his father always had. As a friendly gesture, the Mayor of Lynn gave him the illuminated arms of the Knights of the Garter created by Richard III and Henry VII, bound in red velvet, from the library of Queen Elizabeth.[4] At the next general election in 1768 a local squire announced that he would contest the seat, and since by then Walpole had had enough of Parliament he withdrew from it.[5]

His political career was erratic. He never attained office; he never initiated any legislation; he spoke only half a dozen times. His interest ebbed and flowed with Conway's fortunes and his own success as adviser to leading figures. When he succeeded late in life to the earldom of Orford he did not take his seat in the House of Lords. He made no figure in prints and ballads, although he was intimate with many who were their

---

[3] Walpole to Montagu, 25 March 1761.

[4] It is now at Farmington.

[5] His letter of withdrawal to the mayor, William Langley, 13 March 1767, is the only letter known to or from any one of his constituents. Mr. L. Hall, Archivist of King's Lynn, has very kindly searched the Guildhall records for me and discovered that occasionally the mayor and corporation would respectfully request Walpole to do something, such as to present their addresses of felicitation to the King on his accession or marriage, or the birth of his first child, or to vote for a bill that they believed would improve local commerce, but the people who sent him to Parliament took little of his time.

chief subjects. Yet he was spasmodically influential behind the scenes, and it is upon him more than upon anyone else that posterity has relied for the parliamentary, as well as the social, history of his time, even while it has condemned his virulence and occasionally suspected his integrity.

The political history of the mid-eighteenth century is difficult to follow. The King and his ministers, parties and factions, advance and retreat, while on a confused and darkling plain Pelhams, Grenvilles, Cavendishes, Townshends, Russells, and Yorkes struggle and fight. Peering through the murk are the later historians whose observations on what they have made out lead to equally sanguinary combat among themselves. Most Americans' knowledge of the twenty-seven years when Horace Walpole sat in Parliament is limited to Bonnie Prince Charlie and the '45, Braddock's Defeat, and the Death of Wolfe. As to the leading actors, we have heard of Pitt, the Great Commoner, but few others, even though the Colonists as they moved west and north chose the names of those whom they regarded as their friends for their new towns and villages—Shelburne, Grafton, Conway, Wentworth, Rockingham, Wilkes-Barre. We know even less about the great parliamentary questions of the years 1741 to 1768, apart from those concerned with America—the Stamp Act, and its repeal.

The old labels "Whig" and "Tory" were still used, but largely, it appears, as rhetoric. When Walpole called himself "a settled Whig," "a Whig to the backbone," he meant a man who was opposed to excessive power being in the hands of a single branch of society, the sovereign, Lords, Commons, clergy, bench, or mob. This hatred of authority and of those who wielded it was no doubt part and parcel of his early resentment of his father, a resentment that continued on—that went underground—after they had become close friends. In Horace Walpole's mind, being a Whig had nothing to do with party discipline or loyalty as they are understood today. It had to do with visions. It was giving one's allegiance to a cause, to, he said, "the principles of the constitution as it was settled at the Revolution, the best form of government in the world that I know of, and which made us a free people, a rich people, and a victorious people, by diffusing liberty, protecting property, and encouraging commerce."[6] He kept on each side of his bed copies of Magna Charta and the Warrant for Charles I's execution, on which he wrote "Major Charta." This must have made his cynical Whig friends smile.

When he wrote to the Mayor of King's Lynn announcing his retirement from Parliament, he made a great point of his disinterestedness: he had done nothing, he said, for any constituent and nothing for himself. He certainly had done nothing for any constituent, but it should be added that his failure to do something for himself was not for lack of trying. After the death of his eldest brother he was urged by his friends to ask the prime minister, Henry Pelham, that the patent place in the Customs, from which he received a large portion of his income so long as his two elder brothers lived, be extended to him for his life. He asked Pelham for it twice, once in person and once by letter,[7] and was turned down both times. Six years later he wrote to Newcastle on the same subject and was again turned down. Henry Fox and Lord North later still offered to help him get the extension in order to engage his support, but he refused it, "because," he said, "I would receive no obligation that might entangle my honor and my gratitude, and set them at variance."[8] That is, he was (naturally) eager to have the place, but he would not accept it as a bribe. You may read his "Account of my Conduct Relative to the Places I hold under Government, and towards Ministers," in the posthumous edition of his *Works,* together with his letters to and from people in office. Although he did more to secure his £1,400 a year place in the Customs than he states in his "Account," and he was not as indifferent to money as he liked to make out, by the standards of the time he was quixotically disinterested and far from being the "disappointed jobber" that he has been called.

---

[6] Walpole to Mason, the first draft of his letter of 2 Feb. 1784.

[7] Walpole to Pelham, 25 Nov. 1752. For a brief account of his efforts to secure this place for life, see the Yale Walpole, 29. 327, n. 4. A more extended account is in *Letters from George III to Lord Bute, 1756–66,* ed. Romney Sedgwick (1939), pp. xxix–xliii.

[8] Walpole to Mason, 2 Feb. 1784.

Politics

He rejoiced in having obtained all he ever wanted politically, "the liberty of pleasing myself without being tied to a party."[9] What he did join were factions, which, he explained, depended "on personal character, intrigues, and minute circumstances, which make little noise and escape the eyes of the generality."[10] The factions that Walpole belonged to were the ones most likely at the moment to further the fortunes of Henry Conway, whether they were those headed by the Duke of Bedford, Henry Fox, or Lord Rockingham. From the time that they both entered Parliament in 1741 (when Conway was twenty-one years old and Walpole twenty-four) until Conway retired from it forty-three years later, Walpole was his tireless and vociferous champion, with the exception of the one painful interlude that I have already mentioned. This was when the first Rockingham ministry was formed in 1765. Conway became secretary of state in it, which was the highest political post he achieved. It was the climax of Walpole's effort to play a commanding part in politics. The long and confusing account of the formation of the ministry in his *Memoirs* concludes with this remarkably naive statement: "I first had tried to form a party to overthrow the administration, Bute, Grenville, Bedfords, and all. When I found the Opposition too weak and too foolish to compass that, I turned to the next best thing, dividing Bute and the ministers. In that I succeeded."[11] He did it, we are led to believe, singlehanded.

He made it clear that he wanted no office in the new ministry that he was convinced he had brought into being, but, he wrote, "As disinterestedness was my ruling passion, I did hope that on the change some considerable employment would be offered to me, which my vanity would have been gratified in refusing."[12] He was in bed with the gout when "the last negotiation" about the chief places in the new government was held, and he was "mortified" when Conway told him later that his name had not been so much as mentioned. He excused the in-

---

[9] Walpole to Henry Fox, 19 July 1765.
[10] Walpole to Mann, 26 June 1765.
[11] *Memoirs of George III* (1894), II, 97.
[12] Ibid., II, 149.

attention of the other leaders of their "new party" whom he had either ignored or ridiculed, "But what," he asked posterity, "could excuse this neglect in Mr. Conway? For him I had sacrificed everything; for him I had been injured, oppressed, calumniated. The foundation of his own fortune . . . he owed solely to me. . . . Such failure of friendship, or, to call it by its truer name, such insensibility, could not but shock a heart at once so tender and so proud as mine. . . . I had command enough of myself," Walpole concludes, "not to drop a word of reproach on a friendship so frozen,"[13] but not command enough to refrain from taking posterity into his confidence.

Although faction and the kaleidoscopic politics of the mid-century with its guerilla warfare suited his temperament, he was too volatile to maintain power, even in the only role he aspired to, which was that of prompter. When he converted a situation into a cause, he became extremely active, writing pamphlets and scurrying about collecting, reporting, and analyzing news, and anticipating the enemy's next move. There was always an enemy: Pulteney, Hardwicke, Bute, George Grenville, and there were always buffoons, among whom the Duke of Newcastle was first. Not that many of these characters remained fixed. Enemies could become allies, allies enemies. Even Pitt, who in eloquence surpassed Cicero and who in the year '59 wearied the bells of England with ringing for victories, even Pitt toppled from his pedestal when he accepted a peerage for his wife and a pension for himself. Although Walpole's political friends—both long-term and temporary—respected his ability to discover what was in the wind and frequently sought and acted on his advice, they regarded him with uneasiness. Moderation and temperate action in the heat of battle and concentration on routine business were beyond him. His inner uncertainties shimmered out and disconcerted his associates. His exhortations and flutterings exhausted their patience. His tastes, his celibacy, his independence set him apart from ordinary men; his talk about disinterestedness implied that he considered himself superior to them. He made people feel that he was

---

[13] Ibid., II, 150.

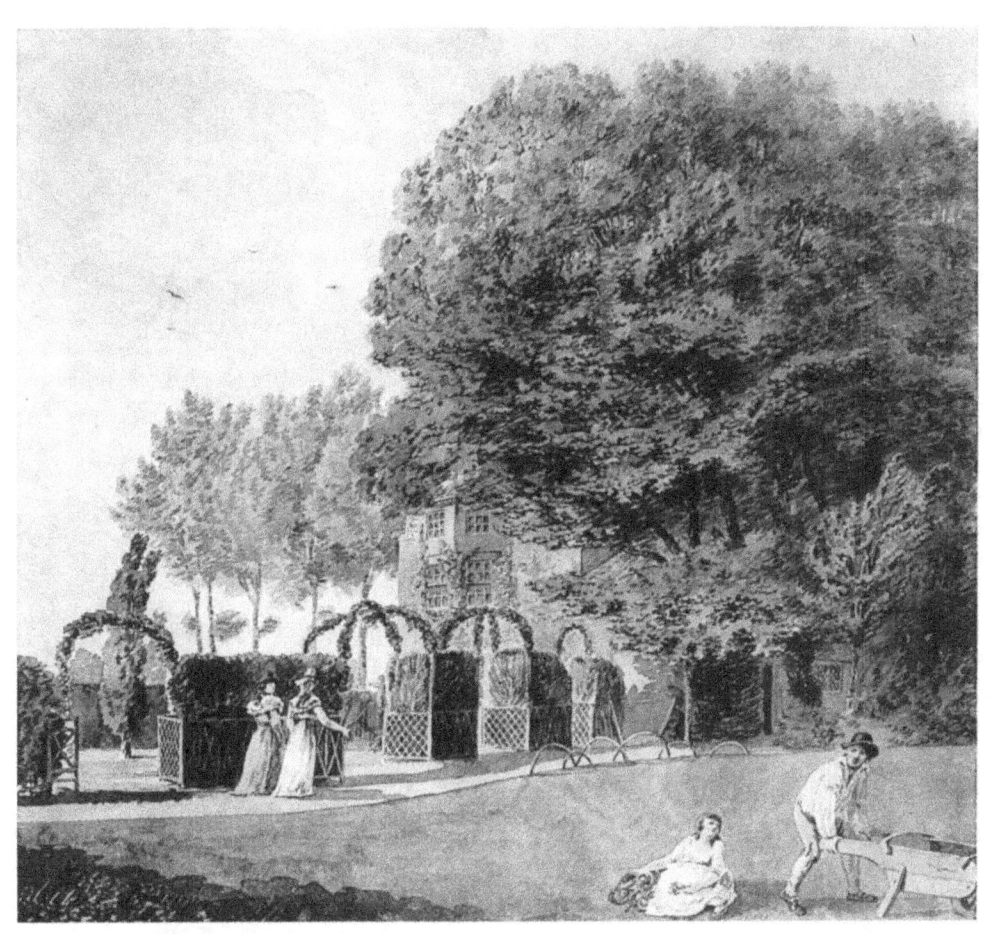

22. THE BERRYS AT LITTLE STRAWBERRY HILL, *by J. C. Barrow,* 1795

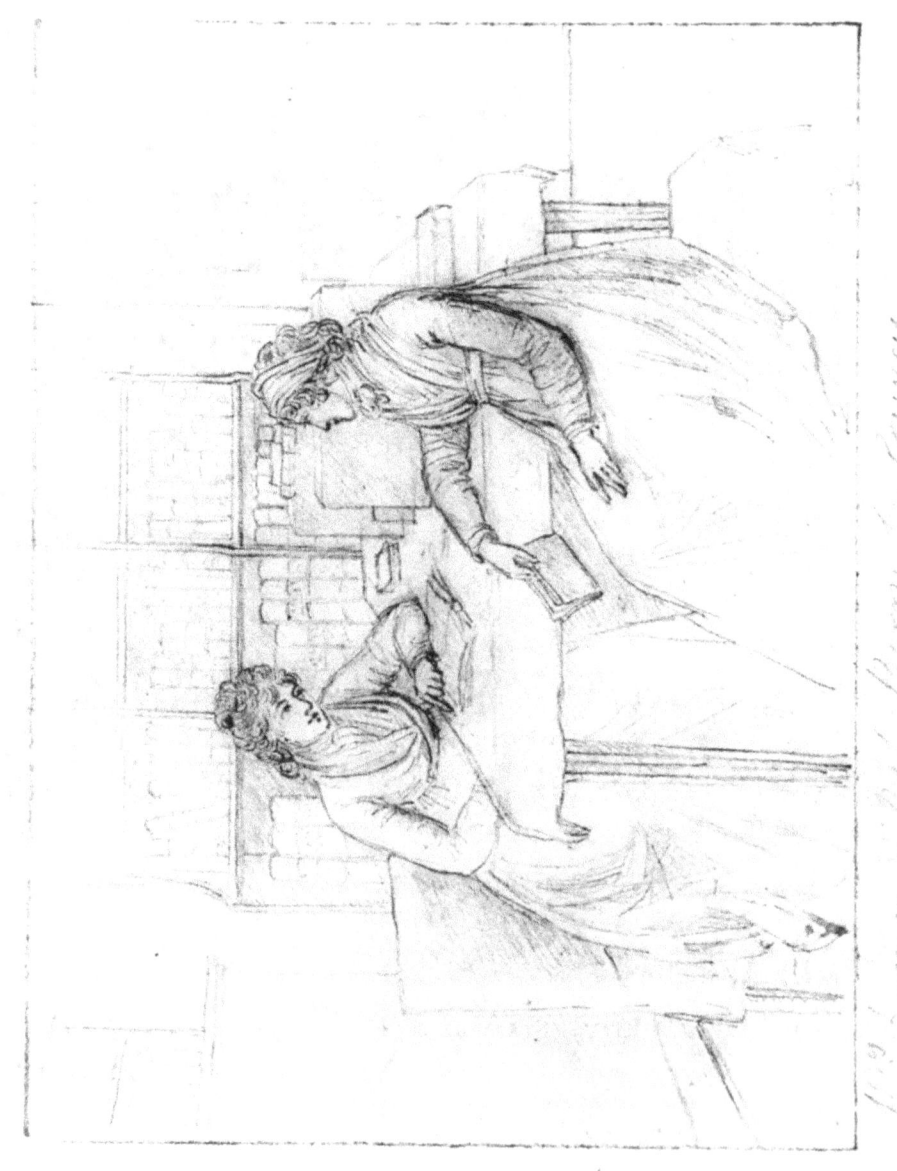

23. Mary Berry and Mrs. Damer, *by Richard Cosway*

24. THE BILL FOR THE ELECTION DINNER

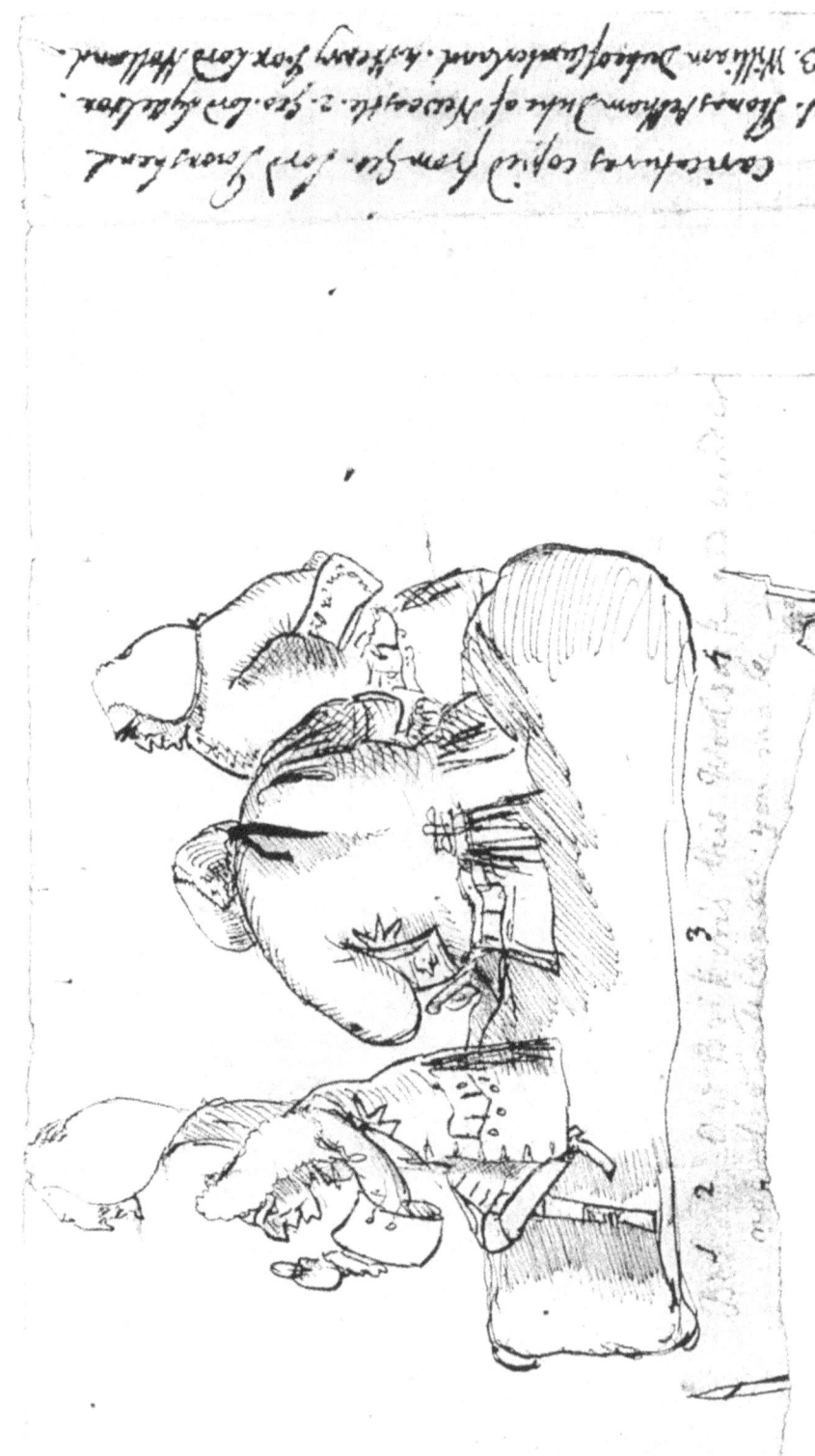

25. CARICATURES OF NEWCASTLE, LYTTLETON, THE DUKE OF CUMBERLAND, AND HENRY FOX, *by George Townshend*

quicker and more discerning than they were; they were afraid of his tongue, as they might well have been. He was no respecter of persons, but spoke up caustically to anyone, and repeated what he said in conversation and in his letters. His friends knew that he was passionately attached to them while they agreed with him, but that a divergence of opinion convicted them in his eyes of irresolution and disloyalty to principle. He himself said that he always leaned most to a man in Opposition,[14] and was on the side of the rebellious. It is not remarkable that when his friends distributed the plums of victory his name was not even mentioned.

He was aware of his faults, and he sought to placate posterity's criticism of them by confession. At the age of forty-two, in one of his fits of candor and disillusionment, he drew up a character of himself in his *Memoirs*. "Horace Walpole," he wrote, "without the least tincture of ambition, had a propensity to faction, and looked on the mischief of civil disturbances as a lively amusement. Indignation at the persecution raised against his father," he explained, "and prejudices contracted by himself, conspired with his natural impetuosity of temper to nourish this passion." With the passing of time, he said, and the removal of the objects of his passion, "maturity of reason and sparks of virtue extinguished this culpable ardor. Balanced for a few years between right and wrong, happily for him virtue preponderated early enough to leave him some merit in the option. Arts, books, painting, architecture, antiquities, and those amiable employments of a tranquil life, to which in the warmest of his political hours he had been fondly addicted, assumed an entire empire over him." "Walpole," he concluded, "had a warm conception, vehement attachments, strong aversions; with an apparent contradiction in his temper—for he had numerous caprices, and invincible perseverance. . . . He had great sense of honor, but not great enough, for he had too much weakness to resist doing wrong, though too much sensibility not to feel it in others. He had a great measure of pride, equally apt to resent neglect, and

---

[14] *Memoirs of George II,* ed. Lord Holland (1846), II, 170.

scorning to stoop to any meanness or flattery. A boundless friend; a bitter, but a placable enemy. His humor was satiric, though accompanied with a most compassionate heart. Indiscreet and abandoned to his passions, it seemed as if he despised or could bear no constraint . . . One virtue he possessed in a singular degree—disinterestedness and contempt of money—if one may call that a virtue, which really was a passion."[15]

I think we may question three of these claims. The first is that he was "without the least tincture of ambition." What he had in mind was his "disinterestedness" and "contempt for money," both of which we may allow up to a point, but apart from them he was a man of overwhelming ambition, "a *nisi prius* nuisance," if there ever was one. In whatever he attempted he wanted to be pointed out by the finger of those passing by, including the fingers of politicians. He knew that he could never be at the head of a ministry, but he saw himself dominating the man who might be.

Before raising the second doubt we must ask what he meant when he said that he had "too much weakness to resist doing wrong." What "wrong"? I think he meant the "lively amusement" of being mischievous, of yielding to a puckish desire to set people he disliked at variance with each other.[16] He could not order and command as his father had done, much as he wished it, but he could confuse and anger and humiliate, and that was a demonstration of power. To disarm posterity's criticism of his unamiable behavior he acknowledged his fault and stated that "this culpable ardor" had been extinguished by "maturity of reason and sparks of virtue." It is here that the second doubt

---

[15] Ibid., III, 159–63.

[16] An instance is the "anonymous Memorial, pretended to have been signed by several noblemen and gentlemen of the first rank and fortune" that Walpole wrote and sent "to five or six particular persons." The Memorial alleged that the future George III was being educated by "low men" of Jacobite tendencies (*Memoirs of George II* [1846], I, 298–302), who had been placed near the Prince of Wales by Pelham and his government. Mr. Romney Sedgwick suggests (and I think justly) that the intended Memorial was inspired in part by Walpole's resentment of Pelham's refusal to assure him his rich place in the Customs for life.

arises: the continuing *Memoirs* make it plain that one confession was not enough to extinguish the passions aroused by politics. Earlier he had apologized for his intemperance in one of his pamphlet wars. "These things," he wrote, "were only excusable by the lengths to which party had been carried against my father—or, rather, were not excusable even then."[17]

The third statement of his "confession" that we may challenge is that the "amiable employments of a tranquil life . . . assumed an entire empire over him." He never lost his itch to express himself politically through others, as Henry Conway, the Duke of Richmond, and Charles James Fox were to find out. He did this in person and by letter. This is how he wrote to the Duke of Richmond: "You have not been a very active opposition, but may plead in excuse that you could do no good. *Now* you can—or never. Give the ministers no respite. Press them with questions and motions, leave their poor heads no time to think of what they ought to think of, the next campaign. Call for papers. Don't mind being refused. Talk of their waste,"[18] and so on for hundreds of words.

What did he mean by "virtue"? I think he meant his "disinterestedness," of course, and also a vague but ardent desire to improve the world. He burned with zeal to right what he thought was wrong, to cure injustice, to befriend the downtrodden, to reform. This zeal made him pro-American in 1775 and pro-Louis XVI in 1793. He was one of those people who put themselves in other people's places and so become identified with them. It was he as well as Admiral Byng who was tried and shot for losing Minorca, and he as well as King Theodore of Corsica who was shut up in the Fleet for debt; "virtue" to him meant charity as well as disinterestedness. He was "balanced," he said, "for a few years between right and wrong"; virtue won out, he believed, by fleeing from the fumes of politics into the sweet air of humanistic studies. But he carried with him his journals and *Memoirs* in which he went on indulging his desire to injure those he disliked.

---

[17] "Short Notes" (1748), Yale Walpole, 13. 21.
[18] Walpole to the Duke of Richmond, 27 Oct. 1775.

Horace Walpole

He chose an epigraph for his first political journal that might serve for all his *Memoirs* as he thought of them. "Nothing extenuate, nor set down aught in malice . . . Othello."[19] He said that his intention was "to let my readers rather into the character of the actors than into the minute events of the drama. The laborious two hundred years hence may draw out a journal of what month the miscarriage happened before Toulon; or on what day the Battle of Dettingen was fought." "The laborious"—what a majestic dismissal of mere fact-finders! Good, plodding, essential people, let them toil away; his mission was the analysis and exposition of character and the revelation of the secret springs of action. Anyone could give posterity the date of the Battle of Dettingen, but only he could reveal the faithlessness of Lord Hardwicke. During the forty-five years that he wrote his journals and memoirs he never wavered from this belief. His *Memoirs,* he said, were his "favorite labor,"[20] yet only Montagu, Gray, Bentley, Mme du Deffand, and probably Conway knew of their existence.

He never, I think, seriously considered destroying them, but he did hedge them about with elaborate restrictions. Three years before he died he wrote a memorandum to guard against their being overlooked after his death: "In the round library of books of prints up two pair of stairs in my house at Strawberry Hill," he wrote, "there is a large wainscot chest marked on the outside lid with a great A. As soon as I am dead, I solemnly desire and enjoin my executrix [Mrs. Damer] to see it strongly corded up without being opened, and the cords to be sealed with her own seal; and I desire her to deposit the key of the chest with the church plate in the church at Houghton in Norfolk, and to take a receipt for it from the vicar and every succeeding vicar with a solemn promise not to deliver the said key till the first earl of Waldegrave that shall attain the age of thirty-five years shall demand it." Only a Lord Waldegrave of that age who was then "Master of Strawberry Hill should take possession of the great chest marked A." Its contents were never to pass out of his family

---

[19] This unpublished manuscript, "Memoires from the Declaration of the War with Spain," is at Farmington.

[20] *Memoirs of George II* (1846), III, 162.

Politics

and they should never be printed. A few months before he died he wrote another memorandum on the same subject, one less like something out of *The Castle of Otranto,* reducing the age when Lord Waldegrave should take possession of the chest to twenty-five and not prohibiting publication. When Chest A was opened by the sixth earl in 1810, it was found to contain, among much besides, twenty-three folio volumes of memoirs and journals covering the years 1746 to 1791. After twelve years of discussion and hesitation the first installment was brought out under the editorship of Lord Holland.

As I have said, those who had known Walpole were astonished to discover that so good-natured a man should have harbored such malevolence, but the next generation shared Carlyle's high opinion of his work. Still later nineteenth-century writers in their own books and when editing other papers of the time borrowed from him freely with and without acknowledgment. In this way his political writings have become enmeshed in the political history of the eighteenth century.

It was natural for the generation following Walpole to condemn him for the *Memoirs:* each generation is in revolt against its immediate predecessor, and there were then alive many whose close relations had been attacked by him; yet before we, five or six generations later, are too self-righteous about him we should remember that he was writing in the age of Junius and in the tradition of Dryden who called Shadwell,

A monstrous mass of foul corrupted matter,

and Pope, who called Hervey,

This painted child of dirt that stinks and stings.

Walpole's description of Lord North, "Two large prominent eyes that rolled about to no purpose (for he was utterly shortsighted), a wide mouth, thick lips, and inflated visage, gave him the air of a blind trumpeter,"[21] is mild by Dryden's and Pope's standards. In the House of Commons Walpole said, "similes and quotations, and metaphors were fallen

---

[21] *Memoirs of George III* (1894), IV, 52.

53

into disrepute. . . . It was not the same case with invectives. . . . Debates, where no personalities broke out, engaged too little attention."[22] People who are familiar with the English eighteenth century have heard enough of the rebel heads rotting on Temple Bar and soldiers being whipped to death for stealing a handkerchief, but we cannot judge Horace Walpole fairly if we think of his background as being only the lilacs and nightingales at Strawberry Hill. There was also what Virginia Woolf called "the presence of obsolete conventions"[23] inherited from an earlier and still more ferocious time, and one of these in the eighteenth century was unbridled personal abuse. I think the *Memoirs* are less remarkable for their savagery than for Walpole's uneasiness about the effect of it upon us. This was something new, and it is part of his long shadow that touches us today.

Twentieth-century historians have conceded that the *Memoirs* are "historical sources of first-rate importance," but some have regarded Walpole with suspicion. These skeptics have spent a great deal of time poring over the printed texts and have decided that Walpole doctored the *Memoirs* after he wrote them to conform to his changed opinions of people and views of government.[24] Had these gentlemen gone back to the original manuscripts, they would have reached the opposite conclusion.

There is no mystery about where the manuscripts are; the great bulk of them are where they have always been since Walpole's death, in the possession of the Earls Waldegrave, who have for the past many years put them generously at the disposal of inquiring scholars.[25] I have

---

[22] *Memoirs of George II* (1846), II, 145.

[23] Virginia Woolf, *The Death of the Moth* (New York, 1942), p. 195.

[24] Carl L. Becker, "Horace Walpole's Memoirs of the Reign of George the Third," *American Historical Review,* XVI (1911), 496.

[25] At Farmington, in addition to the earliest and final journals, are the "Journal for the years 1769–71," which preceded the foul copy of the *Memoirs* for those years, some of the "characters" inserted by Walpole in his transcribed copies of the published *Memoirs,* Bentley's drawings for them, and many preliminary notes and jottings on odds and ends of paper. Lord Ilchester owns the copies of the *Memoirs* made by Lord Holland, the passages cut from Walpole's transcribed copy—the snippets themselves—and one longish passage about Henry and Charles Fox that had been torn from the original *Last Journals.* The late Lord

not collated all the three million words in the manuscripts and the published texts, but I have collated enough of them to be satisfied that Walpole did not tinker with the text in an attempt to mislead us. The "diatribe" on Lord North, for example, which has been cited as an instance of his duplicity, was not an alteration, but an addition, and the panegyric of North in an earlier passage, which Walpole has been charged with carelessly leaving in after he had written the diatribe, was not written by him at all, but was inserted by the first editor of the *Memoirs of George III,* fifty years after Walpole died. Walpole changed a word here and there—who does not on re-reading his manuscript?—but he did not change his statements or bring his views and prejudices up to date. He did add cadenzas on leading personages of the moment that he was writing about, and passages of reflection and comment. Some of these insertions are at variance with what he had written earlier, but far from attempting to conceal his altered views he points out that the *Memoirs* are full of "contradictory opinions." He accounts for them by their being written at different periods and by his changing his mind about the persons concerned in them; there is sometimes a lapse of three or four years between the events and his report of them. "If I had any personal causes for changing my opinion," he wrote, "I have told them fairly that the fault may be imputed to my passions, rather than to those I speak of." He might, he admitted, have made his book "more uniform by correction; but the natural coloring would have been lost; and I should rather have composed than written a history. As it stands an original sketch, it is at least a picture of my own mind and opinions. That sketch may be valuable to a few who study human nature even in a single character."[26] The *Memoirs,* you see, are as much a "sketch" of Walpole as of his time. In fact, he is so prominent in them that the great events of which he writes tend to become merely background for his activity, and the actors in them merely supporting members of his cast.

He has been badly served by the editors of his *Memoirs.* They cut

Ilchester printed this last in *Studies in Art and Literature for Belle da Costa Greene,* ed. Dorothy Miner (Princeton, 1954), pp. 449–59.
[26] *Memoirs of George III* (1894), I, 2–3.

out passages—some of them with scissors—that they thought offensive for one reason or another, and although they said that they had indicated these omissions they did not always do so. Walpole was careful to give the dates when he began and finished each year, but his editors omitted them.[27] Dr. Doran, the editor of the *Last Journals*, inserted newspaper cuttings that Walpole pasted on the manuscript of that work as if they had been written by Walpole himself. One of Doran's footnotes deserves three stars in the editorial Chamber of Horrors: Walpole wrote of a naval engagement in which the English attacked the French with nineteen sail, the correct number. Doran misread the nineteen as thirty-nine and then added a note that Walpole had grossly exaggerated.

It will not be possible to pass final judgment upon the *Memoirs* until a new edition of them is made with a full critical apparatus. When it is published with a text that shows Walpole's preliminary notes (which he wrote on scraps of paper and the backs of letters and cards), the early drafts and the later insertions, when the excisions by the first editors have been restored in so far as they can be, the newspaper cuttings removed from the text, and the text dated and annotated, the reader will see that Walpole was telling the truth when he said that he did not change what he had written to make himself appear wiser or more virtuous than he was. Until this edition appears, students of the *Memoirs* will go on bumping into each other in the dark.

The new edition will not, I think, have a wider audience than the earlier ones. Even with the improvements I have suggested non-specialists of the period will continue to find the *Memoirs* hard going, because Walpole assumed that his readers would be familiar with the politics of the time and because, apart from his "characters," he was not writing at his best. When the Common Reader picks up one of the nine printed volumes he becomes confused by faulty syntax and discouraged by the detailed accounts of the dismissal, resignation, and appointment of minis-

---

[27] Not only did Walpole give them in the foul copies, but in his "Short Notes of My Life," the manuscript of which is now at Farmington. Thirteen of the dates are in the manuscript, but only five were printed by Cunningham, whose text was followed by Mrs. Toynbee.

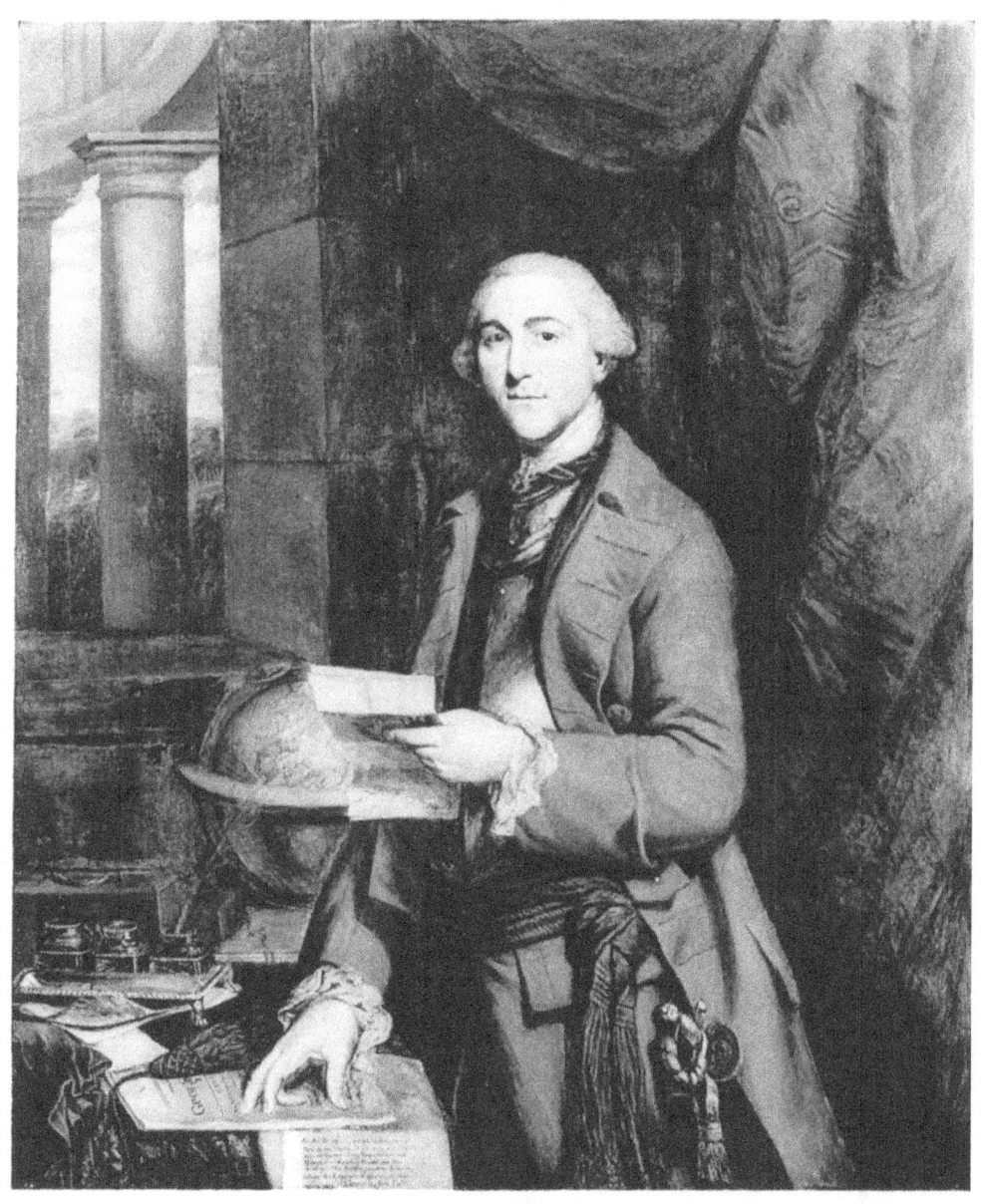

26. HENRY SEYMOUR CONWAY, *by G. Berwick,* ca. 1767

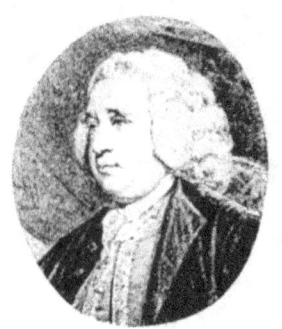

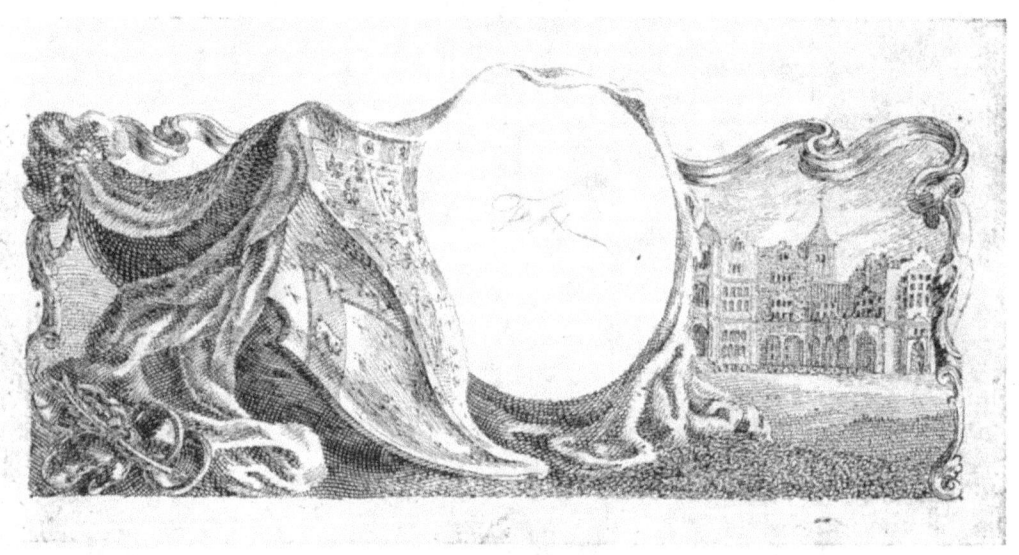

27. HENRY FOX

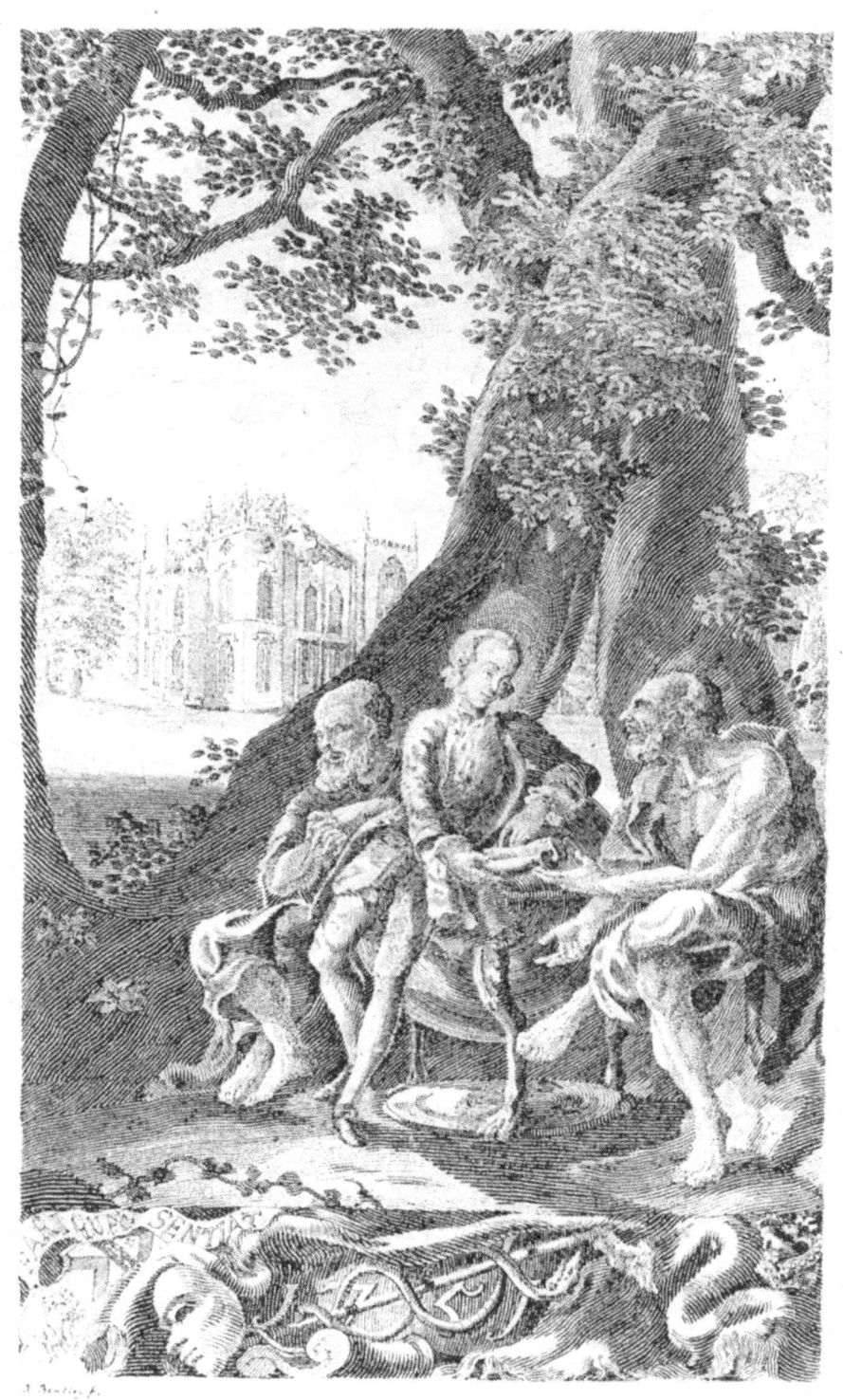

28. WALPOLE, *by Bentley*, ca. 1755

Begun Dec. 26. 1755.

Memoires
from the Death of Mr Pelham to the end of the year 1755.
Book the fourth.

Plus on étudie le monde, plus on y découvre le ridicule. La Bruyère.
Les exemples du passé touchent sans comparaison plus les hommes, que ceux de leur siecle.
Nous nous accoutumons à ce que nous voyons; & je ne sai si le Consulat du cheval de Caligula
nous auroit autant surpris que nous nous l'imaginions. Card. de Retz.

Having never proposed to write a regular history, but to throw together some anecdotes & characters which might cast a light on the times in which I have lived, & might lead some future & more assiduous historian to an intimate knowledge of the men whose councils or actions he shall record, I had determined to lay down my Pen at the Death of that Minister, whose fortune, situation & genius had superinduced a very new complexion over his country, & who had composed a system of lethargic acquiescence, in which the spirit of Britain, agitated for so many centuries, seemed willingly to repose. But as the humbness of that Enchantment has been dispelled by the Evanition of the Talisman, & many of its mischievous principles reviving, I shall once again endeavour to trace the stream of events to their secret source, tho with a pen more unequal than ever to the task. A monkish Writer may be qualified to record an age of Barbarity and Ignorance: Sallust was only worthy to snatch the rapid Episode of Catiline from Oblivion; Tacitus to paint monsters whose vices surpassed caricatura; Livy to embrace whole ages of Patriots & Heroes. Tho no Catiline, I trust, will rise in my pages to deform his country by his horrid glory, tho we have a minister with the monkey-disposition of Heliogabalus, yet happily without his youth or Lusts, & by the character of the age system matured into little mischiefs & unbloody treacheries; Tho we have no succession of incorrupt Senators; yet the times beginning to wear in some lights a more respectable face, it will require a steadier hand & more dignified conceptions than served to catch scize & to sketch out the littlenesses & the trifles that had characterized the foregoing period.

Tho The style of the following sheets will perhaps wear a more serious aspect than I have used before, yet I don't plein know why I should check a smile at transient follies; for as much appropriated as gravity is to an Historian, can I conceive how history can always be faithfull, if always solemn — Is a court a perpetual a Shrine of Virtue, or such a Tribunal of severity? Do not follies predominate in mankind over either Virtues or Vices — & who ever has been conversant in a court, does he not know how strongly the cast of it verges towards ridiculous! Besides, I am no Historian; I write casual memoires; I draw characters; I string anecdotes, which my Superiors the Historians of Britain may enchace into their weighty Annals or pass over at their pleasure. In one point I shall not vary from the style I have assumed, but shall honestly continue to relate the blemishes of the material Personages as they enter upon the scene; & whoever knows the interior of affairs, must be sensible to how many more events the faults of Statesmen give birth, than are produced by their good Intentions.

& I mean, at the time I write, the end of the year 1755.

29. A Page from the "Foul" Copy of the Memoirs

ters, the reports of debates, and the passage or defeat of bills that mean little or nothing to him. One may read the letters with ease and pleasure, even when unfamiliar with the people and events in them, because they are written with wit, grace, and for the most part, good nature. This is not true of the *Memoirs;* Walpole wrote them for us, posterity, but he could not chat with us as he chatted with his friends in his letters, since he did not know us. When he wrote his letters he had his correspondents clearly in mind, they were sitting amicably across the desk from him, but we, posterity, were formidable strangers, who made him stilted and stiff. The non-specialists drop the *Memoirs* and miss the set pieces on Pelham, Mansfield, or whomever, which Walpole flung off when he could burst through his self-consciousness.

Historians of the period must study the *Memoirs,* but they, too, are confused by them, not only by the bad editing, but by Walpole himself. They find his accounts of debates and the maneuvers and machinations of the principal characters invaluable; they quote him constantly; and then when he attacks one of their favorites they quite naturally turn on him with dislike. Since the *Memoirs* were written in passion they evoke passion. By lashing out at nearly everybody in them, Walpole sooner or later angers most of his readers, as he foresaw that he might. Even if you know little and care less about any of the people that he pillories, these unbridled passages tend to turn you against him.

Here is a mild example of what I mean:

"The Countess of Northumberland was a jovial heap of contradictions. The blood of all the Percies and Seymours swelled in her veins and in her fancy, while her person was more vulgar than anything but her conversation, which was larded indiscriminately with stories of her ancestors and her footmen. Show and crowds and junketing were her endless pursuits. She was familiar with the mob, while stifled with diamonds; and yet was attentive to the most minute privileges of her rank, while almost shaking hands with a cobbler. . . . She had revived the drummers and pipers and obsolete minstrels of her family; and her own buxom countenance at the tail of such a procession gave it all the air of an antiquated pageant of mumming. She was mischievous under the appearance of frankness; generous and friendly without delicacy or sentiment."[28]

How do you feel about that? If the blood of all the Percys and Seymours swells in your veins it doubtless strikes you as being in bad taste, but if you have never heard of the lady before, you may be entertained by it and not care whether it is just or not. If you have read her *Journals* you will find confirmation of Walpole's "character" of her, and if you pursue your study of her further you will not find him contradicted anywhere. You may feel that, even so, this is no way for a man to talk about a woman, especially when he is talking about her to posterity. If you are annoyed *and* an historian you may re-examine other passages in the spirit that filled Walpole himself when he set out to prove established historians prejudiced and untrustworthy.

In his *Memoirs* Walpole eluded the censor that guarded his letters. When he was writing to Conway or Lady Hervey or Cole he wanted to keep their respect. Many of his friends were saving his letters, some of which would be printed one day, and that was sobering. He did frequently let himself go in them, especially when writing to Mason, who brought out his worst side, but he usually ended by apologizing or laughing at himself and so toned down his asperities.

Although he was under no such restraint in the *Memoirs,* he fretted about their reception. He did not worry about the facts in them because he knew that he was a superlatively good reporter and that, "the laborious" would find them accurate. The Duke of Grafton when Prime Minister said of him that there was no one from whom he "received so just accounts of the schemes of the various factions" or that "had so good means of getting the knowledge of what was passing."[29] What Walpole worried about were his "characters." They had honorable precedents, such as Clarendon's and Bishop Burnet's, who had also written in passion. Some of his readers would enjoy his severity, but "I am aware," he

---

[28] *Memoirs of George III* (1894), I, 333–34.
[29] *Autobiography* (1898), pp. 140–41; even the cold-blooded Rigby respected Walpole's "political intelligence" (*Bedford Correspondence* [1843], II, 165).

wrote, "that more will be offended at the liberty I have taken in painting men as they are: and that many, from private connections of party and family, will dislike meeting such unflattered portraits of their heroes or their relations."[30] He tried repeatedly to ward off criticism on this score. "Few men," he pointed out, "can sit for patterns of perfect virtue."[31] He had taken posterity into the secret councils of the time and shown us the true nature of its principal actors, yet he feared that his strictures might hurt him as much as the people he was describing and he desperately wanted our high opinion of his work and of himself. He was in the position of a man who has written many letters in anger that he prudently did not post, but who on rereading them is torn between shame of his intemperance and admiration of his wit. The *Memoirs* gave him a sense of power. He could not make history, but he could write it. Posterity would learn from him the events of his time and how they came about. In the library at Strawberry, working secretly at night, he was reaching into the future, settling the reputations of his more powerful political contemporaries forever. He would have the last word.

The savagery of the *Memoirs* has hurt his posthumous reputation; he paid a high price for it while he lived. When his destructive impulses boiled up to the surface, virtue, conscience, stepped in and the conflict between the two made him ill. We are here at Plutarch's frontier of biography beyond which the poets and inventors of fables dwell. There are no documents to guide us, no maps or charts, but we have Walpole's own statements that he realized dimly where his illness came from. He knew that he welcomed it as an excuse to avoid going to the House of Commons. I think, also, that he believed that the gout was a purgatory that it was right for him to endure. When it seized him he found in it no cause for self-pity, but a perverse comfort. He deserved to suffer for his sins.

He had his first attack just after he turned thirty-eight. He had been "very much fatigued in the House" and wanted to escape. As we have

---

[30] *Memoirs of George II* (1846), I, xxix.
[31] Ibid., I, xxx.

seen, he tried to persuade himself that the gout had "come to look for Mr. Chute at Strawberry Hill," but confessed that none of his evasions would do, and that "he still knew where to look for it when he wanted a political illness."[32] Five years later he had a severe attack, again when politics had made him tense and apprehensive, and thereafter the gout came regularly, thirty-five attacks in all, including what he called their "codicils." It was believed at the time that he died of it. There is at Farmington a full and detailed history of his case culled from his letters. Since in the beginning his gout was, I think, stimulated by the tumult in his mind and spirits, the case history indicates the signs of anger, fear, or depression that he showed before each attack.

While still a novice in the gout he confessed that he was as superstitious about naming it as the Romans were about pronouncing the word Death, but as time went on he told his correspondents when the gout struck and where, its progress and decline, its "codicils," and what little he did to combat it. He was speaking for the eighteenth century when he called the gout, "a monster and a mystery" and a harlequin that assumed new and capricious disguises. The eighteenth century was like Caliban crouching before Prospero when threatened with cramps and aches. Walpole was admired for the way he stood up to the tormentor. Except when he was feverish or in great pain and exhausted, he talked about the gout in his most lighthearted way; he was, he said, "Ariel in a slit shoe." Like everyone else in the eighteenth century he believed that the gout was a specific against all other diseases. It became a major preoccupation of his life, his "biennial visitor," whose arrival he looked forward to with dread, but also with fascination, until, finally, he would not be without it. "An insignificant man that grows old," he wrote to Lady Ossory, "wants something to give him a little importance; and with my meager figure, what with its being a little respectable, and what with its being a little comical, I find the gout does not at all succeed ill with me."[33] Years later he told

---

[32] Walpole to Bentley, 16 Nov. 1755.
[33] Walpole to Lady Ossory, 26 Oct. 1769.

Politics

Mary Hamilton and Boswell almost in the same words that "he would not be free of it if he could for he knew how to manage it, he did not know how to manage other distempers."[34]

He had no more faith in physicians than in divines, and would have none of them. Friends and acquaintances made his lot harder by pressing their nostrums upon him. Were he to take any of them, he said, it would be that of the Frenchwoman who urged him to preserve the parings of his nails in a bottle close stopped.[35] He experimented with his diet: Morello cherries and venison pasty proved to be disastrous, "iced" water safe. Silk wrappages about his hands and feet and Dr. James's powders, which he said could not cure death but which he believed he would take if the house were on fire, were all that he finally used.[36]

At the climax of his agitation about the first Rockingham ministry, on the eve of his friends' triumph and his own humiliation, he had his first very bad attack. I believe he knew that his friends were going to ignore him and that in his bitterness and disappointment he unconsciously produced the gout to keep out of the way. The quiet of Strawberry Hill, he wrote, "is not only the best, but my sole medicine. The relief I feel seems to come more from a cessation of politics than of the gout . . . for while I live, I shall never be able to decompound the ideas of the two disorders."[37] And again, "Many of my opinions are fantastic; perhaps this is one, that nothing produces gout like doing anything one dislikes."[38]

As soon as he could he escaped to Paris. His conspicuous success there helped to restore him in mind and health. The shops also contributed to his recovery, since nothing builds up a collector more rapidly than spending a lot of money. Twenty-two cases were needed for all the books and prints and china and bibelots that he bought. Some of them must

---

[34] Walpole to Mrs. Dickenson, 25 Aug. 1790; *Boswell Papers* (1933), XVII, 102.
[35] Walpole to Gray, 19 Nov. 1765.
[36] James's powder was composed of antimony and phosphate of lime.
[37] Walpole to Anne Pitt, 9 Aug. 1765.
[38] Walpole to Lady Hervey, 2 Jan. 1766.

have been very large: case No. 4, for example, contained fourteen smaller cases, of Sèvres and Chantilly from Dulac's.[39] He spent over £ 400 on china alone. "The employments of a tranquil life" in the seclusion of Strawberry Hill he believed were henceforth to be his, undisturbed by the House of Commons.

---

[39] Yale Walpole, 7. 405.

IV

STRAWBERRY HILL

WALPOLE began talking seriously about having a country house three years after he got home from the Grand Tour. He was then what Gray called, "The Friend of London." His days and nights were taken up by the House of Commons, masquerades, balls, White's, shops, Vauxhall, Ranelagh, the theater (which he loved), and the opera (which bored him, apart from the entertainment supplied by the co-owners of his box). We are told the latest sayings of Lady Townshend and George Selwyn, the latest perfidies of the men who caused Robert Walpole's downfall, the forthcoming marriages, the outstanding births and deaths. We read about the battles in Germany and Flanders, the French invasion of England that did not come off, and the Scottish invasion that did. There are references to Walpole's few speeches in the House of Commons and to his successful political squibs. We have recently discovered much about this period of his life that we didn't know before from his unpublished verses (some of which are obscene), and from his "new" letters to Lord Lincoln. There are also the unpublished letters written by his friends to one another: Sir Charles Hanbury Williams, Henry Fox, Richard Rigby, and "Gilly" Williams. They were Sir Robert's bright young men, hard-living, reckless, and cynical. In their accounts of gambling, mistresses, and political maneuver, Horace Walpole turns up as frequently as anybody. Their liking and respect for him are marked.

A few years of that life was enough. He had other things that he wanted to do, such as reading, collecting, writing, and being alone. He loved gaiety, but he held radically different views of what was right and

Horace Walpole

wrong from those held by his London intimates. To debauch a woman on promise of marriage and not marry her, to ruin your tailor's or baker's family by not paying them, he thought was hateful, and the current views and practices of "honor" preposterous. He was like a modern liberal in an ultraconservative club, one who enjoys good living, but who also wants to make the world a better place to live in. This charitable impulse did not mean that he was tied to those who shared his advanced views. He did not want to see too much of anyone and when he did he became peevish and irritable. "I always travel without company," he wrote when still in his twenties, "for then I take my own hours and my own humors, which I don't think the most tractable to shut up in a coach with anybody else."[1] His rule, he said, for keeping his temper in order was never to leave it too long with another person. He traveled alone the rest of his life.

Thanks to his father's gifts of government places, he could live as he pleased. He had a house in Arlington Street, but he wanted one outside of London as well, and in his thirtieth year he rented Strawberry Hill, just west of Twickenham. Twickenham was the perfect place for him to settle, not too near and not too far from London: the improved roads and coaches had brought it to within a two-hour drive. The neighborhood had the added charm of being familiar to him: he had spent a summer there as a boy with Townshend relations, and across the river was Richmond, where his father had had a lodge for hunting over the week ends. Furthermore, it was pleasant living in a place that had always been known for its illustrious people. Twickenham was the Tivoli of London. Walpole wrote some verses about its inhabitants, past and present, that he called "The Parish Register of Twickenham." There were Essex, Bacon, Lord Clarendon, and so on to Lady Mary Wortley Montagu, Pope, and Fielding. "We have very famous people," he wrote, "Clive and Pritchard, actresses; Scott and Hudson, painters; my Lady Suffolk, famous in her time"[2] as George II's rather companionable mistress. He bought Strawberry Hill in 1749, in his thirty-second year.

---

[1] Walpole to Mann, 16 Aug. 1744.
[2] Walpole to Bentley, 5 July 1755.

30. Notes for the *Memoirs*

Expences to Paris Aug. 1769.

carried 82£.

Journey to Dover, including money given to D Hollands serts. 11 — 11 — 0.
to the Custom house officer at Dover — — — — 1 — 1 — 0.
at Dover — — — — 1 — 3 — 6.
to the Boatmen at Dover — — — — 0 — 5 — 0.

The whole Journey from London to Paris, including D Holl's &c. 39 — 10 — 6.

Expences at Paris.

Louis — livres — sous

black sword & belt —	0 — 15 — 0.
black silk stockings —	0 — 12 — 0.
a sword —	5 — 0 — 0.
Prints —	2 — 0 — 0.
cup & saucer —	1 — 12 — 0.
prints —	2 — 15 — 0.
black & gold snuff box —	12 — 0 — 0.
& China — together —	714 livres
China at Sayde's —	528 livres
Ruffles —	312 L. 14 livres
Philip's & Cabaret's bill —	3 — 3 — 17.
Prints, portfol. &c —	32 Liv. 8 S.
Blue & white large cup, cover & saucer	72 — 0 — 0
blue & white & yellow Dejeune	60 — 0 — 0.
Poirier's bill	Louis livres 37 — 14 — 0
packing, expenses	Louis livres 60 — 0
Dulac's bill (one of which lady to the marit's Louis livres 8, 10) bone	Louis 22 — 7 — 0.
postage of letters.	livres Louis 46 — 0 — 10.
Cloaths, Taylor, lodging, coach, footman & all other bills	Louis livres 85 — 15.
rests of the house, mending Chaise, Coachman, footman & hairdresser	Louis 4 — 0

31. A Page of Walpole's Purchases in Paris, 1769

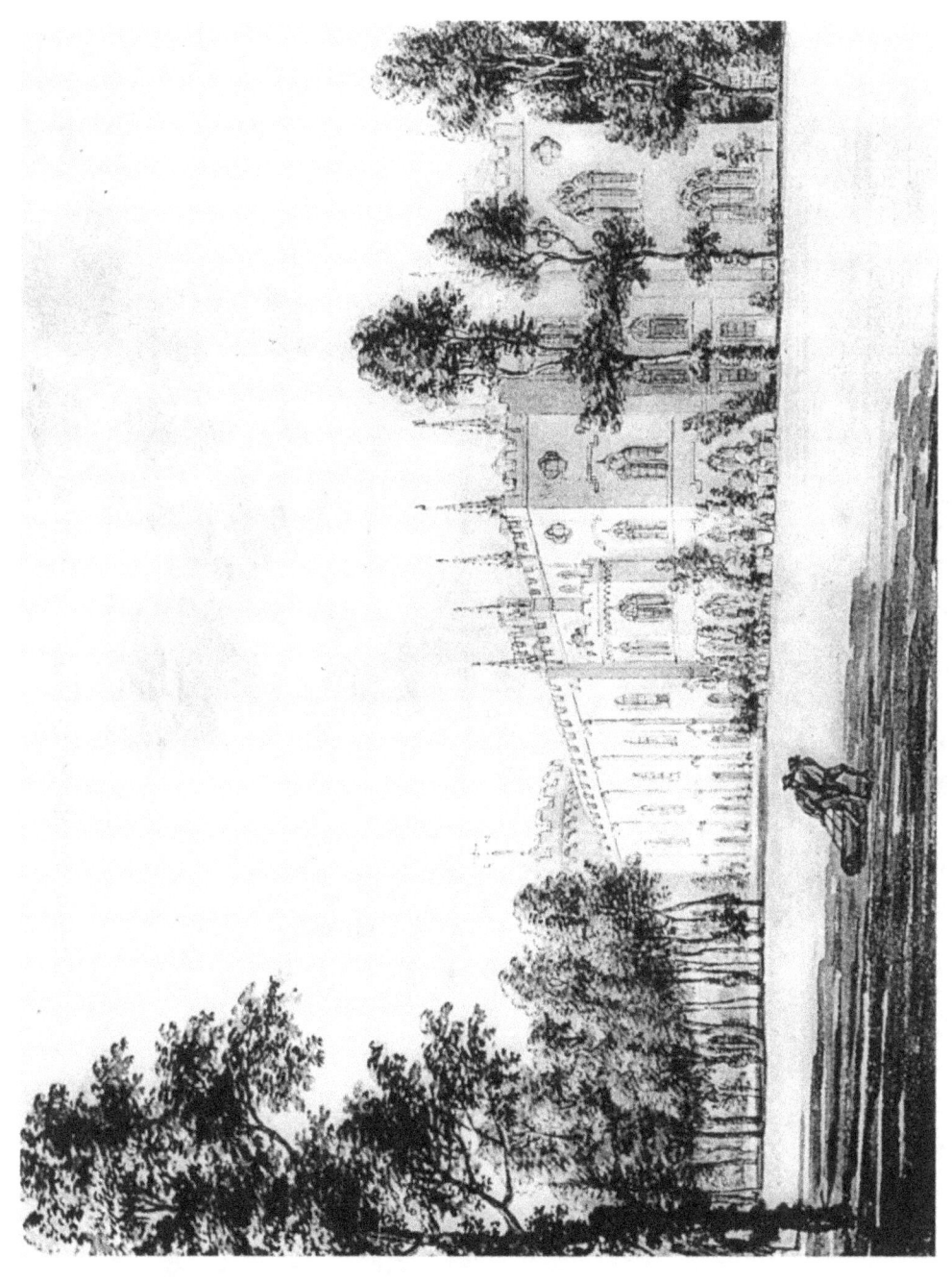

32. STRAWBERRY HILL FROM THE SOUTHEAST, *by Paul Sandby, ca. 1774*

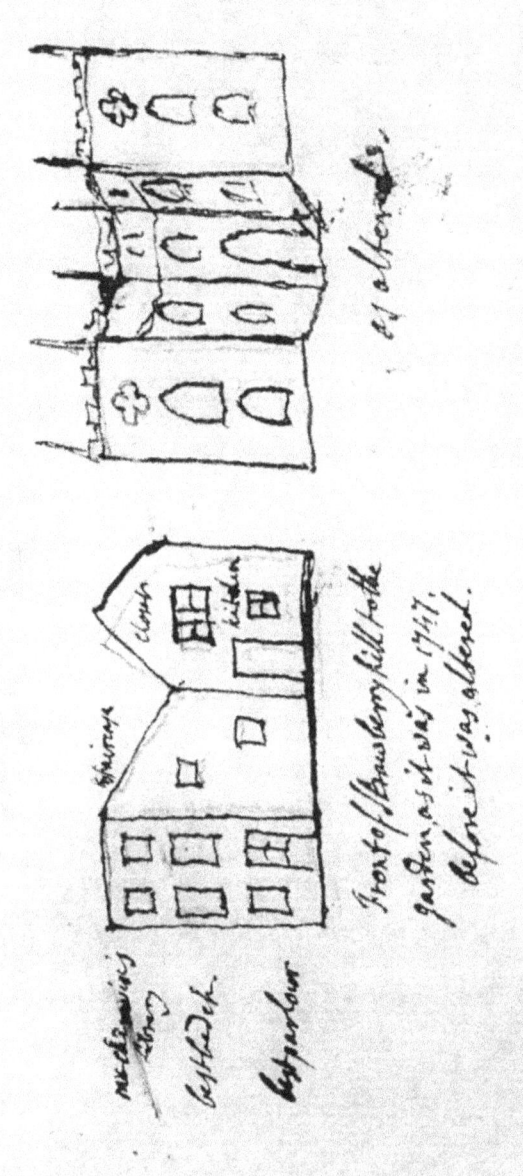

33. STRAWBERRY HILL BEFORE AND AFTER ALTERATION

Strawberry Hill

The house was a cottage that had been built fifty years earlier by Lord Bradford's coachman. Five acres went with it. "Hill" is a misnomer; the highest part of the property is only thirty-three feet above the Thames. The land sloped gently in "enamelled meadows, with filigree hedges"[3] to the river three hundred yards away; a little stream meandered through them. Walpole bought Turkish sheep with four horns and two cows, "all studied in their colors for becoming the view."[4] At the outset the view was Strawberry's most attractive feature. It was animated by coaches and chaises on their way to and from Teddington and Hampton Court; moving up and down the river were "barges as solemn as Barons of the Exchequer";[5] Richmond Hill and Ham Walks bounded the prospect. It was, Walpole said, "a gay and tranquil scene," and he made it more so by setting out one hundred and twenty-two trees at a cost of £9 6s.,[6] and shrubs and flowers, and vegetables. "I am all plantation," he wrote, "and sprout away like any chaste nymph in the *Metamorphosis*."[7] He said that the house itself was so small that he could send it to Mann in a letter. It was to grow and grow, as we shall see. When we study it we are as close to him as when we study his letters and the books that he wrote and owned. When we talk about Strawberry Hill we are talking about Horace Walpole himself.

We first hear of his decision to do it over in the Gothic style in 1749, two years after he moved into it. Why Gothic? He explains in the Preface of his *Description of Strawberry Hill* that the house was "built to please my own taste, and in some degree to realize my own visions." As an undergraduate he had written verses on King's College Chapel, pointing out that it had been built when

> *Art and Palladio had not reached the land,*
> *Nor methodized the Vandal Builder's hand.*[8]

---

[3] Walpole to Conway, 8 June 1747.

[4] Walpole to Mann, 5 June 1747.

[5] Walpole to Conway, 8 June 1747.

[6] *Strawberry Hill Accounts,* ed. Paget Toynbee (Oxford, 1927), p. 1.

[7] Walpole to Montagu, 20 Oct. 1748.

[8] "Verses in Memory of King Henry the Sixth, Founder of King's College, Cambridge."

Horace Walpole

Even then he thought that Englishmen should be proud of their native Gothic. He grew still more patriotic on his travels when he found Frenchmen and Italians condescending to Englishmen as untutored Northerners, rich, vigorous, but deficient in the arts and graces. "Gothic" among the *cognoscenti* was a word of contempt; "Gothic" had become an underdog, and that made it attractive to him. On his return he saw buildings in England as fine as any in Europe. The irregularity of Gothic, with its freedom from restraint and tyranny of rule, suited the "wildness" in himself.

He did not settle on Gothic immediately. Innovation, experiment, revolution were in the air. In addition to Gothic, which he explained was of many kinds, including "the Venetian or Mosque Gothic," there was "the Sharawadgi, or Chinese want of symmetry," in buildings and gardens. Sharawadgi had the allurement of the mysterious: although adepts used the word airily, no one, least of all the Chinese, knew what it meant.[9] There are at Farmington sketches for Chinese summer houses at Strawberry Hill and Holland House, but after Walpole had flirted with Sharawadgi he attacked it and "preached so effectually" against it to Dicky Bateman, its proponent, "that his every pagoda took the veil."[10] The "Mosque Gothic" appears only once among the drawings at Farmington: a Turkish swimming pool with a bashaw, eunuch, and two houris. All this was too exotic. Patriotism won the day; he settled on a late medieval English "castle" with refinements from France and Italy. Such a house had been beyond the wealth and taste of his Norfolk ancestors, but by putting up their arms and the arms of the chief families with which they were allied he would realize the vision of himself as the scion of an ancient Norfolk family. The Armoury was to have, he wrote to Mann, "trophies of old coats of mail, Indian shields made of rhinoceros's hides, broadswords, quivers, long bows, arrows, and spears—all *supposed* to be taken by Sir Terry Robsart in the holy wars."[11] When he got this letter back and copied it for us he added a note on Sir Terry Robsart, "An

[9] It was probably a hoax invented by Sir William Temple.
[10] Walpole to Lord Strafford, 13 June 1781.
[11] Walpole to Mann, 12 June 1753.

ancestor of Sir R. W., who was Knight of the Garter." He, the youngest son of the great Sir Robert Walpole, would have a house worthy of his father and his ancestors.

John Chute and Richard Bentley encouraged him in his Gothicism. The three of them made up what Walpole called "The Committee." They proceeded to enlarge the original cottage and to transform it with wooden battlements and pointed windows and quatrefoils and pinnacles. There was in this a certain amount of aesthetic twitter, but the Committee were serious. They were not moved by fashionable boredom, as it has been said that the eighteenth-century medievalists were. They were anything but bored. "One must have taste to be sensible of the beauties of Grecian architecture," Walpole said, "one only wants passions to feel Gothic."[12] The Committee had discovered beauty in the older English architecture and they determined to revive it. Their spirit was the same as that of the American antiquaries who early in this century discovered the beauties of our Colonial period, formed a dining club, and called themselves "The Walpole Society." The Committee were not alone in the field, but they regarded their rivals as well-meaning fumblers: Lord Brooke's Gothic at Warwick Castle was "woeful"; Saunderson Miller's church tower at Wroxton fell down, although his improvements at Hagley had "the true rust of the Barons' Wars"; Kent, Walpole said, failed to conceive either the principles or graces of Gothic.[13] The field was wide open to the Committee.

To get what they wanted they went back to the late English Gothic buildings themselves, or rather, to the prints of them in the sumptuous histories of churches and counties in the library at Strawberry Hill. The Committee pored over these prints, especially those of tombs, "for you know," Walpole said, "the great delicacy and richness of Gothic ornaments was exhausted on small chapels, oratories, and tombs."[14] The Committee picked and chose and adapted. They saw no impropriety in merging the tombs of John of Eltham, Earl of Cornwall, in Westminster

---

[12] "Anecdotes of Painting," *Works* (1798), III, 94.
[13] Ibid., III, 490.
[14] Walpole to Cole, 11 Aug. 1769.

Horace Walpole

Abbey and of Thomas, Duke of Clarence, at Canterbury to produce the chimney piece in the library at Strawberry Hill. Prince Arthur's tomb in Worcester Cathedral, as illustrated in Sandford's *Genealogical History of the Kings of England* (1677), was beautiful in itself and it had a place at Strawberry Hill because Prince Arthur, like Strawberry's creator, was descended from Cadwallader, last King of the Britons. Details of it inspired the Strawberry wallpaper in the entrance hall and on the staircase.[15] When finished, Strawberry exhibited, Walpole explained, "specimens of Gothic architecture, as collected from standards in cathedrals and chapel tombs," and showed how they might be "applied to chimney pieces, ceilings, windows, balustrades, loggias, etc."[16] Strawberry Hill was an eighteenth-century museum in which were displayed examples of Gothic detail—in ways that would have made the original architects stare.

Walpole and his friends had no idea how Gothic buildings were constructed, nor did they care. What they were after was atmosphere; they were not concerned how their workmen achieved it. Stresses and strains and all that were left to one William Robinson, Clerk of the Works at Greenwich Hospital. Walpole did not include him among the architects in his *Anecdotes of Painting,* and the twenty-five pounds that he gave him after the first rooms were built looks like a tip, but Robinson had his uses: he knew how to build an eighteenth-century house which, although it might wear out, would not fall down. The fabric of Strawberry Hill was lath and plaster: "Gilly" Williams said long before its master died that Mr. Walpole had already outlived three sets of his battlements.[17]

---

[15] Walpole's copy of Sandford has a note by him on the plate of the tomb and one by Bentley indicating the change of scale that was needed for the transition. On that print we see the Committee in actual operation, anticipating what William Morris was to make commonplace in the next century. For a description of other translations, see W. S. Lewis, "The Genesis of Strawberry Hill," *Metropolitan Museum Studies,* V, Pt. 1 (New York, 1934), 66–86.

[16] "A Description of Strawberry Hill," *Works* (1798), II, 395.

[17] Yale Walpole, 4. 251, n. 19, a note furnished by Miss Berry to Mme du Deffand's letter of 25 June 1769, where she inquired about the new building at Strawberry Hill and concluded "*Oh! vous travaillez pour la postérité pour votre mémoire.*"

Strawberry Hill

There was nothing pedantic about the Committee. "I did not mean," Walpole wrote, "to make my house so Gothic as to exclude convenience and modern refinements in luxury. The designs of the inside and outside are strictly ancient, but the decorations are modern."[18] This eclecticism enabled him to have a gallery with the ceiling from Henry VII's Chapel in Westminster Abbey, gold network over looking-glass from Chantilly, and crimson Norwich damask. The carpets in the Gallery and elsewhere were Moorfields; in still other rooms there were Axminsters and Wiltons; Aubusson tapestry was used on beds and chairs all over the house. Bentley designed Gothic furniture, but Walpole also had "a thousand plump chairs, couches, and luxurious settees covered with linen of blue and white stripes adorned with festoons."[19] To enrich the "gloomth" he sent a man to Flanders to buy painted glass. The man came back with four hundred and fifty pieces showing "scriptural stories, stained in black and yellow . . . birds and flowers in colors, and Flemish coats of arms,"[20] which were called "the achievements of the old counts of Strawberry."[21] Gloomth, gaiety, novelty, romantic visions, and comfort—all were found at Strawberry Hill.

The east end of the house was finished in 1754, but Walpole went on adding rooms and outbuildings for nearly forty years. He was driven in part by his ever-expanding collections, in part by his instinct to magnify and adorn his dearest possession. Ultimately, the main house had twenty-two rooms, a modest number compared to Houghton, but making a house too large to send in a letter. The new rooms were larger than the old; whereas the early China Closet was only about ten by twelve feet, the later Gallery was fifty-six feet long and fifteen feet wide; the early Little Cloister was perhaps fourteen feet long, the Great Cloister, fifty-six. Each room had its name: the Holbein Chamber, the Star Chamber (a pun: it had a glass star in the ceiling), the Long Gallery, the Drawing Room in the Great Tower, and so on. Since Walpole had

---

[18] "A Description of Strawberry Hill," *Works* (1798), II, 397.
[19] Walpole to Mann, 12 June 1753.
[20] "Anecdotes of Painting," *Works* (1798), III, 159 n.
[21] Walpole to Mann, 18 Oct. 1750. Many of these were sold in 1842.

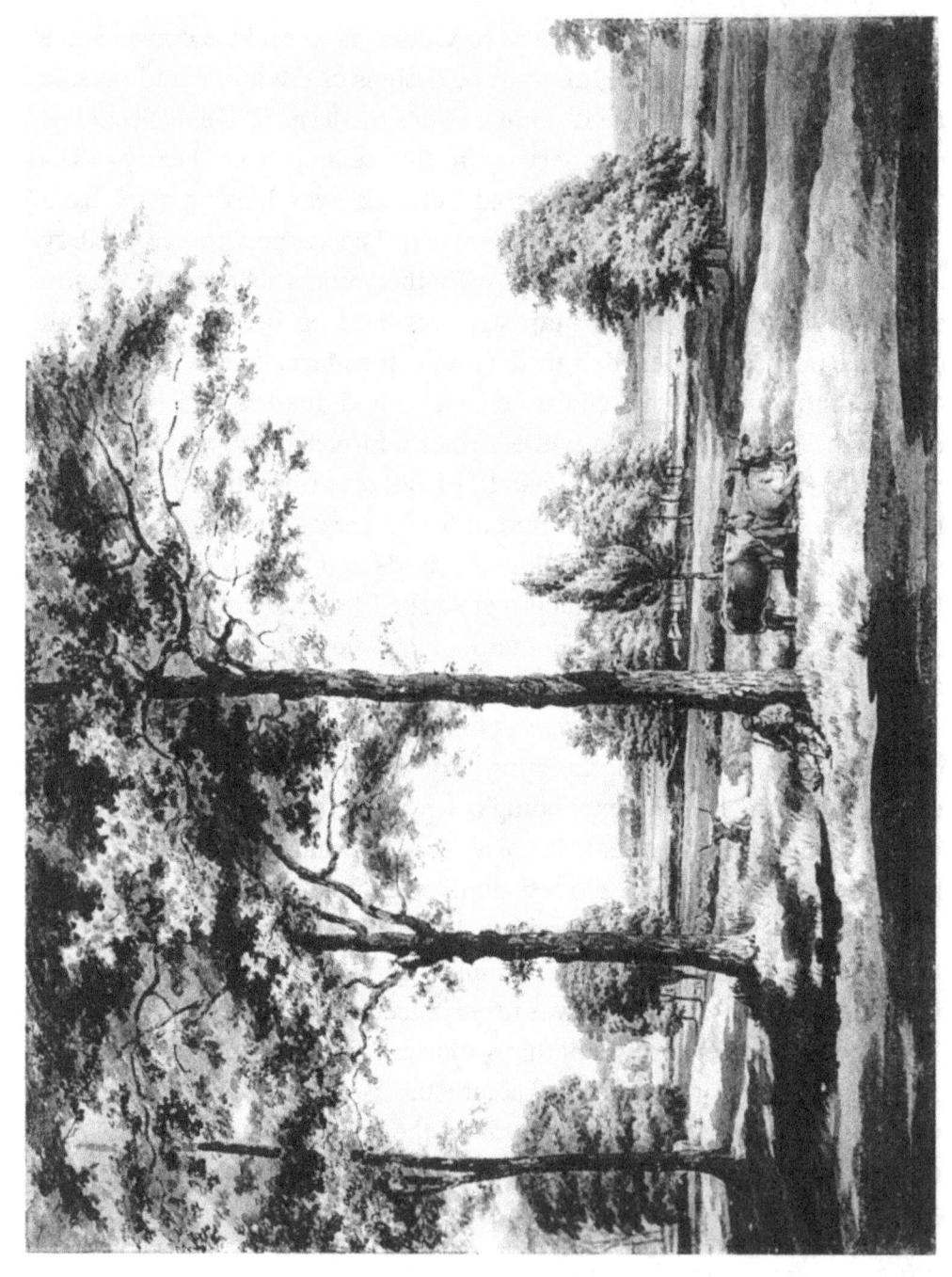

34. VIEW OF RICHMOND AND TWICKENHAM FROM STRAWBERRY HILL,
by William Pars, 1772

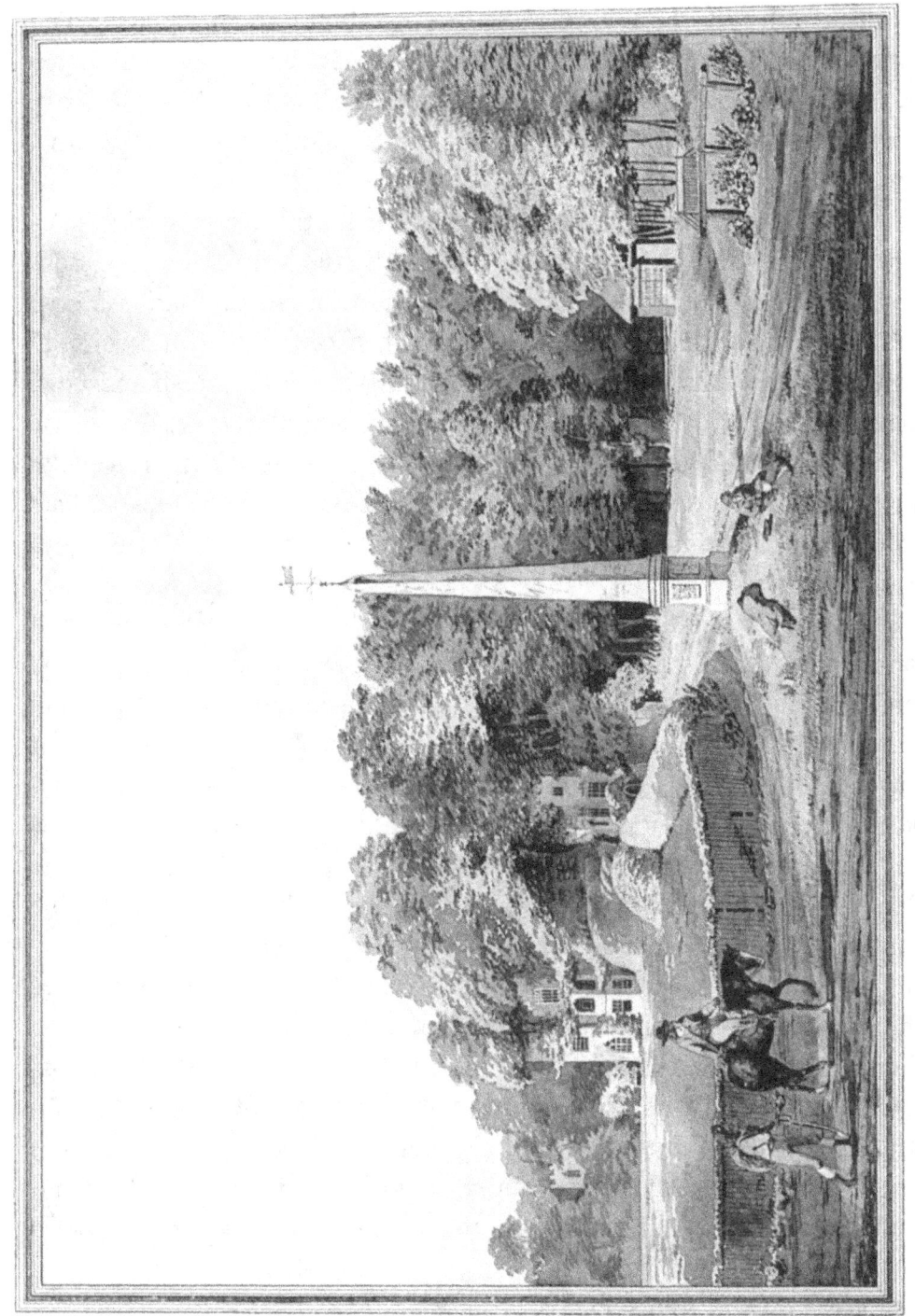

35. STRAWBERRY HILL FROM THE EAST, *by James Malton, ca. 1791*

his meals all over the house, there was no dining-room as such. The names of the rooms changed from time to time: the Great Parlour became the Refectory, the Yellow Bedchamber the Beauty Room: the Tribune was first called the Cabinet and then the Chapel. No house was ever more alive.

It is easy to make fun of Strawberry Hill: the Committee's ignorance is so evident, their intention so naive, the whole thing so contrived. We may say what we like, but of more interest, I think, is how the eighteenth-century visitors felt about it. Strawberry Hill "worked" for them. They thought that they were seeing something fresh and new, something rather over their heads, perhaps, but since Mr. Walpole was doing it, it must be taken seriously. They accepted his attempts to evoke the past, and they found in the discarded relics of former ages that he brought together an awakened appreciation of early English artists and craftsmen.

Strawberry's influence spread at once. The Committee were asked to provide Gothic improvements for their friends—"a fictitious steeple" for Nicholas Hardinge at Kingston, fourteenth-century farms for Lady Suffolk and Sir Thomas Seabright, a gateway for Dr. Trevor, Bishop of Durham, "a menagerie" for Lord Strafford. The clergy turned to Walpole for help. The Bishop of Ely sought his advice about the east window there, and Walpole's name was invoked in a quarrel that divided the Chapter on the subject of replacing the organ; he helped to restore the tomb of William of Hatfield, Edward III's second son, in York Minster; but his greatest opportunity was missed when the Bishop of Rochester and the Dean of Westminster consulted him about an altarpiece for the choir of the Abbey. His solution of their problem was the Market Cross at Chichester, which he had already adapted for Lord Strafford's menagerie. The Market Cross was "to be elevated on a flight of steps, with the altar in the middle, and semi-circular arcades to join the stalls, so that the Confessor's chapel and tombs may be seen through in perspective,"[22]

---

[22] Walpole to Mason, 10 July 1775.

but, fortunately, the courage and imagination of the Dean and Chapter were unequal to the opportunity that Walpole offered to them.

Even today the sympathetic visitor to Strawberry Hill can sense something of the magic and make-believe that Walpole tried to catch. The early rooms communicate it more distinctly than the later ones, perhaps because they are smaller and more intimate, perhaps because they have kept more of their painted glass, perhaps because through two of them you can still walk out into the garden. The garden has changed more than the house, but its stretches of turf and the trees in the distance carry us back to the eighteenth-century water-color drawings of them. The garden must have softened the most skeptical visitor then as now.

The spirit of revival that shaped the house had no place in the garden. On the contrary, we find revolution there. When Mann assumed that it would be Gothic as well as the house, Walpole put him straight at once. "Gothic is merely architecture," he explained, "and as one has a satisfaction in imprinting the gloomth of abbeys and cathedrals on one's house, so one's garden, on the contrary, is to be nothing but *riant,* and the gaiety of nature."[23] Until the eighteenth century, English gardens had conformed to the classical order of straight walks and symmetry; they had obelisks, pyramids, and "topiary works." Walpole would have none of them. The chief feature of his garden was the lawn, which swept east to the road bordering the river and south to the fields between "the mansion" and Little Strawberry Hill, the cottage that he let Mrs. Clive, the actress, and her brother have and where, after her death, he installed the Berrys. A small walled garden to the west of the Round Tower must have been very pretty. It had a circular pool, which he called Po-Yang, and borders of annuals. Strawberry was famous for its lilacs, tulips, jonquils, acacias, and syringas. Walpole planted a little wood and made two discreet cascades. Here and there one came on entertaining objects, a great oak bench, designed by Bentley in the shape of a shell,

---

[23] Walpole to Mann, 27 April 1753.

71

a Gothic screen to "the Prior's garden," Bernini's *Apollo and Daphne* in bronze, and the sleeping Morpheus in plaster. Like the house, the grounds grew and grew until the original five acres became forty-six.

There were various outbuildings: a cottage with a "tea-room" and library, a Chapel at the end of a short winding path in the little wood, the Printing Press, and, finally the New Offices, containing a stable for seven horses and six bedrooms for servants. By the time the New Offices were built, Walpole's taste had become purer. He confessed to the "imperfections and bad executions of my attempts; for neither Mr. Bentley nor my workmen had *studied* the science."[24] Later still he said that "every true Goth must perceive" that the early rooms "are more the works of fancy than of imitation."[25] When he built the New Offices he abandoned his antiquarian researches and chose what he called "a collegiate style."[26] It was executed by James Wyatt, who had made his reputation as a Goth at Lee Priory, which Walpole described as "a child of Strawberry, prettier than the parent."[27]

He had few misgivings about the objects that filled the house and forced him to build on room after room. As you read his *Description of Strawberry Hill* and the 1842 sale catalogue, you get an impression of indiscriminate clutter. The walls were crowded with pictures and drawings, the closets and cabinets with china, glass, snuffboxes, rings, and "curiosities." Gradually one can sort out certain concentrations of interest, of which the most important were classical antiquities, English coins and enamels, and English prints. Less has been written about the high quality of these collections than about the curiosities that the public preferred and that lent themselves to ridicule.

Like most eighteenth-century collectors, Walpole began with classical antiquities. "I am far gone in medals, lamps, idols, prints, etc.," he

[24] Walpole to Thomas Barrett, 5 June 1788.
[25] Walpole to Mary Berry, 17 Oct. 1794.
[26] Walpole to Cole, 1 June 1776.
[27] Walpole to Mary Berry, 27 Sept. 1794. The offices were designed by James Essex, but he died before they were built.

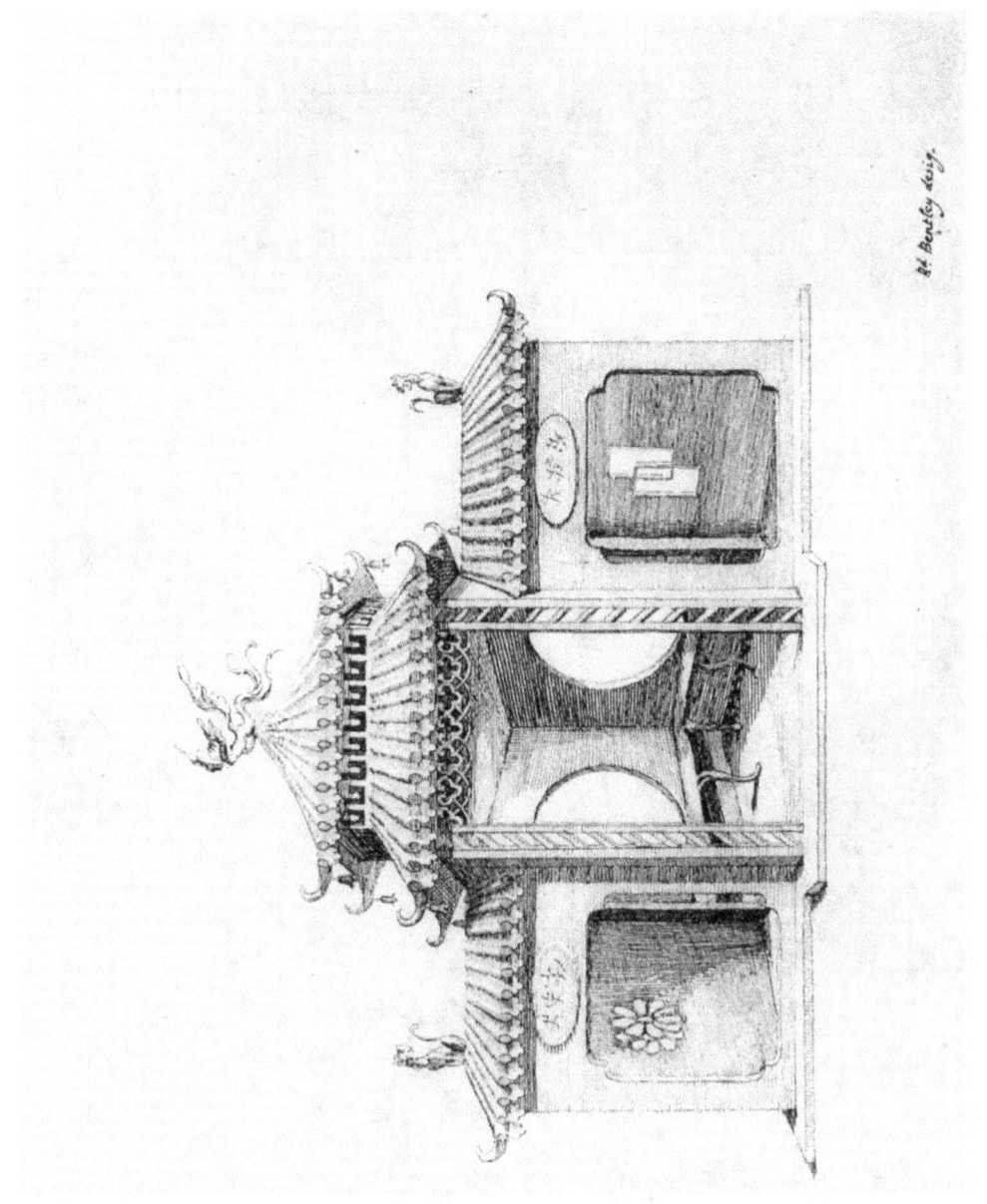

36. THE CHINESE SUMMER HOUSE, *by Bentley*

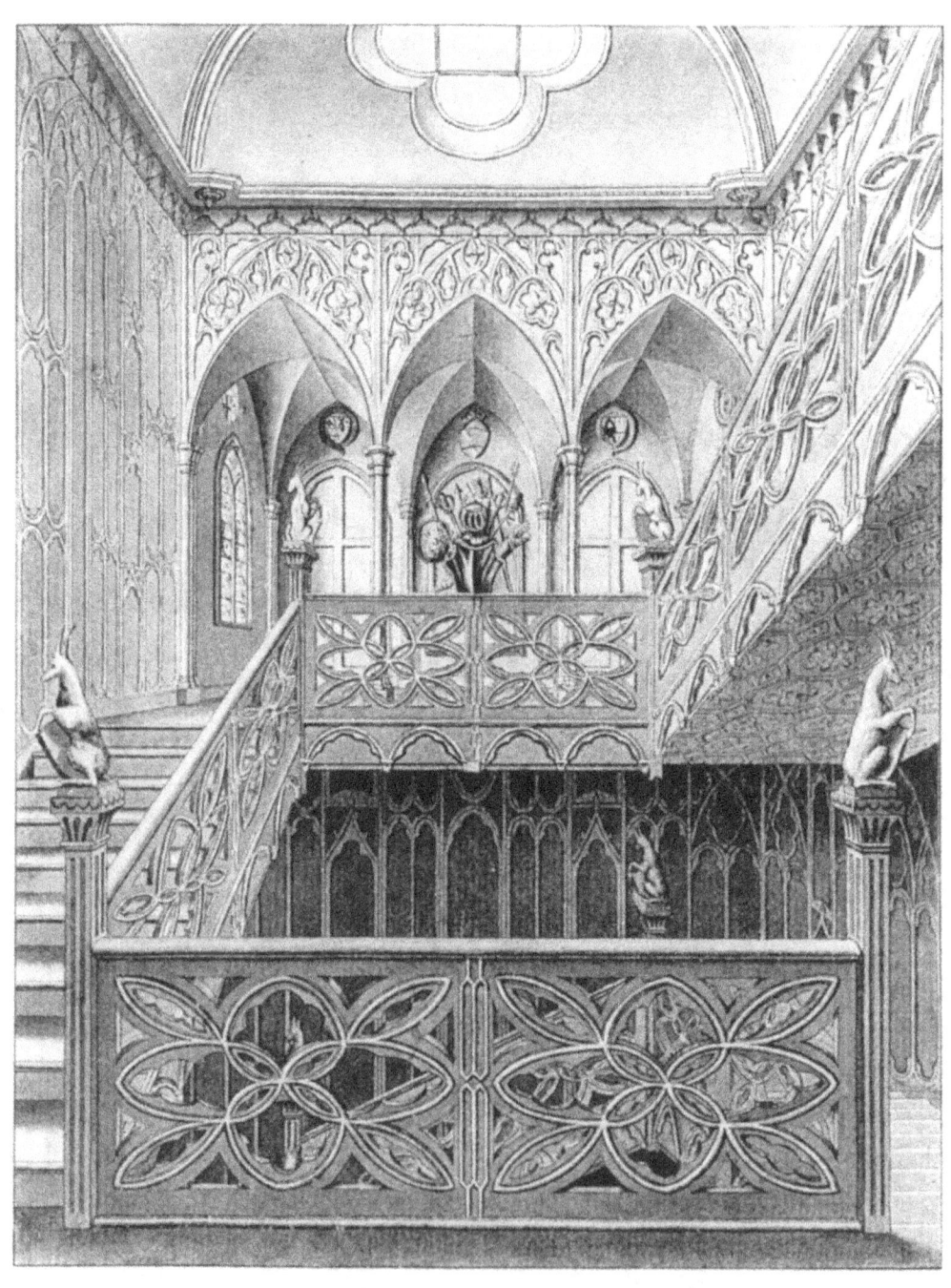

37. THE ARMOURY, *by John Carter,* 1788

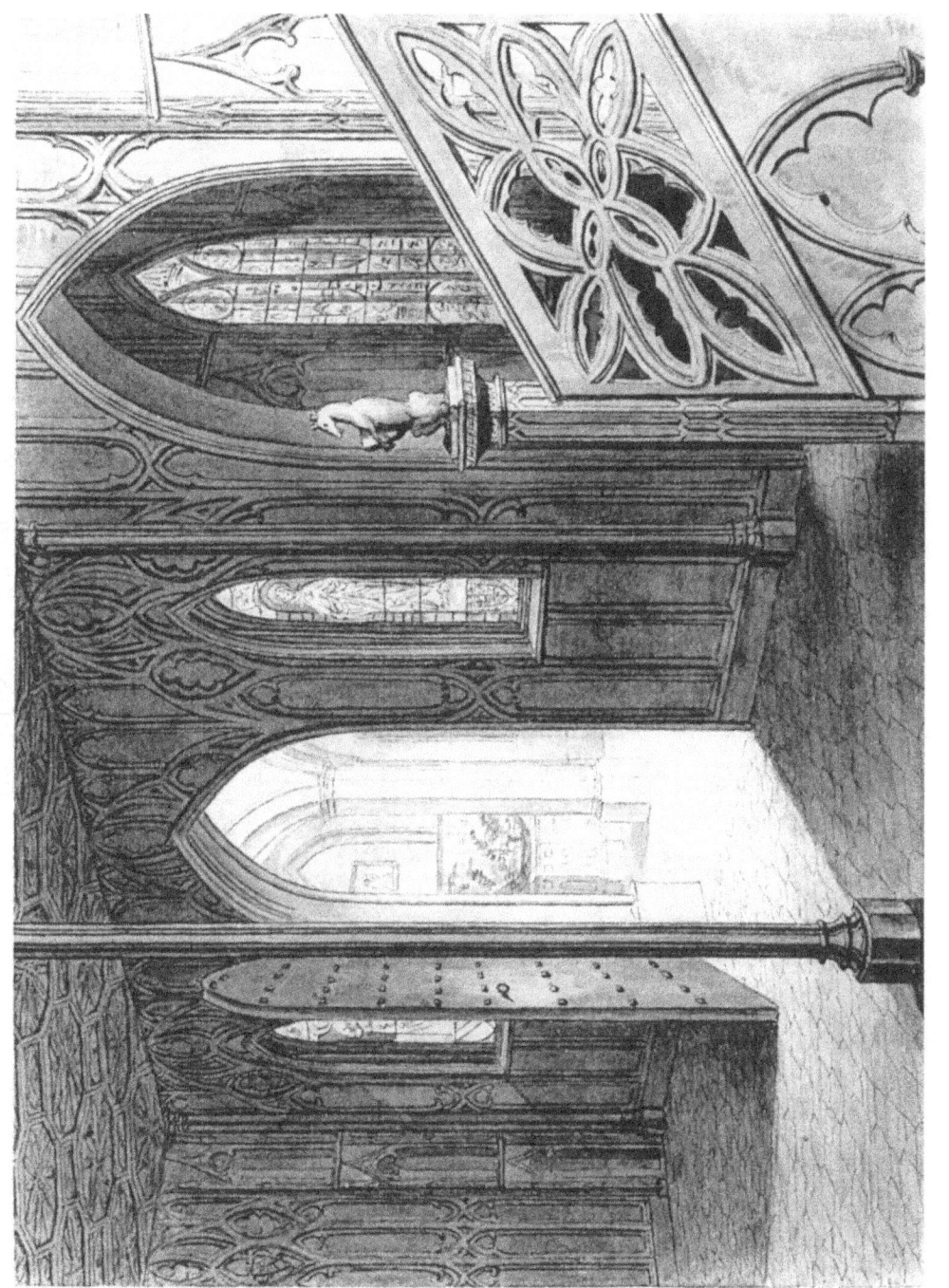

38. The Little Cloister and Hall, *by John Carter, 1788*

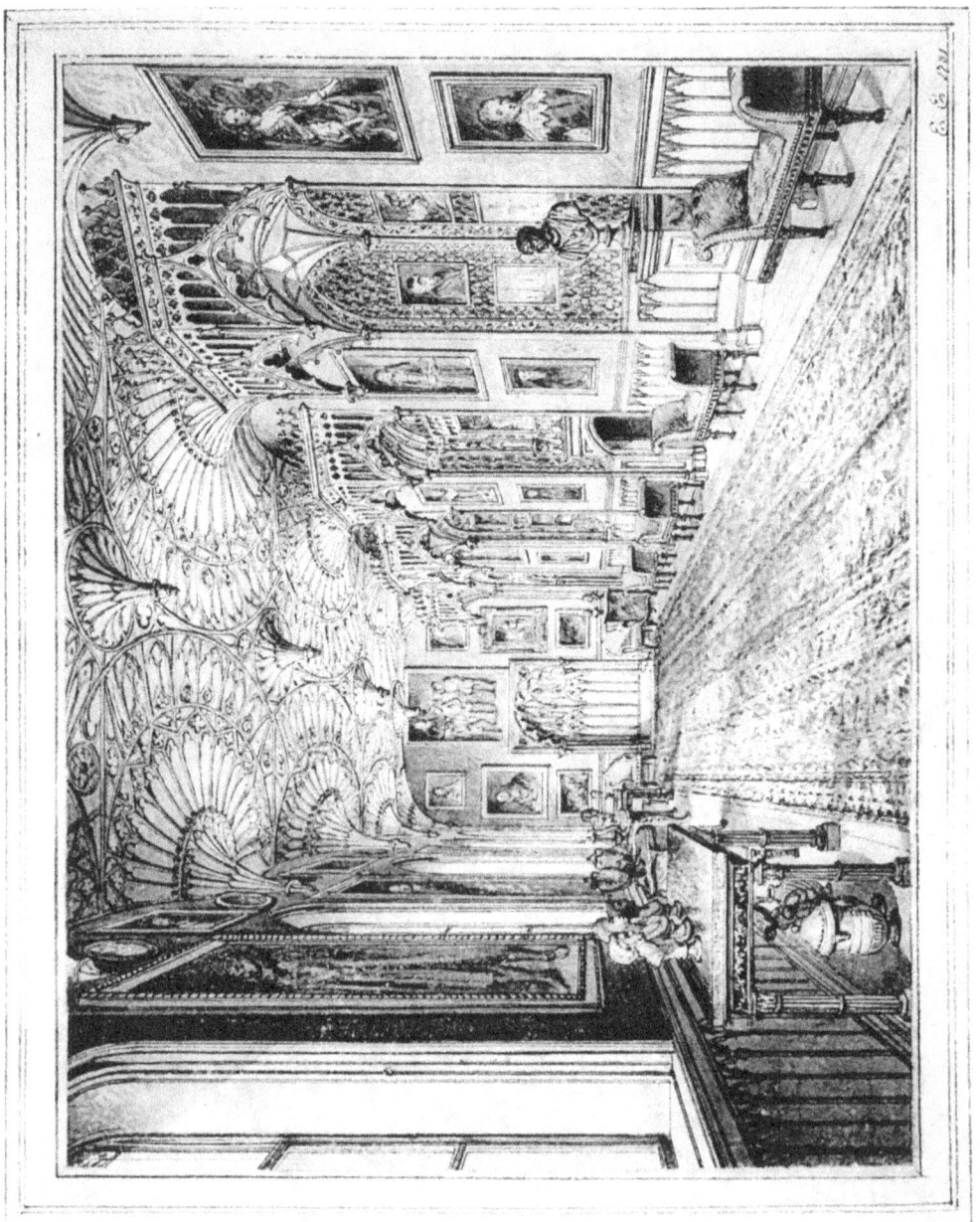

39. THE GALLERY, *by Edward Edwards, 1781*

wrote from Rome; "I would buy the Colosseum if I could."[28] He swept up hundreds of Greek and Roman coins and medals in gold, silver, and brass, as well as bronze Floras, muses, hermaphrodites, bulls, and harpies, cameos, intaglios, and smelling bottles, but with the purchase in 1744 of Conyers Middleton's extensive collection, his concentration on classical antiquities ended. Greece and Rome yielded to England, a change of taste that was followed by British antiquaries in general as the eighteenth century wore on.[29]

He had already begun his second big collection, English coins and medals, and when, at the age of twenty-four, he bought many of the best pieces in Lord Oxford's sale, he became one of the leading English numismatists. He went on to English miniatures and enamels. He admitted that the King and the Duke of Portland rivaled him in this field, but his collection of Isaac and Peter Oliver, Holbein, Nicholas Hilliard, and Samuel Cooper put him first. Then there were the drawings and prints of English heads, twelve thousand of them, arranged in reigns from King Arthur—no less—to the middle of George III's reign, many of which have notes in Walpole's hand. He had virtually complete collections of Hollar, Faithorne, Vertue, and Hogarth. Among his dozens of oils he was particularly proud of the portraits of Henry V, VI, VII, and VIII.[30] Better known today are Reynolds's *Ladies Waldegrave* (Walpole's great-nieces)[31] and his conversation piece of George Selwyn, "Gilly" Williams, and Lord Edgcumbe,[32] Hogarth's *Sarah Malcolm*[33] and his sketch of *The Beggar's Opera*,[34] and Romney's *Lady Craven*.[35]

---

[28] Walpole to Conway, 23 April 1740.

[29] Of the sixty-three contributions to the first volume of *Archaeologia* in 1770, fifty-two dealt with British antiquities; in the 1790 volume all the contributions did so.

[30] The one that he believed showed the marriage of Henry VI (now at the Toledo Museum of Art) is no longer thought to be Henry VI. The portraits of Henry VII and Henry VIII with their children are now at Sudeley Castle in the possession of Mrs. Dent Brocklehurst.

[31] Now at the National Gallery of Scotland.

[32] Now at the Bristol Art Gallery.

[33] Now at the National Gallery of Scotland.

[34] Now at Farmington.

[35] Now owned by Mr. Richard Martineau of Eton College.

Horace Walpole

His friends were represented throughout the house by the presents that they made him, about one hundred and sixty of them. They range from Mann's gift of the bronze bust of Caligula with silver eyes that shows the Emperor at the beginning of his madness to "three pieces of rocks made of rice," which came from Mrs. Clive's brother, Mr. Raftor. Donors to the Strawberry Museum got full credit for their generosity, no matter what they gave.

Walpole's lack of critical reserve about the talents of his friends and relations appears in his collection of their drawings and etchings. Ladies and gentlemen showed him their sketch books and received his extravagant praise. The flattered artists then gave him their etchings of peasants brooding in the manner of Parmigianino or pointing to cows in the manner of Salvator Rosa. Walpole pasted these works with his own hands into a superb folio of crimson morocco elaborately gilt. Posterity, he said, would envy him the possession of such a volume.[36] The Strawberry Press printed title pages for the gifts of Lord Harcourt, Lady Louisa Augusta Greville, and Isabella Byron Lady Carlisle. Even more notable than these artists were Lady Lucan, Henry Bunbury, Lady Diana Beauclerk, and Mrs. Damer. They had soared, he said, "above their modest timidity" and had reached almost to the sublimity of Raphael and Shakespeare. Mrs. Damer was not inferior to Praxiteles. Walpole designed an ebony cabinet for Lady Diana Beauclerk's drawings of gypsies and children;[36] he went further and built a tower with a hexagonal closet to house her drawings for his *Mysterious Mother*. "Oh, such drawings!" he wrote, "Guido's grace, Albano's children, Poussin's expression, Salvator's boldness in landscape, and Andrea Sacchi's simplicity of composition might perhaps have equalled them had they wrought all together very fine."[37] In the dawn of an era of English painting that he hoped would rival the brightest schools of the past its men and women of high rank were furnishing proofs of genius that he delighted to display at Strawberry Hill. He could be as intemperate in praise as in censure.

---

[36] It is now at Farmington.
[37] Walpole to Mason, 18 Feb. 1776.

Strawberry Hill

The library was not a large one by eighteenth-century standards, only about eight thousand volumes. Walpole was not a bibliophile; he scorned the mysteries of what is today called bibliography and he had little curiosity about textual variants. He bought a few books for their bindings and rarity and for their association with earlier owners, but not many. He bought his books to read, which he did with a pencil or pen in his hand. About a third of them have his crosses and lines and notes in their margins; passages that struck him as particularly memorable he copied into his "Books of Materials." His notes occur most often in memoirs, letters, and English topography, genealogy, and heraldry: he was fond of recording anecdotes, pointing out family relationships, and adding odd circumstances. Also he took pleasure, as we all do, in correcting misstatements, particularly when the author was "learned." Much of this annotation found its way into his letters and works, but its chief interest lies, I think, in seeing what phrases and sentences and sentiments struck him with sufficient force to compel him to stop and make a mark or write a note. These marginalia bring us close to Walpole himself. One of the last of them is poignant as well as characteristic. It is a note in Murphy's *Travels in Portugal* (1795): Was the Cathedral of Batalha built after a design by an English architect? The Commonplace Book in which Walpole wrote his note is tightly bound; he must have had to bend over it and, while he laboriously carved out his note, to force his gouty left hand down upon the book to keep it open.[38]

The Strawberry library had all the English and Latin classics—Shakespeare, Milton, and Dryden; Virgil, Horace, and Ovid—many times over. His favorite French books centered around Mme de Sévigné. English topography, the history of counties, towns, and churches, had a large section to itself, and so had noble authors and books on the arts. The library was weak in law, medicine, and philosophy. It was surprisingly strong in controversial theology. Walpole liked to read about the squabbles of clerics and the sort of thing that he found in Bayle—a statement by an abbot of Leicester that he had seen at Jerusalem a finger of

---

[38] This Commonplace Book is now at Farmington.

the Holy Ghost and the snout of a seraphim, and the discovery that cater-pillars were tried and excommunicated at Lausanne in 1479. He also made collections of contemporary publications and must have been a great comfort to his bookseller, from whom after 1760 he bought hundreds of poems, pamphlets, and plays as they came out. He had them bound, ten or twelve to a volume, with his arms on the sides and "Poems of Geo. 3," "Tracts of Geo. 3," and "Theatre of Geo. 3" lettered on their spines. He made a table of contents in each volume and frequently added on the title page the month when the piece appeared. He would paste pertinent cuttings from newspapers on the flyleaves of the bound volumes. These poems, plays, and tracts with his notes and cuttings were to supplement his own journals and letters and to furnish posterity with materials for the study of his time. Finally, there were enormous books of battles and royal ceremonies and hundreds of portfolios and bound volumes with thousands of prints from Italian, Flemish, and Dutch masters and hundreds of their drawings.[39]

What interested the casual visitor most were the "curiosities." "In his villa," Macaulay wrote, "every apartment is a museum; every piece of furniture is a curiosity; there is something strange in the form of the shovel; there is a long story belonging to the bell rope," and he singled out "Queen Mary's comb, Wolsey's red hat, the pipe which Van Tromp smoked during his last sea fight, and the spur King William struck into the flank of Sorrel"[40] at the Battle of the Boyne. Walpole bought these "relics" because they evoked visions, but he did so with his tongue in his cheek. "You would laugh if you saw in the midst of what trumpery I am writing," he once wrote. "Two porters have just brought home my purchases from Mrs. Kennon the midwife's sale: Brobdignag combs, old broken pots, pans, and pipkins, a lantern of scraped oyster shells, scimitars, Turkish pipes, Chinese baskets, etc., etc. My servants think my

[39] For the library, see Allen T. Hazen, *A Catalogue of Horace Walpole's Library,* 4 vols., New Haven (in preparation); and W. S. Lewis, *Horace Walpole's Library* (Cambridge, England, 1958).

[40] In the *Edinburgh Review* (Oct. 1833); *Critical and Historical Essays* (1907), I, 331–46.

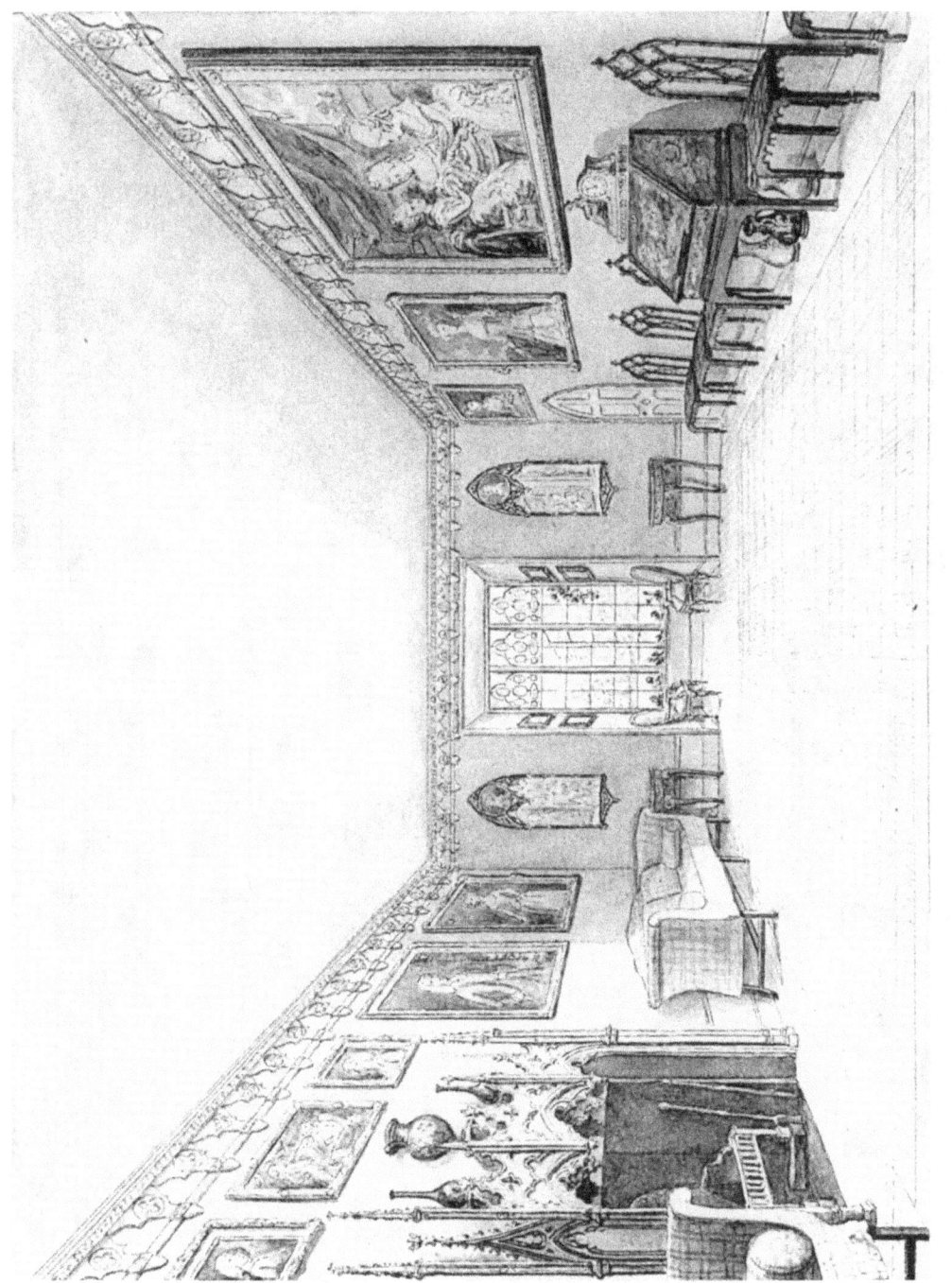

40. The Great Parlour (Refectory), *by John Carter*

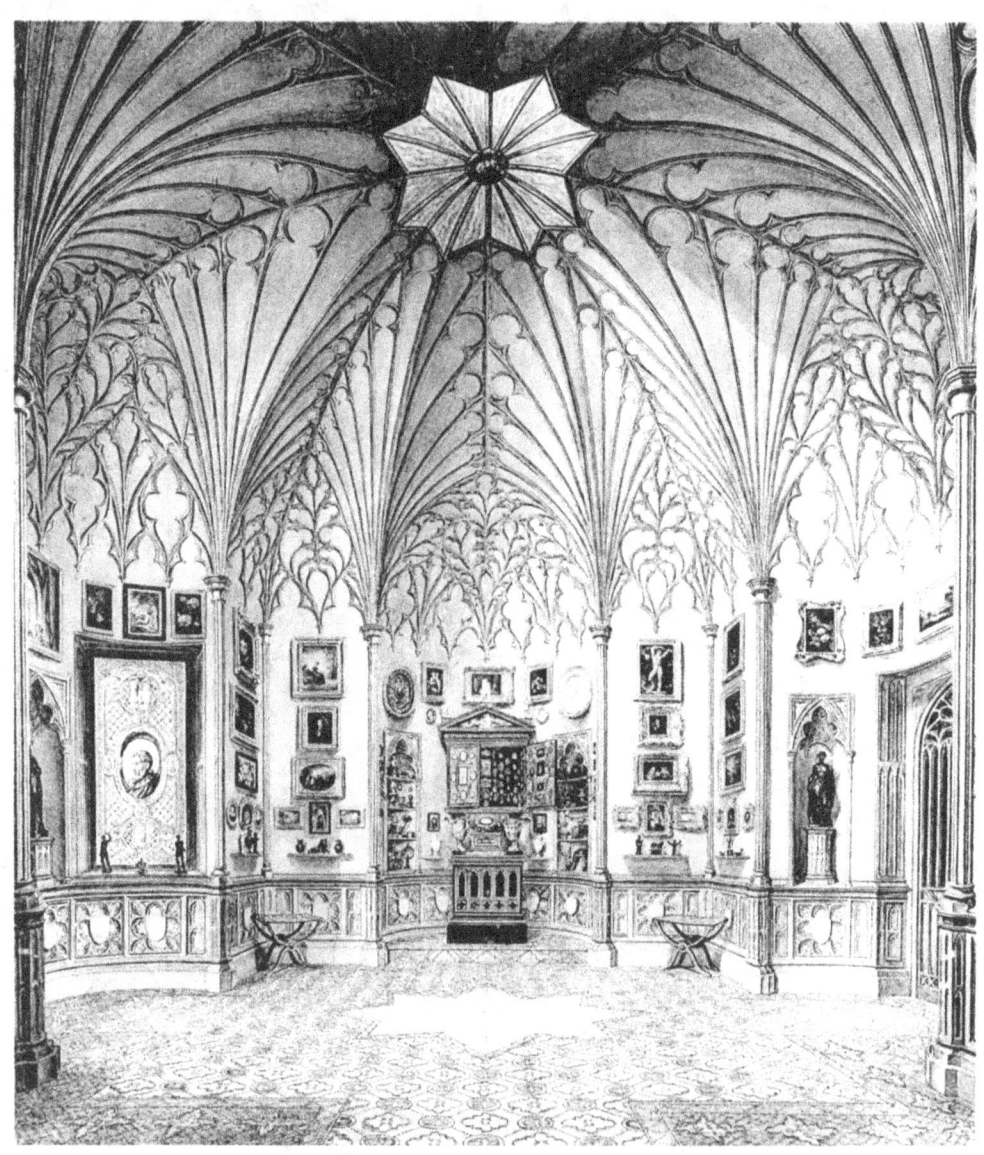

41. THE TRIBUNE

head is turned, I hope not: it is all to be called the personal estate and movables of my great-great-grandmother. . . . P.S. I forgot that I was outbid for Oliver Cromwell's nightcap."[41]

The fame of Strawberry Hill, the house, its gardens, contents, and its creator, spread far and wide during his life. He enjoyed this celebrity, particularly the admiration of foreigners. On one occasion he entertained the ambassadors of France and Spain. Strawberry was not large enough for crowds of guests, nor did he want them, because, apart from the expense of entertaining them, they would have made impossible the combination of intimacy and fairyland that he sought. So on this occasion there were only a dozen. Much thought went to achieve the right mixture of elegance and surprise, and he had luck in the weather. "Everything succeeded to a hair," he wrote.

"A violent shower in the morning laid the dust, brightened the green, refreshed the roses, pinks, orange-flowers, and the blossoms with which the acacias are covered. A rich storm of thunder and lightning gave a dignity of coloring to the heavens, and the sun appeared enough to illuminate the landscape, without basking himself over it at his length. During dinner, there were French horns and clarinets in the cloister, and after coffee I treated them with an English and to them very new collation, a syllabub, milked under the cows that were brought to the brow of the terrace. Thence they went to the printing-house, and saw a new fashionable French song printed. They drank tea in the gallery, and at eight went away to Vauxhall."[42]

As time went on, Strawberry became so popular that its creator shuddered when the bell rang at the gate.[43] To make his house less accessible he printed tickets for admission and rules to govern the visitors while they were there. No one was refused a ticket who applied properly,

[41] Walpole to Conway, 12 Feb. 1756. Walpole paid £15 19s. for these objects as appears from the receipted bill of his purchases now in the British Museum (Add. MSS 35,335).
[42] Walpole to Montagu, 18 June 1764.
[43] Walpole to Cole, 14 June 1769.

but only one company of four was permitted a day, between twelve and three from the first of May to the first of October, and the visitors had to apply in advance.[44] The tickets and rules were for strangers and friends of friends. When they came Walpole kept out of the way, leaving the conduct of the tour to his housekeeper, who expected to pocket a guinea from each guest on his departure. It was different with someone whom he wanted.

Those who were taken round the house by Walpole himself never forgot it. He hobbled ahead pointing out objects of particular interest, opening a locked cabinet to place an ivory or cameo carefully in the hand of a flattered visitor while telling a story about it or holding forth on its special significance. There was perhaps a dog at the master's heels or beside him on a sofa; squirrels came to the windows to be fed; canaries sang in their cages; pots of tuberoses and heliotrope and bowls of pot-pourri were in all the rooms, and after dinner a pot of frankincense was produced. The sulky Swiss men servants were a discordant note, the housekeepers were perhaps too full of character, but nothing, a neighbor said, would have surprised the housewives of Twickenham more than a change in Mr. Walpole's household.[45]

He brought out a short catalogue of the house as early as 1760; his last catalogue, greatly enlarged, came from the Press in 1784. This he called *A Description of the Villa of Mr. Horace Walpole, Youngest Son of Sir Robert Walpole, Earl of Orford, at Strawberry Hill, near Twickenham, Middlesex, with an Inventory of the Furniture, Pictures, Curiosities, &c.* It is a large quarto of eighty-eight pages, but it soon required further pages of "Additions" and "More Additions." The Preface to it, like all of Walpole's prefaces, is propitiatory. He was afraid that it would look "a little like arrogance in a private man to give a printed description

---

[44] Careful track was kept of those who came and also of those who had tickets and did not come. The worst offenders, apart from those who "saw with their fingers," were those who had a ticket, did not come, and did not return the ticket. Such a one was a Mr. Blakiston, who had a ticket for the 19th of August 1786. He neither came nor returned it, and when he brought it a week later Walpole recorded in his list of visitors that he was not admitted.

[45] Laetitia Matilda Hawkins, *Anecdotes ... and Memoirs* (1822), I, 97.

of his villa and collection, in which almost everything is diminutive." In answer to possible criticism of purists who should object to the mixture of portraits, French porcelain, and Greek and Roman sculpture in a house affecting "obsolete architecture," he concluded, "I do not mean to defend by argument a small capricious house." During his life he gave away few copies of the *Description,* because, he said, "If the visitors got the book into their hands, I should never get them out of the house, and they would want to see fifty articles which I do not choose they should handle and paw."[46] Instead, he left over eighty copies (out of the 200 printed) to friends on his death. These bequests suggest the eighteenth-century practice of leaving money for mourning rings, which was then going out. A copy of his *Description* was more intimate and personal than a ring, because Strawberry Hill was not only himself, but his wife, family, mistress, and endlessly satisfying companion. No bequest that he could have made would have been more personal.

He was torn between a desire to entail Strawberry upon a branch of his family and to let it go after his death to those who would buy his beloved collections partly, perhaps, because he had owned them. On the one hand he saw himself as the creator of a "castle" filled with treasures that he would settle upon younger relations and that would increase their importance in the world. This appealed to his vanity and self-love, but he realized that entails are broken.[47] On the other hand, there is the immortality that is gained through the sale room and its catalogue. In the end Walpole had it both ways: his relations lived at Strawberry for ninety-one years, and his collections have passed into the hands of those who have put an ever-higher value upon them.

The thirty-two days' sale in 1842 was perhaps the most written-about auction ever held in England. The catalogue of it went through eight editions. Robins, "the King of Puffery," spent money on an Introduction by Harrison Ainsworth and woodcuts by Delamotte, but econ-

---

[46] Walpole to Lady Ossory, 15 Sept. 1787.

[47] As early as 1754 he wrote "The Entail, A Fable," which tells how a butterfly established itself in a rose and summoned a caterpillar to settle it upon his family, only to have it destroyed by "a wanton boy."

omized on his cataloguers, with the result that the library was so badly described that booksellers and collectors forced him to withdraw the two-days' sale of prints and books and expand them to a ten-days' sale a month later in London. Copies of the catalogue were available in Paris and Leipzig as well as in London and at Strawberry Hill, and Robins, the auctioneer, saw to it that advance articles on the sale appeared in the newspapers and magazines. All this had just the wrong effect on *The Times,* which day after day insisted that what was being sold was rubbish and that Walpole, far from being what Robins called him, "the mighty master who planned and matured this wondrous whole," was "merely a great fool among the lesser fools of his ignorant age." Parodies of the catalogue appeared offering such objects as Homer's staff and wallet, "The bridge of the fiddle on which Nero played while Rome was burning," and a pimple from Oliver Cromwell's nose. *The Athenaeum* and others came to Walpole's defense, all of which increased the crowds that went down to see the house and its contents.

The sale was an enormous success. The total reached, over £33,000, was considered absurdly high. Apart from a few of the finest coins, manuscripts, and prints, which were bought by the British Museum, and the collection of tracts bought for Buckingham Palace, everything went to dealers or the great private collectors. During the century and more since the sale, objects from it have turned up frequently, and so have many others alleged to have been in it. Owners are sanguine in the matter of pedigree, and when a picture or chair or set of china in a famous house has been assigned an interesting association succeeding generations seldom question it. We can be sure of the pictures if their original stretchers have survived, because Walpole wrote his identifications on them. On objects that he was especially fond of, such as Lady Diana Beauclerk's cabinet and the snuffbox bequeathed to him by Mme du Deffand, he added a plaque or an inscription. Thanks to the manuscript catalogue of the library, the 1842 sale catalogue, and Mr. Hazen's researches we know virtually every printed piece at Strawberry Hill. During the three years that I have been writing these lectures, fifty-three volumes with his bookplate have turned up from places as far apart

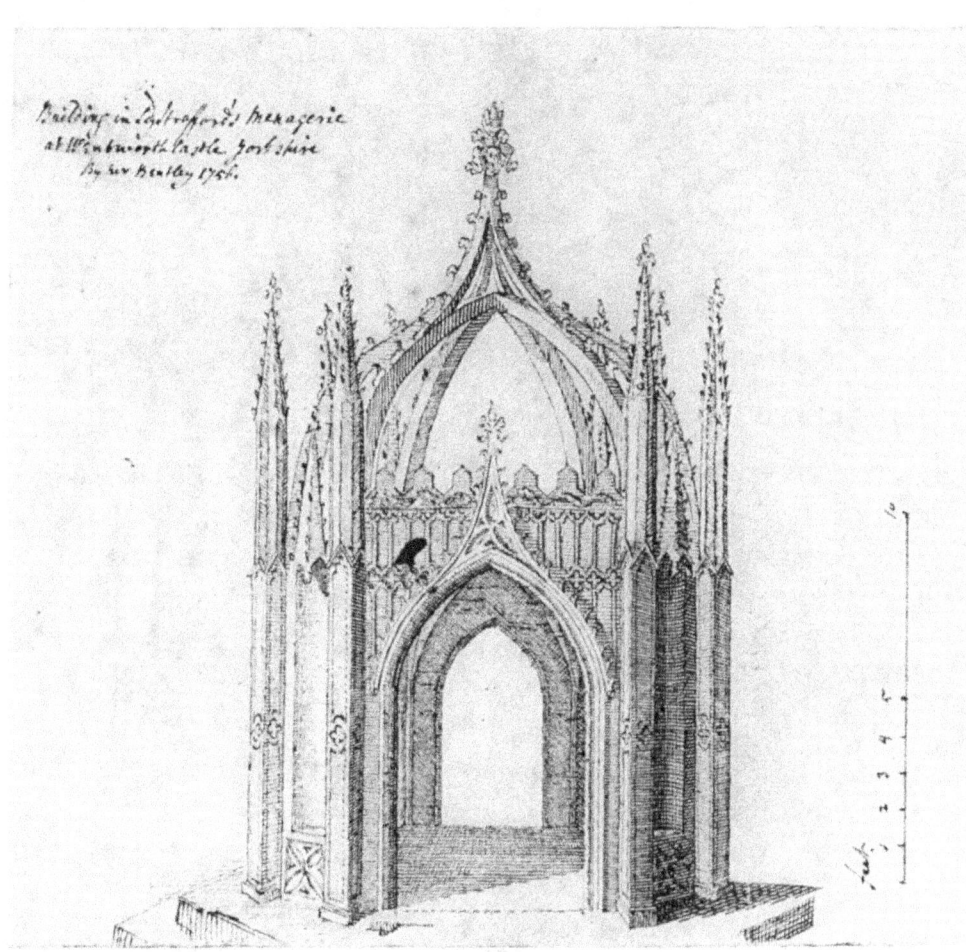

Building in Ld Strafford's Menagerie
at Wentworth Castle gost spire
By Mr Bentley 1756.

42. LORD STRAFFORD'S MENAGERIE, *by Bentley,* 1756

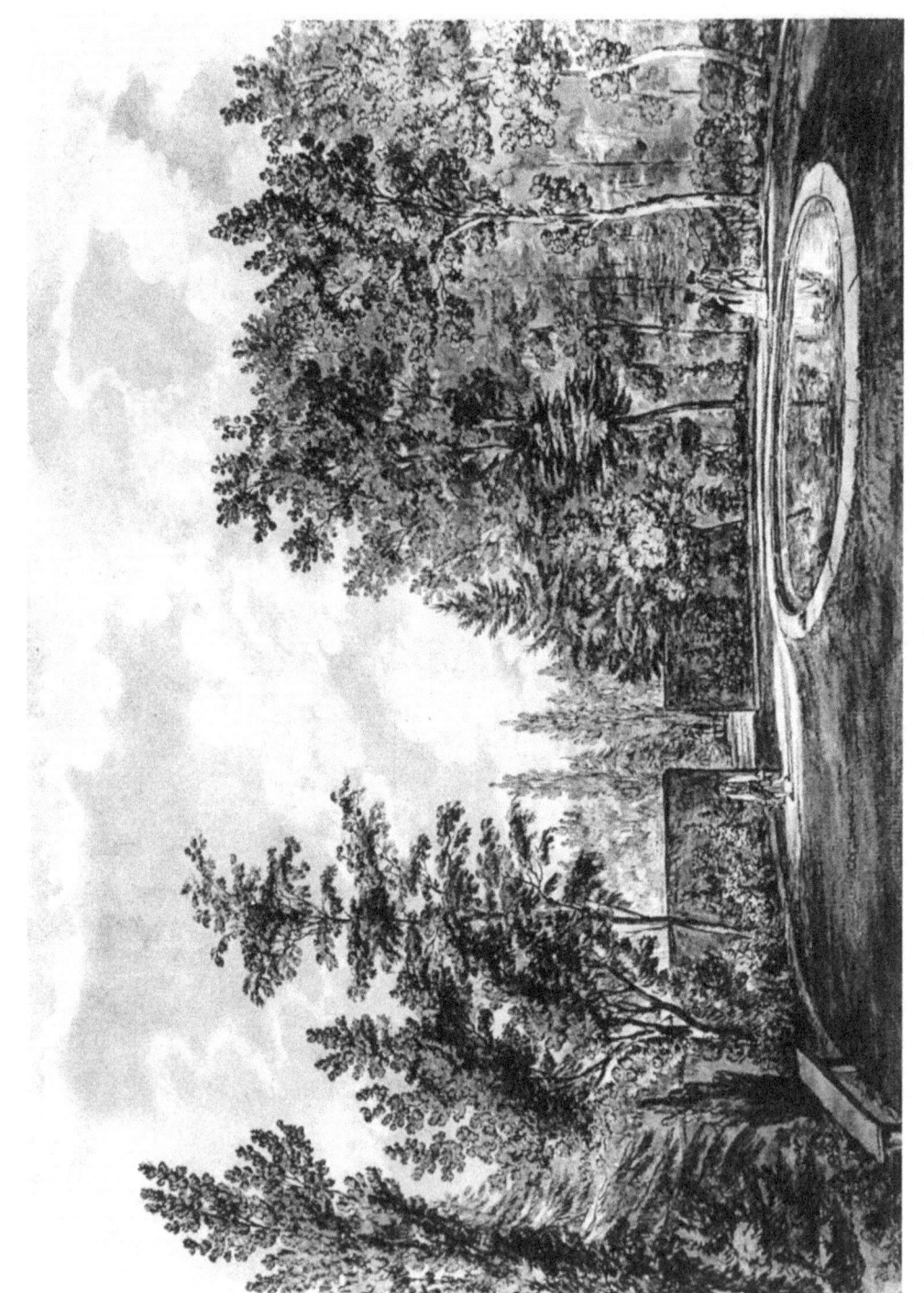

43. View in the Garden

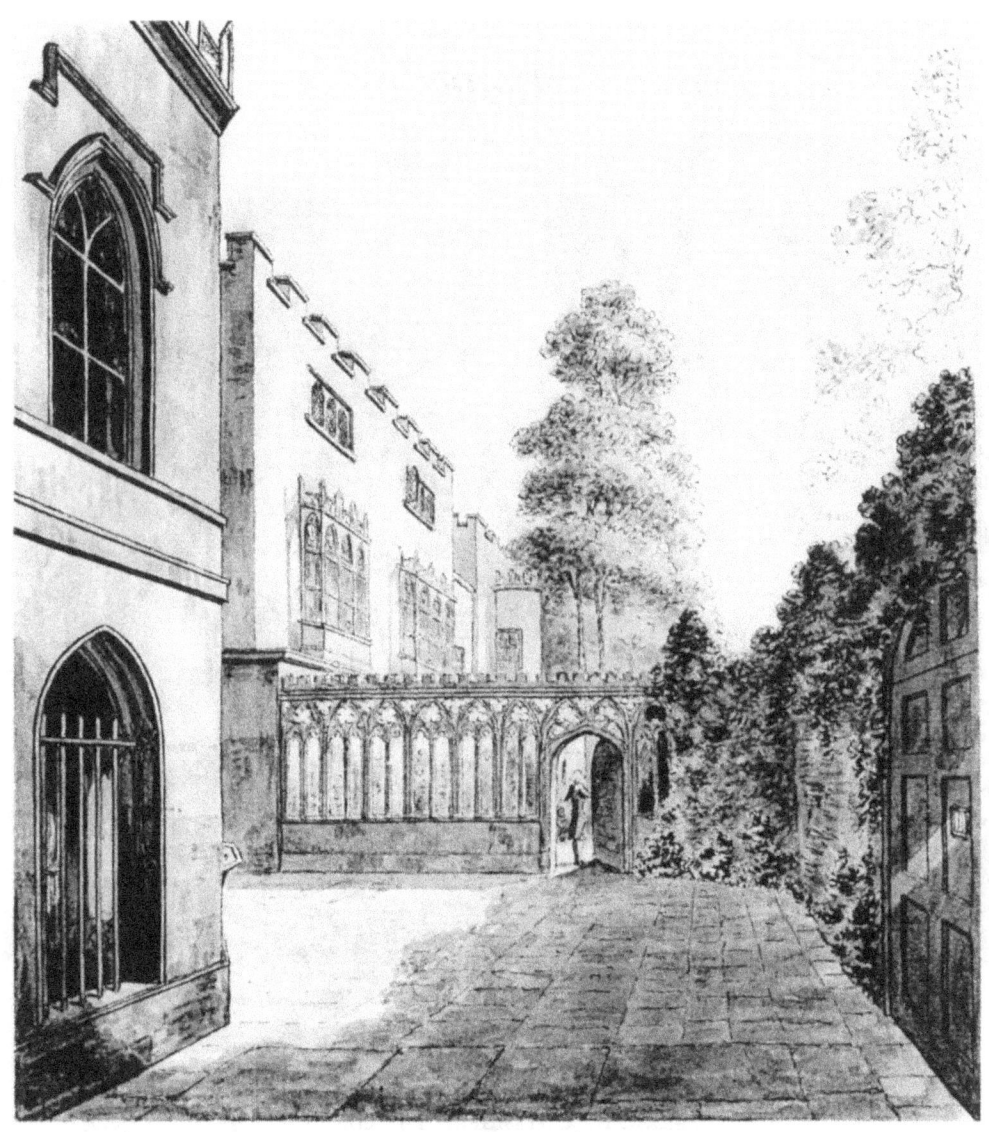

44. THE SCREEN TO THE PRIOR'S GARDEN, *by Edward Edwards,* 1781

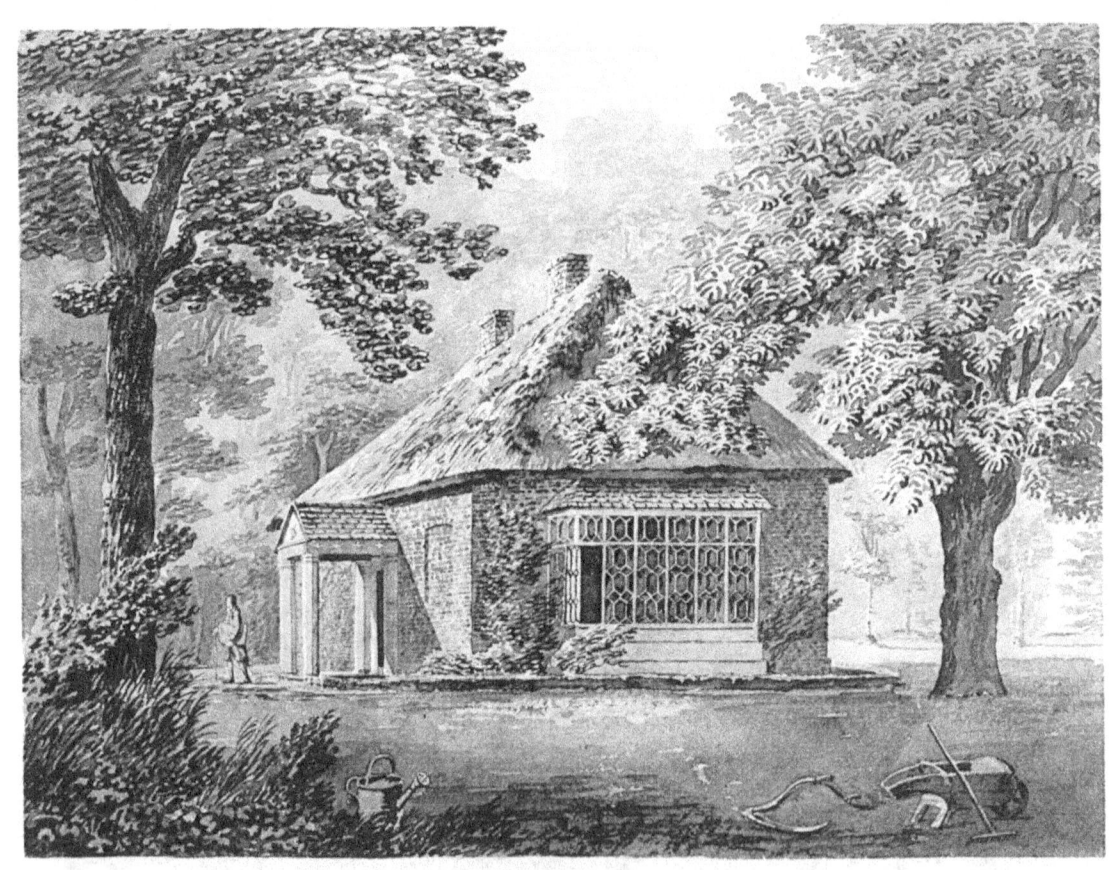

The Cottage,
drawn by J. C. Barrow,
1795.

45. THE COTTAGE IN THE GARDEN

as The Hague and Hollywood, all of them "right" except two. His belief that the contents of his house would be one of his strongest links with posterity has been confirmed.

The influence of Strawberry Hill on public taste went, as we know, far beyond the Committee's fondest hopes. Their "Gothic" caught on, became fashionable, and inspired better architects later.[48] It ultimately spread round the globe, from Lee Priory and Fonthill to Government House at Sydney; Gothic towers have only just ceased being built on American campuses. The eighteenth- and nineteenth-century descendants that have survived have acquired the dignity of national monuments, and when the other day a fine one was pulled down in Bridgeport, Connecticut, there was lamentation in the land.

Against all probability Strawberry itself has survived. Walpole left the life tenancy of it to Mrs. Damer, but she found it too expensive to keep up[49] and relinquished it to the ultimate heir, Lord Waldegrave, Walpole's great-nephew. Although it went through a troubled period of decline, and the 1842 sale swept away its contents, the house remained in the possession of one of the great Victorian hostesses, Frances Lady Waldegrave. Her last two (of four) husbands and her own flamboyance brought it back into fame. Strawberry received its final Gothic touch when a Victorian drawing room, reputed to have cost over £100,000,[50] joined the Round Tower to the Offices.

The property passed out of the Waldegrave family in 1888. It is now owned by the Congregation of St. Vincent de Paul, who use it as a training college (St. Mary's) for teachers. Their pride in it is matched by the affectionate care with which they continue to repair the battlements, and the patience with which they receive visitors who, in Wal-

---

[48] As Sir John Summerson has said, Walpole "opened the door to the architecture of the Picturesque," and "demonstrated for the first time a loyalty to mediaeval precedent which appeared, on the face of it, to be as fastidious as that of any classical architect to the precedents of Rome." *Architecture in Britain, 1530–1830* (1953), p. 243.

[49] Lord Granville Leveson-Gower, *Private Correspondence, 1781–1821,* ed. Castalia Countess Granville (1916), II, 366.

[50] *The Antiquary,* XVIII (1888), 78.

pole's tradition, apply for admittance. The house has survived poverty and neglect, riches, "improvements," and a German fire bomb that fell on the Gallery in May 1941. Greater London has cut off its prospects of the Thames and Richmond Hill, its books and pictures and curiosities are scattered about the world, yet in it one can still sense its creator's presence, just as he hoped that we should.

V

LORD ORFORD'S WORKS

THERE are three portraits of Walpole by Reynolds. In all three he is wearing a gray velvet suit with ample ruffles at the wrists and is standing by a high table, on which his right elbow rests lightly. His thin right hand with its long tapering fingers is raised to his cheek; his head is tilted to the right, a slightly oblique effect that is offset by the questioning gaze of his large and brilliant eyes: an arresting, not a handsome man.

The face in the three versions is strikingly different. In the first, which was painted in Walpole's thirty-ninth year, it is open and boyish. In the third, which was done only five years later, we see a man of the world. The second is the one engraved by McArdell. Walpole said that it was "reckoned very like," and Mann, that it had "all his air." To me it is the least pleasing of the three: the eyes are more apprehensive, the jaw is belligerent; Reynolds has added a frown. It was painted in 1757, at the time of Walpole's first major political disappointment, when he was, you remember, "balanced between right and wrong." On the table are carefully chosen accessories: the print of the Roman eagle at Strawberry Hill, an ink pot and quill, a roll of manuscript, and three books. We can be sure that Walpole selected these details, but Reynolds probably placed him so that he could pick up the quill without shifting his position. Between them, they made it clear that Reynolds was painting a writer.

On the back of McArdell's print that hung in his bedroom Walpole

83

copied a passage that he found in de Thou's autobiography, a passage that is extraordinarily applicable to himself:

"In far distant times, one will look with wonder on the green turf that covers the grave where my ashes are buried, and will say: 'It was his lot to be born in a bed of down, blessed with ample means, with favor and resources surpassing those which nowadays all wonder at from their earliest years: the glories of his time, his natural ambition, and the fresh fame of his illustrious father, all gave grounds to hope that he would excel the example of his ancestors which he strove to imitate; yet, despite all this, he preferred to seek the obscure, easeful retreats of the Muses, to shun the rocks and storms of Court and to despise the insubstantial vanities that men contend for: he chose the ivy and the laurel that grow wild rather than the spoils of battle or triumphs that batten on a hungry peace.' "[1]

How struck Walpole must have been when he came upon that passage! It bristles with parallels to his own life, of which perhaps the most remarkable is his taking it for granted that he would be talked about "in far distant times." Why should he be? For his *Memoirs* and letters, of course, but also for his contributions to the arts, literature, and antiquities. He became a successful and influential author, "the elegant and ingenious Mr. Walpole," at an early age.

By 1757 he had written two or three dozen personal essays and several political pamphlets. Although these pieces came out anonymously, according to eighteenth-century practice, Walpole was not one to hide his light under a bushel, and the public that mattered soon learned they were his. He had also written a great deal of verse, which he knew was not outstanding. When only nineteen he wrote,

---

[1] The print is now owned by General Sir Henry Jackson, K.C.B., who kindly lent it to me for study. I am indebted to the Warden of All Souls, Mr. John Sparrow, for the translation of this inscription from the Latin.

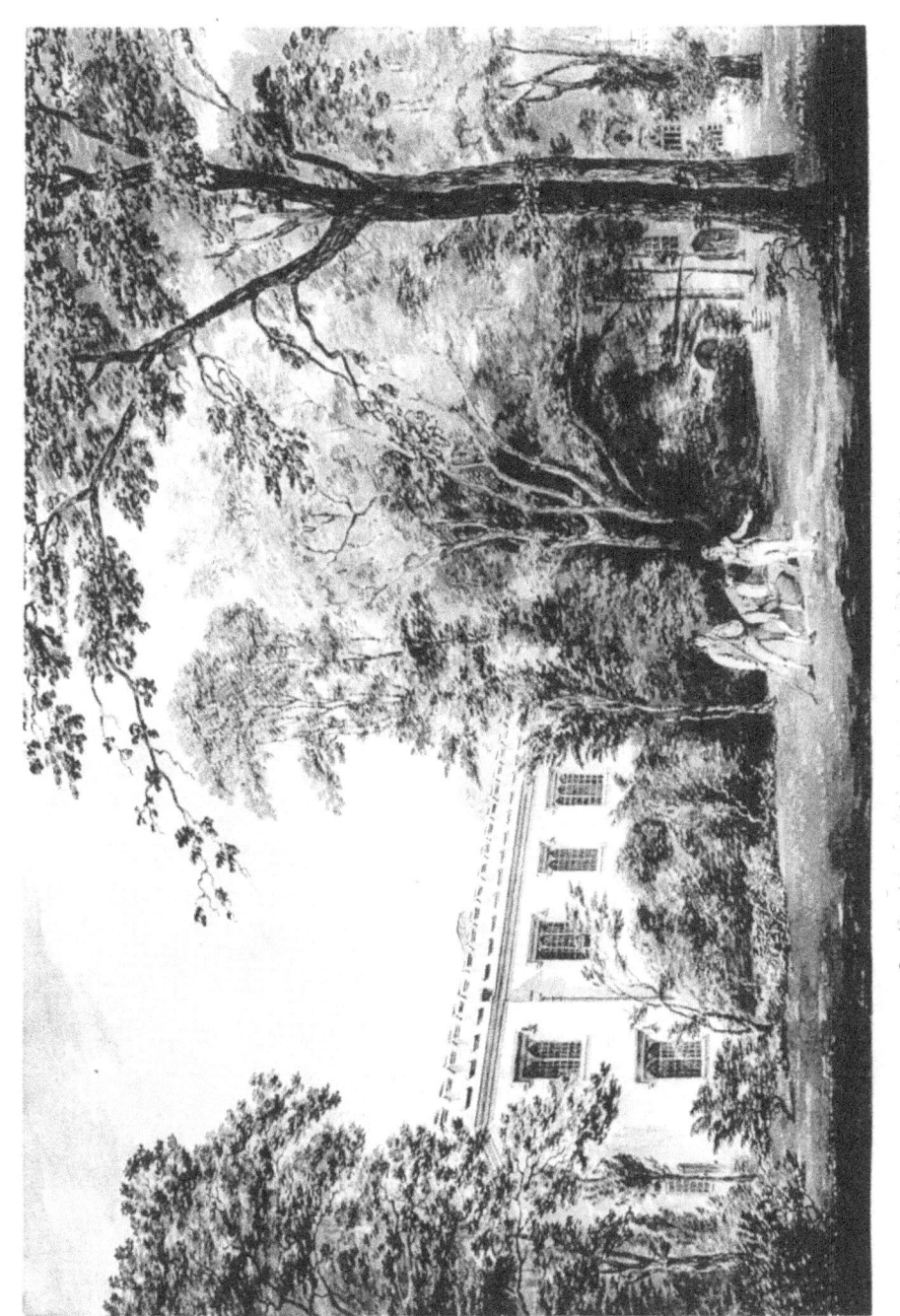

46. THE NEW OFFICES, *by J. C. Barrow, 1791*

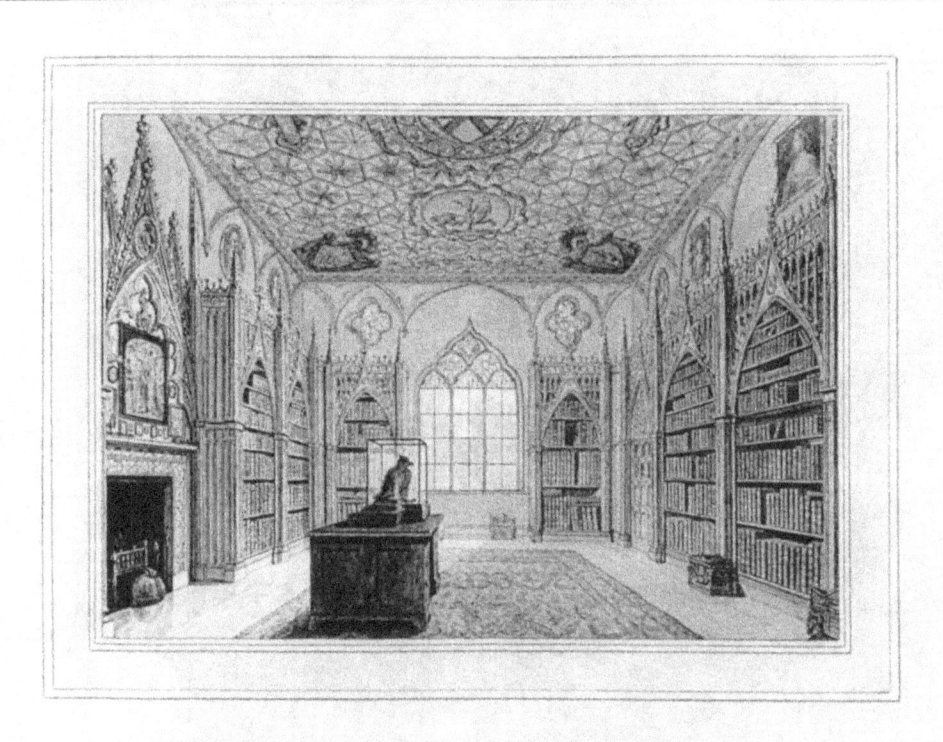

Rule for replacing a Book.

Each Volume is lettered on the infide; the firft Numeral refers to the Divifion, and the fecond to the Shelf: alfo, on many, the Number of the Book as placed on the Shelf is noted.

If any Perfon fhould take a Book out of the Library, they are particularly requefted to fet down their Name on this Slate, and the Title of the Book.

A. S. D.

47. THE LIBRARY, *by John Carter*

Lord Orford's Works

Seeds of poetry and rhyme
Nature in my soul implanted;
But the genial hand of Time
Still to ripen'em is wanted:
Or soon as they begin to blow,
My cold soil nips the buds with snow.[2]

Nevertheless, the seeds continued to sprout as long as he lived. He printed some of his verses at his press[3] and had them included in his posthumous *Works*. Others that he sent to friends in letters were copied and handed about until they got into the newspapers and magazines, where they were frequently reprinted. Gibbon said that they were "marked by taste, lightness, and by the tone of a man of condition who seems to toy with the Muses."[4] Hazlitt and Macaulay scorned them, yet one must be very stern not to like the verses to children and about pets.[5]

In 1757 and his fortieth year Walpole opened the press at Strawberry Hill. It was to be for his own pleasure and convenience; he would bring out only books and trifles by his friends and himself and unpublished manuscripts of antiquarian interest. He would control their distribution. He let Dodsley, the leading London publisher, sell some; others he sold for charity—the poor of Twickenham, a learned and indigent tailor, his friend Bentley—but most he gave away. His political pieces continued to appear anonymously in London. Strawberry was not to be defiled by them.

The Press has to its credit the first editions of more books of lasting

---

[2] Walpole to West, 3 Jan. 1737.

[3] In his *Fugitive Pieces in Verse and Prose* (1757), and "detached pieces" written on special occasions.

[4] Edward Gibbon, *Miscellaneous Works* (1815), p. 156.

[5] Professor David Nichol Smith rescued two of them for the *Oxford Book of Eighteenth Century Verse* (1926), "Countess Temple Appointed Poet Laureate to the King of the Fairies," and "To Lady Anne Fitzpatrick, when about Five Years Old, with a Present of Shells." W. S. Lewis, *Horace Walpole's Fugitive Verses* (1931), gives one hundred and thirty verses from the *Works* and letters; many more have turned up since.

interest than any other private press in England before or since. It began with Gray's "Bard" and "The Progress of Poesy" and closed with Hannah More's verses to the Bishop of London thirty-two years later. Thirty-four books in all were printed at it and several dozen "detached pieces," which were mostly complimentary and occasional verses. Walpole left the choice of type, paper, and printers to those in the book trade. He said that he hoped the results would show "all the beautiful negligence of a gentleman." This was to forestall criticism of typographical errors and technical failures, but the Press had few "negligences." Walpole decided what was to be printed and the size of the edition, but he never attempted to set type himself. After his first printers had run off for debt or because they had got girls with child, he acquired Thomas Kirgate in 1765. Kirgate printed all the remaining pieces (including some forgeries).[6] As a printer he was no more distinguished than his predecessors, but he was discreet, and in time he became his master's secretary, librarian, and curator of prints. The best that Updike could say of the Press typographically was that its edition of Lucan was "worthy of moderate praise."[7] Yet collectors of printing from Walpole's day to ours have been glad to own its books, which have a certain modest elegance of their own.

With the establishment of the Press and the dedication of Strawberry Hill to the Muses, Walpole entered on a ten-year stretch of serious writing for the public. During this period he brought out his five chief books other than his *Memoirs* and letters. These in the order of their appearance are *A Catalogue of the Royal and Noble Authors of England with Lists of Their Works, Anecdotes of Painting in England, The Castle of Otranto, Historic Doubts on the Life and Reign of King Richard III,* and *The Mysterious Mother.* Although they are varied in subject, they have the three qualities that are also in the *Memoirs* and letters, Walpole's desire to inform, to entertain, and to innovate. "You will laugh at my earnestness," he wrote to Cole about the *Castle of Otranto,* "but if I have amused you, by retracing with any fidelity the manners of ancient

---

[6] These were first detected by Mr. Allen T. Hazen in his *Bibliography of the Strawberry Hill Press* (New Haven, 1942).

[7] Daniel Berkeley Updike, *Printing Types* (1922), II, 140.

days, I am content, and give you leave to think me as idle as you please."[8]
To retrace with fidelity the manners of ancient days, the wish to inform,
is as obvious a quality of Walpole's writing as is his wish to entertain, and
it appears in everything that he wrote, including his fiction. The third
quality is less obvious. It is his determination to strike out into something new; to express what he called his "wildness": he had to be different from other men in his writing as well as in his life. I have spoken
of his works as "pioneer," but a friend has given me a more up-to-date
word for them. This word is "off-beat," a word, if I understand it, that
describes independence and rebellion against the conventional and
stereotyped.

These three qualities, the desire to inform, to entertain, and to innovate, are all found in *A Catalogue of the Royal and Noble Authors of
England,* which Walpole printed in 1758, in two small volumes. His
preliminary remarks to it are, as usual, intended to forestall criticism.
The book was, he said, "a present of some curiosity, though perhaps of
no great value." He had discovered in Bayle's *General Dictionary* odd
and artificial divisions of authors: Balthazar Bonifacius made a collection of those who had been in love with statues; Ravisius Textor, of
men who died laughing. Such catalogues were formerly common in Germany and Holland. Walpole hoped that his book would be acceptable to
the noble families descended from the authors in it; future editors of
their works would find it of assistance. He apologized for the freedom he
had taken with some historic names whose descendants still existed, ex-
cusing himself as a citizen of the republic of letters who must be at liberty
to say what he thinks; his catalogue should not be taken too seriously; it
was written to amuse; he would not defend it.

This preface does not explain why he, "a quiet Republican,"[9]
should have spent five months sweeping up the little pile of royal and
noble writings that he conceded were of small value apart from Bacon,
Clarendon, and a few others. I think that he was drawn by the lure of
antiquarianism, the escape from the vexatious present into what he called

[8] Walpole to Cole, 9 March 1765.
[9] *Memoirs of George II* (1846), I, 377.

"the ages that do not disappoint." Let Henry Fox and Rigby be as treacherous as they pleased, he could always lose himself in the Wars of the Roses. Patriotism also came into it: he wanted to point out that English princes and peers could write. Furthermore, the new Strawberry Hill Press should have an extensive and novel work by himself. He had been collecting books by royal and noble authors for years, and by supplementing his account of them with borrowings from earlier antiquaries he made up a work that was not only odd, but in the learned European tradition. Finally, he knew from writing his *Memoirs* the sense of power that the biographer enjoys while sitting in judgment on lives and characters. The biographer's subjects are at his mercy; he can create and destroy, inflate and maim; the biographer assumes the authority of a judge and hands down verdicts for posterity's guidance. "I seem to myself a doorkeeper at the Temple of Fame," he once wrote. Admitting and rejecting kings and noblemen was an agreeable undertaking for a high-strung younger son in rebellion against authority.

Walpole was an accurate biographer, but an emotional critic. He praised the neglected and dismissed the famous. The patrons of Caxton, Lords Worcester and Rivers, both of whom had the added merit of losing their heads, would have been, he said, the brightest luminaries of a more polished age. Bacon he punished in four short sentences and did not name his works because he had stooped "to the little ambition of power." As for Clarendon, his "majesty and eloquence, his power of painting character, his knowledge of his subject, rank him in the first class of writers," yet his justification of Charles I counterbalanced these excellences. We stumble through the *Catalogue of the Royal and Noble Authors,* confused by its epigrams and our ignorance of facts that Walpole assumed his readers knew, but we see clearly his desire to inform, to entertain, and to do something novel.

He recorded that he wrote this book in less than five months,[10] and much of it with people in the room[11]—that is, he wanted it understood

---

[10] Yale Walpole, 13. 29.
[11] Walpole to Gray, 18 Feb. 1768.

Painters &c.

from the News papers, or Hogarth's print of Churchill. Aug. 17. 1763.

The SISTER-ARTS.
An Epigram.

TO various Things, just as they Like,
We oft the Arts compare;
But who'd have thought the Sisters like
A Bull-Dog and a Bear?
[St. J. Cron.]   AMBROSE.

In a catalogue of the pictures belonging to the Earl of Peterborough, which were at his house at Millbank & at Drayton, some of which were afterwards sold, particularly to Ld Pembroke, & most of which are now Lady Eliz. Germain's. mention is made of a portrait of the Earl of Sandwich by his creed. I never heard of her. The view of Drayton was painted by Carter, equally unknown to me.

Sheets of Zuccarelli, Servandoni, & others, in a coll. of pamphlets in my library, class B. shelf 6. no 12. Casanova born in England. 26.

Sr Thomas Reeves Kt of Holyport near Maidenhead Berks, heir of Sr Thomas Reeves Ld Ch. Justice Reeves, has drawn a vast number of heads of painters in Indian Ink, chiefly from the collections of Dr Meade, & has etched a few things, which are not so indifferent as his drawings; & he has discovered a secret for preserving miniatures, which he has communicated to the Society of Arts and Sciences, & which they have found to stand the trial. He married the heiress of one Gregor, who had been steward to Sr William Morrice. The house at Holyport was Gregor's, & was gothicized by him. In it are two excellent heads, tho a little damaged, most indubitably of Holbein in his most delicate manner, they are an elderly man & Woman. Near Sr Thomas Reeves's is a very old Timber house, belonging to Mr Meade, fellow of a college in Oxford, & said to have belonged to Nel Gwynne.

Zincke by his first Wife, who was very handsome, had a son & a Daughter. for the son he bought a place in the Excellers office. The Daughter dying, he retired to South Lambeth, where he quitted business, & married a German Woman by whom he had had 3 or 4 children. She was extravagantly [illegible] & led him a miserable life.

48. A PAGE FROM ONE OF THE "BOOKS OF MATERIALS," 1759

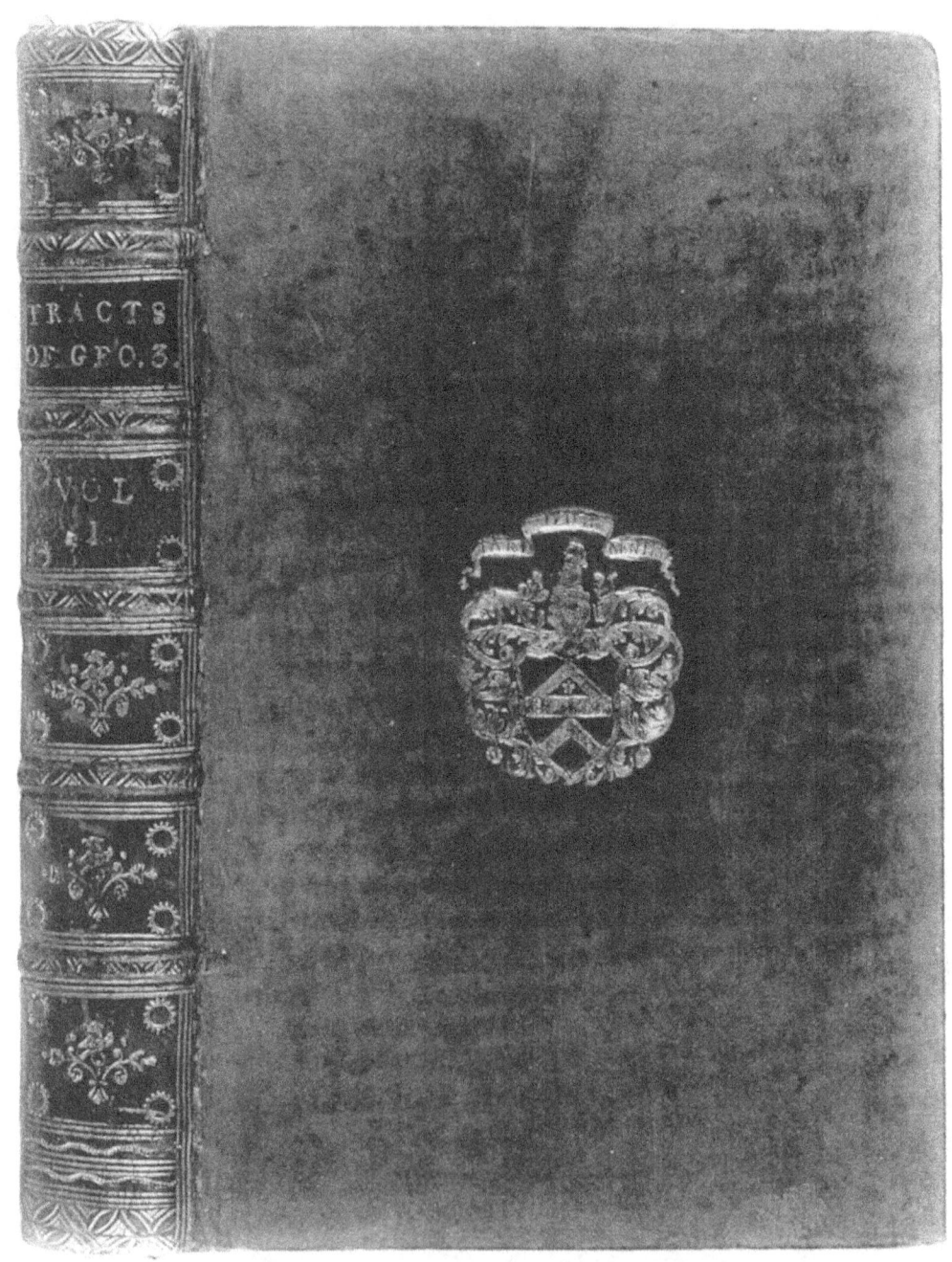

49. VOLUME I OF WALPOLE'S "TRACTS OF GEO. 3"

Mr. Walpole is very ready to oblige any curious Persons with the Sight of his House and Collection; but as it is situated so near to London and in so populous a Neighbourhood, and as he refuses a Ticket to nobody that sends for one, it is but reasonable that such Persons as send, should comply with the Rules he has been obliged to lay down for showing it.

Any Person, sending a Day or two before, may have a Ticket for Four Persons for a Day certain.

No Ticket will serve but on the Day for which it is given. If more than Four Persons come with a Ticket, the Housekeeper has positive Orders to admit none of them.

Every Ticket will admit the Company only between the Hours of Twelve and Three before Dinner, and only one Company will be admitted on the same Day.

The House will never be shown after Dinner; nor at all but from the First of May to the First of October.

As Mr. Walpole has given Offence by sometimes enlarging the Number of Four, and refusing that Latitude to others, he flatters himself that for the future nobody will take it ill that he strictly confines the Number; as whoever desires him to break his Rule, does in effect expect him to disoblige others, which is what nobody has a right to desire of him.

Persons desiring a Ticket, may apply either to Strawberry-Hill, or to Mr. Walpole's in Berkeley-Square, London. If any Person does not make use of the Ticket, Mr. Walpole hopes he shall have Notice; otherwise he is prevented from obliging others on that Day, and thence is put to great Inconvenience.

They who have Tickets are desired not to bring Children.

This Ticket, on being delivered to the Housekeeper, will admit Four Persons, and no more, on *Thursday Aug 4th* 1774, between Twelve and Three, to see Strawberry-Hill, and will only serve for the Day specified.

N. B. The House and Garden are never shown in an Evening; and Persons are desired not to bring Children with them.

Ho. Walpole

50. TICKET AND RULES FOR SEEING STRAWBERRY HILL

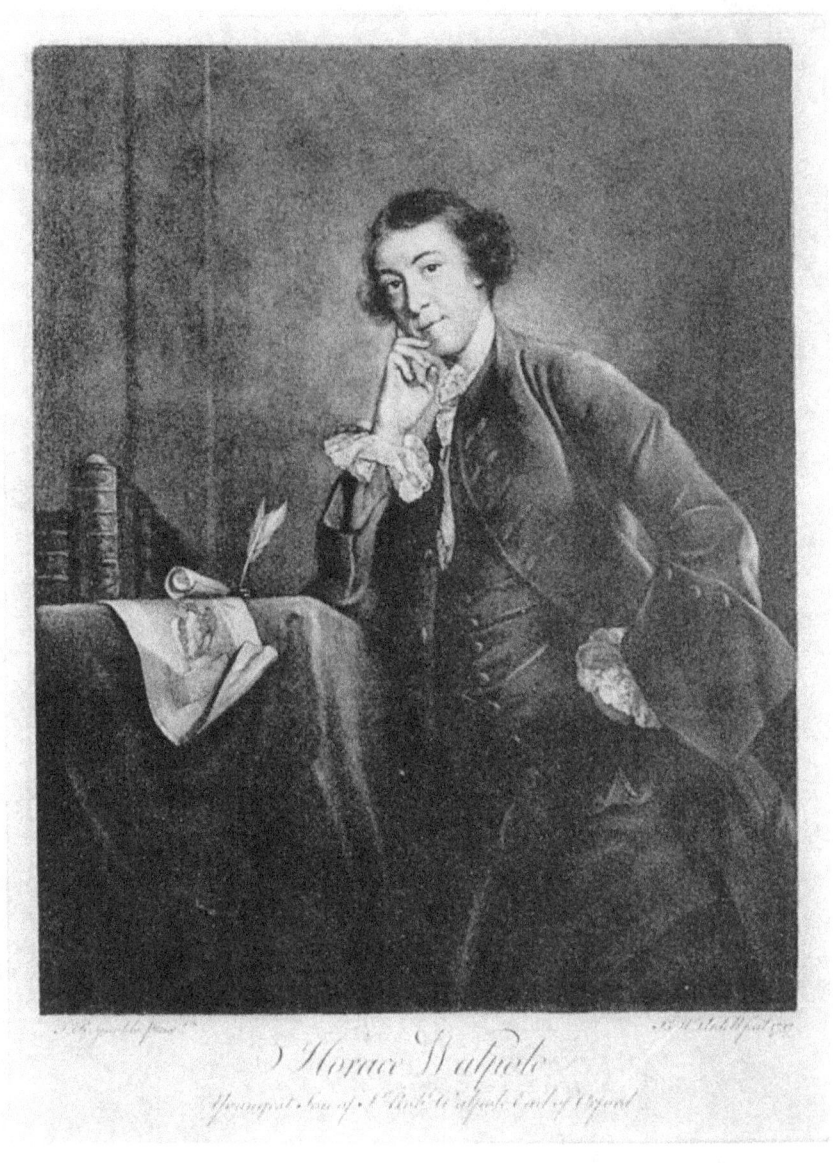

51. HORACE WALPOLE, *by James McArdell, after Reynolds,* 1757

that it had been dashed off. He gave away most of the first edition, which was of three hundred copies. It was eagerly read and lent by antiquaries, who were delighted to have Mr. Walpole join their fraternity. With great deference and many expressions of gratitude they sent him corrections and additions for his next edition. He thanked them meticulously, promised to make use of their help should a new edition be called for, and then put their notes aside. "If I write tolerably," he told Gray, "it must be at once; I can neither mend nor add."[12]

The applause of the learned was gratifying; he liked being a bird of brilliant plumage among crows. In the antiquarian world he was pointed out by the finger of those passing by, which made the fifteenth century a vastly more congenial place to live in than the House of Commons. When Dodsley published two thousand copies of the *Royal and Noble Authors* Walpole's reputation as a writer was established. Fame involved him in various controversies, but he shrugged off the disagreeable as best he could. The *Noble Authors* went on being reprinted until by the nineteenth century it was in every gentleman's library.

The *Anecdotes of Painting in England* was preceded by several works on the arts. Walpole called the first of them *Aedes Walpolianae, or A Description of the Collection of Pictures at Houghton Hall in Norfolk, the Seat of the Right Honourable Sir Robert Walpole, Earl of Orford,* but he explained in his Introduction that it was more of a catalogue than a description. When Sir Robert was forced into retirement he took most of his pictures with him to Houghton. They made life there tolerable for Horace, who escaped to them from the dinner table where he said were men who were "mountains of roast beef" out of whom streamed gravy, and who no doubt looked upon him with equal distaste. He pleased his father by rehanging the pictures,[13] and he finished the catalogue of them that he had begun seven years earlier at the age of eighteen.

---

[12] Ibid.

[13] William Coxe, *Memoirs of the Life and Administration of Sir Robert Walpole* (1798), I, 762.

Horace Walpole

The collection was probably the greatest in England. In it were twenty Van Dycks, nineteen Rubenses, eight Titians, five Murillos, three each of Veronese, Holbein, and Rembrandt, two each of Velasquez and Raphael, a Leonardo, a Michelangelo, a Hals, and scores of lesser hands. Great masters hung about Horace from his birth.

His wish to innovate, to inform, and to entertain is as clear in the *Aedes* as in his later works. It was the first book written by an Englishman on a private English collection of pictures. As for its instruction, Walpole points out in his Introduction that knowledge of pictures "is only to be learned from pictures themselves," and that the books on the art "only served to perplex it. No science," he said, "has had so much jargon introduced into it as painting . . . the vanity of the professors, and the interested mysteriousness of picture merchants, have altogether compiled a new language."[14] Entertainment is provided in the *Aedes* by a history of painting from Apelles to Sir Peter Lely. Opinions and verdicts are tossed off as if they were confetti. The genius of Luca Giordano, we learn, "was like Ovid's, flowing, abundant, various, and incorrect";[15] what was notable in Camillo Procaccini was "the variety of tints in his flesh, the odd disposition of his lights on the verges of the limbs, and his delighting in clustering groups";[16] the Dutch were "drudging mimics of Nature's most uncomely coarsenesses."[17] Walpole's final judgment about the masters was that "all the qualities of a perfect painter never met but in Raphael, Guido, and Annibal Caracci,"[18] which is close to the opinion Mr. Berenson told us was held by Italians as recently as seventy years ago.[19]

---

[14] "Aedes," *Works* (1798), II, 226.

[15] Ibid., II, 233.

[16] Ibid., II, 232.

[17] Ibid., II, 226.

[18] Ibid., II, 236.

[19] Bernard Berenson, *Essays in Appreciation* (1958), p. 148: "When I first came to Italy nearly seventy years ago, it was Carlo Dolci, it was Domenichino, it was Guido Reni, who really spoke to Italians and tourists, although of course *il Divino Raffaello* remained enthroned and all but inaccessible, high up in the Empyrean."

Lord Orford's Works

The *Aedes* concludes with "A Sermon on Painting," written for the entertainment of Sir Robert, and in it we find a fourth characteristic of Walpole's works, the desire to improve: Horace the Innovator, Instructor, and Entertainer is followed by Horace the Evangelist who wished to make the world a better place to live in. Let painting and devotion unite "to aid the doubting, to strengthen the weak, to imprint the eternal idea on the frail understanding."[20] The sermon was preached before his father at Houghton by his chaplain and went so well that it was repeated before Horace's brother Robert and his mistress in their chapel. It ends with a tribute to Moses, a patriot who lay neglected after his services to his people. Sir Robert must have been much amused: dressed up as Moses he was one of the first of many underdogs to be championed by his youngest son. Horace published one hundred copies of the *Aedes* in 1747.[21] It is full of typographical errors, which he corrected himself in ink before giving away virtually the entire edition to friends, but it is the book that he chose to hold when he had Eccardt paint him. On going back to Houghton some years later he confessed that his description of its pictures seemed to him poor and that "the majesty of Italian ideas almost sinks before the warm nature of Flemish colouring. Alas! Don't I grow old? My young imagination was fired with Guido's ideas—must they be plump and prominent as Abishag to warm me now?"[22]

He produced other catalogues. When George Vertue died Walpole bought all of his notebooks from Vertue's widow, together with Vertue's manuscript catalogues of Charles I's, James II's, and the Duke of Buckingham's pictures. Walpole wrote advertisements to them in which he deplored the dispersal and loss to the nation of King Charles's collection and hoped that these catalogues might "incite more elegant imitations."

---

[20] "Aedes," *Works* (1798), II, 282.

[21] Although in his "Short Notes of My Life" Walpole said he printed two hundred copies, Mr. Hazen has, I think, proved that he printed only one hundred. Later editions were published in 1752 and 1767 (*Bibliography of Horace Walpole* [New Haven, 1948], p. 28).

[22] Walpole to Montagu, 25 March 1761.

Horace Walpole

He said that the accession to the throne of George III, a young prince devoted to the arts, and the new glory of English arms and eloquence must inspire Englishmen to paint not just portraits, but subjects worthy of their country. The establishment of the British Museum, of which Walpole was an original trustee, would promote the study of painting by attracting collections "wont to straggle through auctions into obscurity." Men would collect with redoubled spirit and pleasure when they reflected that they were doing so for their country and would have their names recorded as national benefactors. All honor to the patriots who should give their pictures to the nation—a sentiment echoed in the Gallery where we are now assembled.

He thought and spoke of himself as being apart from those who, like Vertue, or "the picture merchants," earned their livelihood in the arts. The word "amateur" had not yet come into use, either as "one who loves or is fond of" something, or as a "dabbler, or superficial student."[23] To call Walpole an amateur, as people frequently do, sometimes with one meaning in mind and sometimes with the other, is to apply to him a word that would not have been understood in 1747. Writing criticism and history was open to everybody. Walpole had the highest reputation in his own day as an art historian and critic, and he has it today. His success was owing to his passion for pictures, drawings, and prints, great sensitivity to color, an excellent "eye," and a fabulous memory.

The English had been collecting pictures for generations, but to see them you had to go to country houses. This Walpole did with the ardor of an explorer. At the age of eighteen, he found at Cornbury "a prodigious quantity of Van Dycks," but had not time to describe any of their dresses. At Easton Neston "in an old greenhouse is a wonderful fine statue of Tully, haranguing a numerous assembly of decayed emperors, vestal virgins with new noses, Colossuses, Venuses, headless carcasses and carcassless heads."[24] He went on visiting country houses

---

[23] The earliest illustration of the first usage in the *Oxford English Dictionary* is 1784, of the second, 1807.

[24] Walpole to Montagu, 20 May 1736.

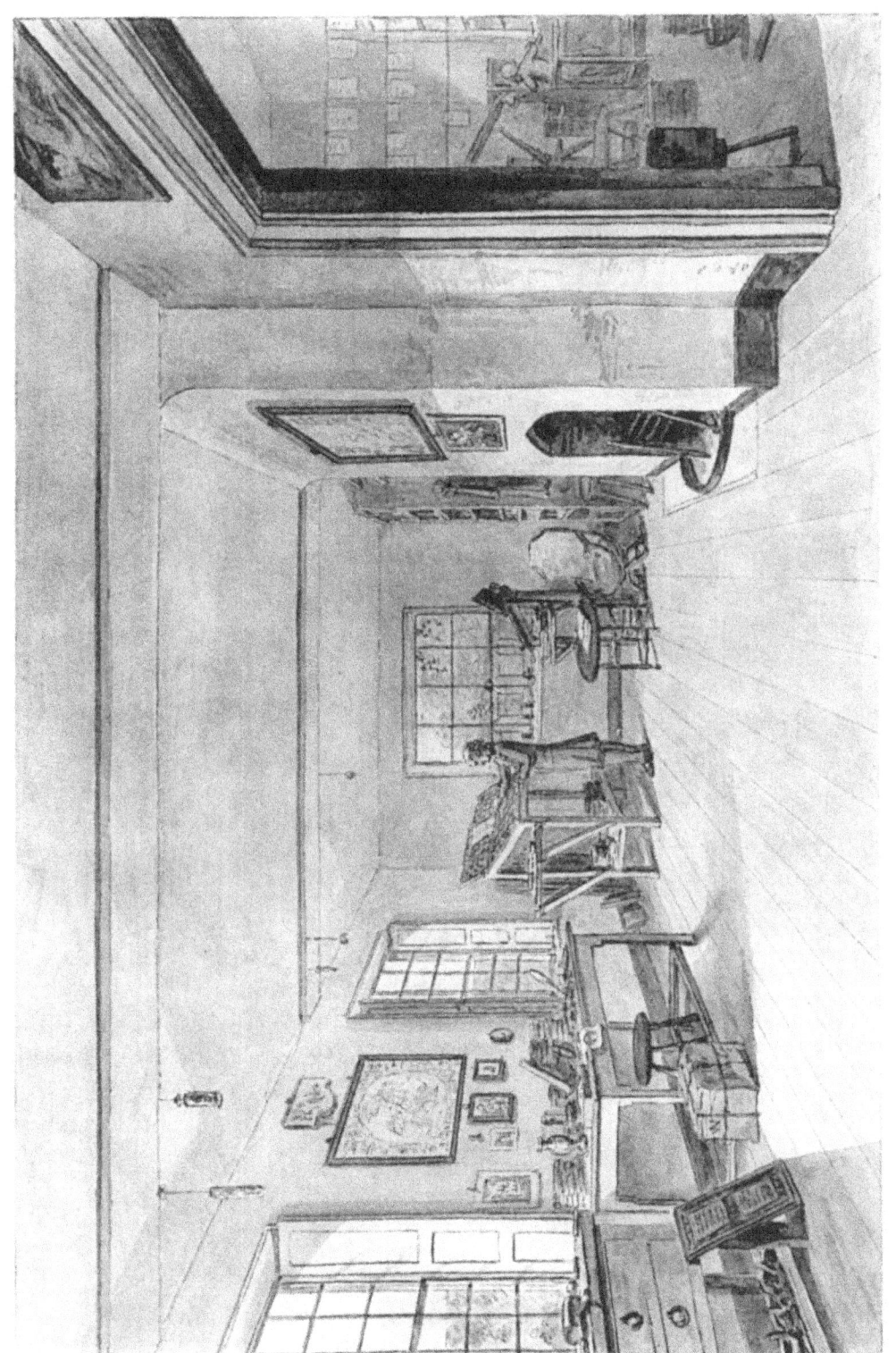

52. THE PRINTING HOUSE, *by John Carter*

M. ANNAEI LUCANI

PHARSALIA

Cum Notis HUGONIS GROTII,

ET

RICHARDI BENTLEII.

Multa ſunt condonanda in opere poſtumo.
In Librum iv. Nota 641.

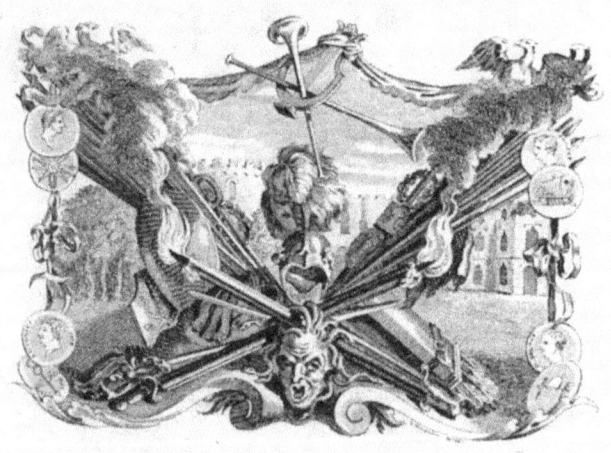

'STRAWBERRY-HILL, Mpcclx.

53. **The Strawberry** *Lucan*

for sixty years, recording what he found in his notebooks.[25] Everywhere were important pictures unknown to the world at large and often unknown to their owners. One could never tell where one might find an authentic Holbein or Van Dyck. They might be in dark passages, porters' lodges, or housekeepers' sitting rooms; he even found them in Kensington Palace. They were often in bad condition owing to damp and neglect, but sometimes he could persuade their owners to have them cleaned and rehung in drier rooms and better light. He recorded anecdotes relating to the subjects of the portraits and their family connections, and made notes on their dresses, ornaments, and heraldic devices. Not all of his attributions are accepted today, but he rescued many fine pictures that might otherwise have been lost. The iconographical history of England hung unread in country houses until Horace Walpole appeared.

His desire to inform and to entertain appears in his *Anecdotes of Painting in England; with some Account of the principal Artists and incidental Notes on other Arts; collected by the late Mr George Vertue; and now digested and published from his original MSS by Mr Horace Walpole.* He used the word "anecdotes" in its earlier sense of "secret, private, or hitherto unpublished narratives or details of history." Vertue had spent a lifetime visiting and cataloguing English collections, copying pictures, attending sales, searching parish registers and wills for births, marriages, and deaths. All this went down, higgledy-piggledy, into thirty-nine notebooks. Walpole put Vertue's work in order, verified his references to books, and supplemented them with many additions and observations of his own. The English Walpole Society's faithful transcriptions of Vertue's chaotic notebooks[26] show what a skillful editor the new owner of them was.

He spent nearly two years preparing the *Anecdotes* for the Strawberry Hill Press. There were ultimately five slim quarto volumes of them,

---

[25] These are now at Farmington. Paget Toynbee extracted and edited from them "Horace Walpole's Journals of his Visits to Country Seats, etc." for *The Sixteenth Volume of the Walpole Society* (Oxford, 1928), pp. 9–80.

[26] In their volumes for 1930, 1932, 1934, 1936, 1938, 1947, and 1955.

including the *Catalogue of Engravers,* all profusely illustrated with plates. This book is Walpole's major historical work next to his *Memoirs* and letters. It was an instant success. Gibbon spoke of his "minute curiosity and acuteness."[27] Strangers wrote to him with gratitude and volunteered additions and corrections for the next edition. It was no wonder that this work was so popular: it was new, informative, and entertaining. Throughout it are passages that are a far cry from "the cant of the virtuosi," such as the one on Holbein's drawing of Sir Thomas More. "It is," Walpole pointed out, "Sir Thomas More in the rigor of his sense, not in the sweetness of his pleasantry—Here he is the unblemished magistrate, not that amiable philosopher whose humility neither power nor pity could elate, and whose mirth even martyrdom could not spoil."[28] The *Anecdotes,* Lionel Cust said, "laid the foundations for an historical study of the Fine Arts in England, which to this day has proved the chief authority for reference upon this subject."[29]

Walpole aspired to be the English Montfaucon as well as the English Vasari, and at one time he had reason to think that his dream of compiling a work for England like Montfaucon's *Monumens de la Monarchie Françoise* might be fulfilled. When George III came to the throne the *cognoscenti* believed that he would be a patron of the arts and learning. Walpole sent Bute, then prime minister, a set of his and Vertue's catalogues of the royal collections and offered his services as "a virtuoso and antiquarian" in the new reign. Bute gave him hopes of royal patronage for an English Montfaucon, which would have been novel, instructive, and entertaining, but nothing came of it, even though Walpole addressed some flattering verses to the King and sent them to Lady Bute. He also planned a history of Gothic architecture in England that was to be written by leading authorities on the subject, including himself. There were to be sections on "the art, proportions and method of building, and the reasons observed by the Gothic architects for what they

---

[27] Gibbon's *Journal,* ed. D. M. Low [1930], p. 103 (26 Dec. 1762).
[28] "Anecdotes of Painting," *Works* (1798), III, 61.
[29] *The Third Volume of the Walpole Society* (1914), p. 122. Similar statements appear in later volumes by Katharine A. Esdaile and Sir Henry Hake.

did." Walpole's contribution was to be the section on Gothic ornament. Other sections were to be on the costs of building, the wages of workmen, and the comparative value of money and provisions at the several periods.[30] This work, in five mammoth volumes, was later carried out by Richard Gough in his *Sepulchral Monuments in Great Britain,* with full acknowledgment to Walpole for his plan of the book.

Walpole took his role of English Vasari seriously. He went to exhibitions and recorded his comments and judgments in the margins of his catalogues. We can see his entrance into the room, bowing, smiling, tripping along on his toes as if the floor were wet, staring at the badly lighted pictures stuck one upon the other up to the ceiling, identifying, rhapsodizing, condemning. No fear of strangers here. His praise could make the reputation of a new man. Far up in the shadows he might spot one—Opie, for example, or Morland. He was always hoping for something even better, but Constable and Turner—like Wordsworth and Coleridge—were just too late for him. "I have been at all the exhibitions," he wrote, "and do not find that we are got an inch nearer Raphael than we were."[31] It was discouraging to have it generally believed that the bright new day had been ushered in by Benjamin West.

The Castle of Otranto was printed anonymously in London. The title page of the first edition states that it was "Translated by William Marshal, Gent. from the original Italian of Onuphrio Muralto, Canon of the Church of St Nicholas, at Otranto." The Preface says that the work "was found in the library of an ancient Catholic family in the north of England," and that it was printed at Naples in the black letter in 1529. The Preface goes on to show that the novel must have been written between the first and last crusades; it points out the art of the author in his handling of the domestics, and states that "the scene is undoubtedly

[30] This outline appears in Walpole's letter to Cole of 11 Aug. 1769. Cole sent the letter to Gough, who printed it in his Introduction. Still another ambitious work that Walpole contemplated was on London streets. It was to be similar to G. F. Poullain de Saint Foix's *Streets of Paris,* but it got no further than many notes in his "Books of Materials," from the Harleian Manuscripts, Stow, and other earlier antiquarian sources.
[31] Walpole to Mason, 7 May 1775.

laid in some real castle." *The Castle of Otranto* was an immediate success, and Walpole thereupon came out in the open. "It was an attempt," he wrote in the Preface to the second edition, "to blend the two kinds of romance, the ancient and the modern," and he reverted with pride to the deportment of the domestics. His rule, he said, was nature and his master Shakespeare; the castle was Strawberry Hill.

There were twenty-one editions of the book in the eighteenth century, including those published in Dublin, Paris, Amsterdam, Parma, and Berlin. Several were illustrated; a few were even printed on vellum. There have been at least fifty editions since 1800, seventeen of them in the present century. One of the latest is a translation made by a French youth of seventeen just before he was captured in the Resistance and killed by the Germans.

It is said in English literature courses that *The Castle of Otranto* survives because it is the most influential of the early "Gothic" novels, but publishers would not go on bringing it out if that were all there is to it. For two hundred years people have *liked* the book; why, it is not so easy to say. If you open it at random you will read something like this: " 'Traitor,' said Manfred, 'how camest thou here? I thought thee in durance above in the court.' " How can one read much of that? The answer, I think, is that you want to see what is going to happen next. There is never a dull moment. A giant helmet with sable plumes falls from heaven and crushes to death the fifteen-year-old heir to the tyrant of Otranto; a portrait sighs, heaves its breast, and steps from its frame; a marble bust bleeds, Death rises from its prayers in an oratory, the elements and the moon work for the good against the evil, the sable plumes of the helmet nod and wave in moments of crisis. There are subterranean vaults with trap doors, caves in woods, mysterious knights, heralds, trumpets, mortal combat. Each dialogue ends with a violent interruption that opens a new scene of alarm; everyone's life hangs in the balance every minute. Sir Walter Scott found the finale "grand, tragical, and affecting,"[32] and concluded that "The applause which cannot be denied to him who can excite

---

[32] Introduction to his edition of *The Castle of Otranto* (1811), p. xxxii.

extort from him ! He buried Spenser ; and which
was more remarkable, was heir to Sir Roger
Williams *, a brave Soldier, whom he brought
to a religious and penitent death. But what
deserved most, and must have drawn the Queen's
affection to him, was his extreme attention to
the security of her person: Each year he † pro-
moted some Acts of Parliament for the defence
of it; and alone persisted in unravelling the

*. He had been one of the standing Council of
Nine, appointed to provide for defence of the Realm
against the Spanish Armada. Biograph. vol. 4.
p. 2287. He wrote a valuable history of the wars
in the Low-Countries in which he had served with
great reputation, and where he was one of the in-
troducers of a new military discipline. Camd.
Epist. p. 350. He fought a Spanish Captain who
had challenged his General, Sir John Norris, assaulted the Prince of Parma's camp near Venlo,
and penetrated to his very tent; and made a brave
defence of Sluys. Fuller in Monmouth, p. 52.
James the First lamented his death so much, that
he wished rather to have lost five thousand of his
own subjects; and intended to write his epitaph.
Bacon-papers, vol. 1. pages 296. 355.

† Lord Clarendon in answer to Sir Henry Wot-
ton, p. 188.

VOL. I.   L   mys.

*A Spanish Captain having challenged the General, Sir
A Roger fought him; afterwards assaulted &c.

54. A PROOF SHEET FOR THE SECOND EDITION OF
The Royal and Noble Authors, 1759

Antique, *Elizabeth*'s Head is taken from a Statue
of an old Woman in the *Villa Borghese* at *Rome*,
the Colouring is much higher than his usual manner; the *Virgin*'s Head and the young *Jesus* are
particularly delicate.   5 Feet 7 Inches high, by 4
Feet 3 Inches ½ wide.

Over the Doors, Two pieces of Cattle, by *Rosa di
Tivoli*.

The CABINET.

Twenty One

IS Twelve Feet ½, by Twenty-two ½.   Hung with
Green Velvet.   Over the Chimney is a celebrated
Picture of *Rubens*'s Wife, by *Vandyke* ; it was fitted
for a Pannel in her own Closet in *Rubens*'s House.
She is in Black Sattin with a Hat on, a whole Length,
the Hands and the Drapery are remarkably good.

Rubens's Family, by *Jordano* of *Antwerp* ; *Rubens* is
playing on a Lute, his first Wife is sitting with
one of their Children on her Lap, and 2 others before
her.   There are several other Figures and Genii in
the Air.   5 Feet 9 Inches high, by 4 Feet 5 Inches ½
wide; this Picture belong'd to the Duke of *Portland*.

A Winter Piece, by *Giacomo Bassan*.   3 Feet 8
Inches ½ high, by 5 Feet 11 Inches ¾ wide.

A Summer Piece, by *Lionardo Bassan*.   3 Feet 8
Inches ½ high, by 5 Feet 11 Inches ¾ wide.

                                                       Boors

55. The *Aedes,* 1747

Journey to Rousham, Ditchley, Blenheim, July 17th 1760.

Rousham, Sr Charles Cotterel's, was a small old indifferent house, built
by a Dormer; much improved for General Dormer, by Kent, in four
years; with the garden. Head of Ds of Norfolk divorced for Adultery; d
by Sr Peter Lely, but finished smooth like Carlo Dolci. D. Iohanna
Dormer Duquessa de Feria, æt. 25. The library a good room, totally
by Kent, a half kind of gothic; odd cieling, does not seem to belong to
the room; chimney with ionic pillars; fine pict. of Gen. Dormer by
Vanloo. good collection of books & prints. the garden of 25 acres; the
best thing I have seen of Kent. gothic buildings, arcade from ancient
baths, temples, old bridge, palladian do. river, slender stream winding
in a stone channel thro grass walks in wood, cascades overgrown with
iury; grove of Venus of Medici. the whole, sweet. — several portraits by
                                                        Lely & Kneller.
Ditchley, Ld Litchfield's, built by last Lord, very good house except
salon, which too small, bad carved figures, painted olive; chimney & a
buffet, each in a corner. fine Hall, basreliefs by in marble, ornaments
by Kent, cieling & side pieces by him, not so bad as his common. Head of old Sr Henry
Lee, with Dog who saved his life, by corn. Iansen. the motto, more faithfull than
favoured. He was æ Eliz! knight for 30 yrs, by vow, & then resigned it to the
Earl of Oxford. four heads of old men, said to be his brothers — but I dont find
he had any; they are good pictures. Sr Ch. Kirk killed at Isle of Rhee, good. Sr
Chr. Hatton. Sr Hen. Lee, again, whole length; old fat man, with a stick &
the garter, good. Anc Es of Lindsey, with an urn; by Sr P. Lely, good.
D. & Ds of york, Types Mary & Anne, children, 3 qrs. the Duke's head & one hand
by Lely, good; all the rest by some wretched Scholar of his.
Blenheim. execrable within, without, & almost all round. most of the Rubens's
spoiled by the sun. a fine lively head by Holbein. Ld Strafford & Leer. a copy.
a pict. called Ds of Northm & Nell Gwyn, is a copy of a picture at Wilton of Mrs Morton

56. ONE OF WALPOLE'S "JOURNEYS"

I cannot pass over the Princess Eleanor, so much celebrated by our legendary historians for sucking the poison out of her husband's wound, without mentioning the crosses erected to her memory, which Vertue with great probability supposed were built on the designs of Peter Cavalini, a Roman sculptor, and whom from various circumstances he discovered to be the architect of the shrine of Edward the Confessor.

The reader, I am persuaded, will be pleased to see how ingeniously my author traced out this hitherto unknown fact.

The original inscription on the tomb ran thus :

Anno milleno Domini cum septuageno
Et bis centeno, cum completo quasi deno,
Hoc opus est factum, quod Petrus duxit in actum
Romanus civis : Homo, causam noscere si vis,
Rex fuit Henricus, sancti praesentis amicus.

The words *Petrus duxit in actum Romanus civis* were discernable 'till very lately. Some old authors ascribe the erection of the shrine to Henry himself, others, to Richard de Ware the Abbat, elected in 1260. It is probable that Both were concerned. The new Abbat repaired to Rome immediately on his election to receive confecration from Urban IV. At that time, says Vasari, flourished there Peter Cavalini, a painter and the inventor of Mosaic, who had performed several costly works in that city. About four years before the arrival of Abbat Ware, that is in 1256, had been erected a splendid shrine for the martyrs Simplicius and Faustina, at the expence of John James Capoccio and his wife, adorned with twisted columns and inlaid with precious marbles exactly in the taste, though not in the precise form of that of St. Edward. Nothing is more probable than that a rich Abbat, either at his own expence, or to gratify the taste of his magnificent master should

Vol. I.   E   engage

✗ The remains of this shrine with its beautifull twisted mosaic columns are now in a chapel erected for them at Strawberry hill.

57. FROM WALPOLE'S COPY OF THE *Anecdotes*

the passions of fear and of pity must be awarded to the author of *The Castle of Otranto*."[33]

Walpole explained to Cole that the story was inspired by his dream of "a gigantic hand in armor" on the uppermost banister of a great staircase. He wrote it in less than two months to keep his mind off politics. The subject, he said, "was very natural for a head filled like mine with Gothic story."[34] It has not been noted, I think, that the Romantic Movement was indebted to Walpole's political disappointment for the most popular of its Gothic tales.

He wanted to tell a story in a new way. He was bored with the insipidity of Richardson and the coarseness of Fielding and Smollett. "I have not written for this century, which wants only cold reason," he told Mme du Deffand.[35] The "wildness" of his nature produced *The Castle of Otranto* as well as Strawberry Hill and its gardens. He complains in his Preface to the second edition that "the actions, sentiments, and conversations of the heroes and heroines of ancient days were as unnatural as the machines employed to put them in motion." What he wanted to do was to make his characters "think, speak, and act as it might be supposed mere men and women would do in extraordinary positions," and as they do in inspired writings. When the villain cries, "Am I to be bearded in my own palace by an insolent monk? thou art privy, I guess, to their amours," he believed that he had accomplished this feat and so did nearly all of his contemporaries. How could he, the most natural of writers, have thought so? My belief is that he accepted the artificiality of the fiction he had chosen as composers of grand opera and ballet accept the artificiality of those arts. If we also accept it, we find that the style which at first seems to us comic becomes rather pleasant and even stirring, and that we no more laugh at it than we laugh at *Siegfried* or *Swan Lake*. We see what Walpole means when he says that he has made his characters talk and act like mere men and women. We enjoy the gleams of human nature that wink about in the dark.

[33] Loc. cit., p. xxxvi.
[34] Walpole to Cole, 9 March 1765.
[35] Walpole to Mme du Deffand, 13 March 1767.

Horace Walpole

The success of his novel encouraged him three years later to make a bid for something still bigger. This was his blank-verse tragedy, *The Mysterious Mother*. Since his ambition and hopes were boundless, we may assume that while he was writing it he dared to believe that his "cold soil" was thawing at last and that his spirit was being released in verse that might carry him to the heights he aspired to—beyond Pope, beyond Dryden, right on——why not? An enthusiastic reviewer of *The Castle of Otranto had* likened him to Shakespeare. While he wrote deep into the night, the literature of the world about him in the Gothic "gloomth," anything might happen.

He set his play in the dawn of the Reformation; the scene is a castle, of course. There are pictures of ancient manners and allusions to historic events; there are two villainous friars, a faithful friend, a faithful porter, damsels, orphans, and mutes. The plot turns on a double incest. Sixteen years before the play begins, its chief character, the Countess of Narbonne, took the place of a girl she knew her son was about to seduce and now sixteen years later she fails to stop him from marrying their daughter. The friars are caricature, but the passion of the countess and her son comes through. As usual, Walpole tried to forestall possible criticism. The subject, he said, was "so truly tragic in the two essential springs of terror and pity" that he had to write it. To palliate the countess's crime and to raise her character he bestowed upon her, he tells us, "every ornament of sense, unbigoted piety, and interesting contrition." Although he protested that the subject was too "horrid" for the stage, he wished to see it acted, but there was no one equal to playing the Countess. She has yet to be performed.

He printed fifty copies of the play at Strawberry Hill, most of which he kept. The few that he gave away circulated rapidly. Transcripts were made of them, handed about, and eagerly read. The bluestockings were shocked, just as the first readers of the *Memoirs* were. That the good-natured Mr. Walpole should reveal such depths! Yet public interest in his play was so sustained that thirteen years later he allowed Dodsley to publish it in London to forestall a pirated edition. Four more editions came out before 1800, after which *The Mysterious Mother* was not reprinted until 1924. Students of our literature have neglected it; a mistake, I think, because it is perhaps superior to any other tragedy written at the time. Byron called Walpole "the author of the first romance and of the last tragedy of our language, and surely worthy of a higher place than any living writer, be he who he may."[36] Walpole later considered three other subjects for tragedies, Sir Thomas More, Anne Boleyn, and Don Carlos, but he found insurmountable difficulties in writing any of them. The last appealed to him strongly: "How many capital ingredients in that story!" he said. "Tenderness, cruelty, heroism, policy, pity, terror!" The reason he gave up "this fruitful canvas" was that the passion in it was also incestuous.[37]

The twentieth century has been initiated into the mysteries of the unconscious and needs no gloss on *The Mysterious Mother,* but one point should perhaps be noted for what it may be worth. When Walpole came to arrange his works for posthumous publication he printed his "Epitaph on Lady Walpole," with its praise of her sensibility, charity, and unbigoted piety, immediately after *The Mysterious Mother.*

His most ambitious biography was *Historic Doubts on the Life and Reign of King Richard III.* He had become convinced that Richard had been traduced by malicious and ignorant historians; that is, Richard was an underdog. When two eminent antiquaries called his attention to what they believed was the coronation roll which showed that Edward V, far from having been murdered in the Tower by his uncle Richard, had walked at his coronation, Walpole determined to clear Richard of "the mob-stories" that put him "on a level with Jack the giant-killer."[38] In his Preface he waved away possible criticism: his attempt, he said, was "mere matter of curiosity and speculation" of an idle man; he was ready to yield to better reasons, but not to "declamation." Unfortunately, the coronation roll turned out to be a wardrobe account of no relevance, and Walpole's case collapsed with it.

Dodsley published the first edition of twelve hundred copies and

---

[36] Preface to *Marino Faliero* (1821).
[37] Walpole to Jephson [Feb. 1775].
[38] "Supplement to the Historic Doubts," *Works* (1798), II, 186.

started a second of one thousand the following day. The book caused a furor. Gray and Cole stood loyally by, but Walpole was attacked by Hume, Gibbon, the President of the Society of Antiquaries, and others. The effect on him of these assaults was to make his doubts certainties: he went on answering his critics in his tartest manner for twenty-five years. The cause of Richard III is as possessive as the cause of whoever is currently said to have written the works of Shakespeare. Fresh champions spring up from time to time, only to discover that Walpole has preceded them. Present-day experts on the fifteenth century are divided in their opinions of Richard's guilt and doubtless always will be,[39] since the subject releases emotional forces.

Why did Walpole get so excited about Richard III? An explanation has recently been given to me by Dr. M. J. Mannheim that goes deeper than Walpole's stated wish to rescue Richard from the cupidity of the Lancastrian historians. This is that Walpole loved and hated his father; part of him regarded his father as a monster; Richard was a monster; by defending Richard, Walpole was atoning for his suppressed hatred of Sir Robert. We are here at the point in biography beyond which, Plutarch tells us, there "is nothing but dark unpassable bogs, or Scythian cold, or frozen sea."

Finally, there are Walpole's little known *Hieroglyphic Tales.* They are the most off-beat of all his works: Gulliver out of Mme d'Aulnoy on a planet not yet made. They were written, he says in his Preface, "a little before the creation of the world, and have ever since been preserved, by oral tradition, in the mountains of Crampcraggiri, an uninhabited island not yet discovered" by clergymen not yet born. They are therefore a step beyond the *Castle of Otranto,* whose supernatural phenomena are three-dimensional. In the *Hieroglyphic Tales* Walpole bursts into the fourth dimension of time. He had read in Bayle that the Greeks had "a controversy about things that never were nor shall be, whether some are not possible." "The merits of an Hieroglyphic Tale," he noted in one

---

[39] See, for example, Appendix J, "The Princes in the Tower," in *The Complete Peerage,* Vol. XII, Pt. II (1959).

NO.

Mr. WILLIAM TOMKINS,
At Mr. Turner's, Surgeon, in St. Martin's Lane.

122 A small landſkip, the morning.

123 Ditto, the evening,

124 * A Thiſtle and Butterflies.

Mr. XAVIER VESPRE,
In Thriſt-Street, Soho.

125 * A picture upon glaſs : a firſt attempt in that way.

Mr. WALE,
In Little Court, Caſtle-Street, Leiceſter-Fields.

126 The head of Pompey ſhown to Cæſar,

127 Philip, his ſlave, making his funeral pile.

Mr. WEBB,
In St. Martin's-Lane.

128 A lady, whole length,

129 A gentleman, half length,

130 A piece of flowers.

Mr. WEST, *a Penſilvanian, lately arrived.*
In Caſtle-Street, Leiceſter-Fields,

131 Angelica and Medoro, an hiſtorical picture, *} Theſe are much admired,*

132 It's companion, Cymon and Iphigenia, *} but are very tawdry in the manner of Bartocio.*

133 A gentleman, whole length. *General Monckton*

Mr. WILDING,
At the Golden Head, in Sutton-Street, Soho.

134 Miniature of a child.

Mr. RICHARD WILSON,
In the Great Piazza, Covent-Garden.

well. 135 A small landſkip, with a ruin,

136 Ditto, it's companion,

✕ He was ſon by a second Wife of a Quaker, by profeſſion a Cooper, ſettled in Oxfordſhire, whence he went to Penſilvania, where his ſon Benjamin was born, who having great propenſity to drawing, was sent to Italy by a contribution of different perſons.

58. NOTES IN AN EXHIBITION CATALOGUE

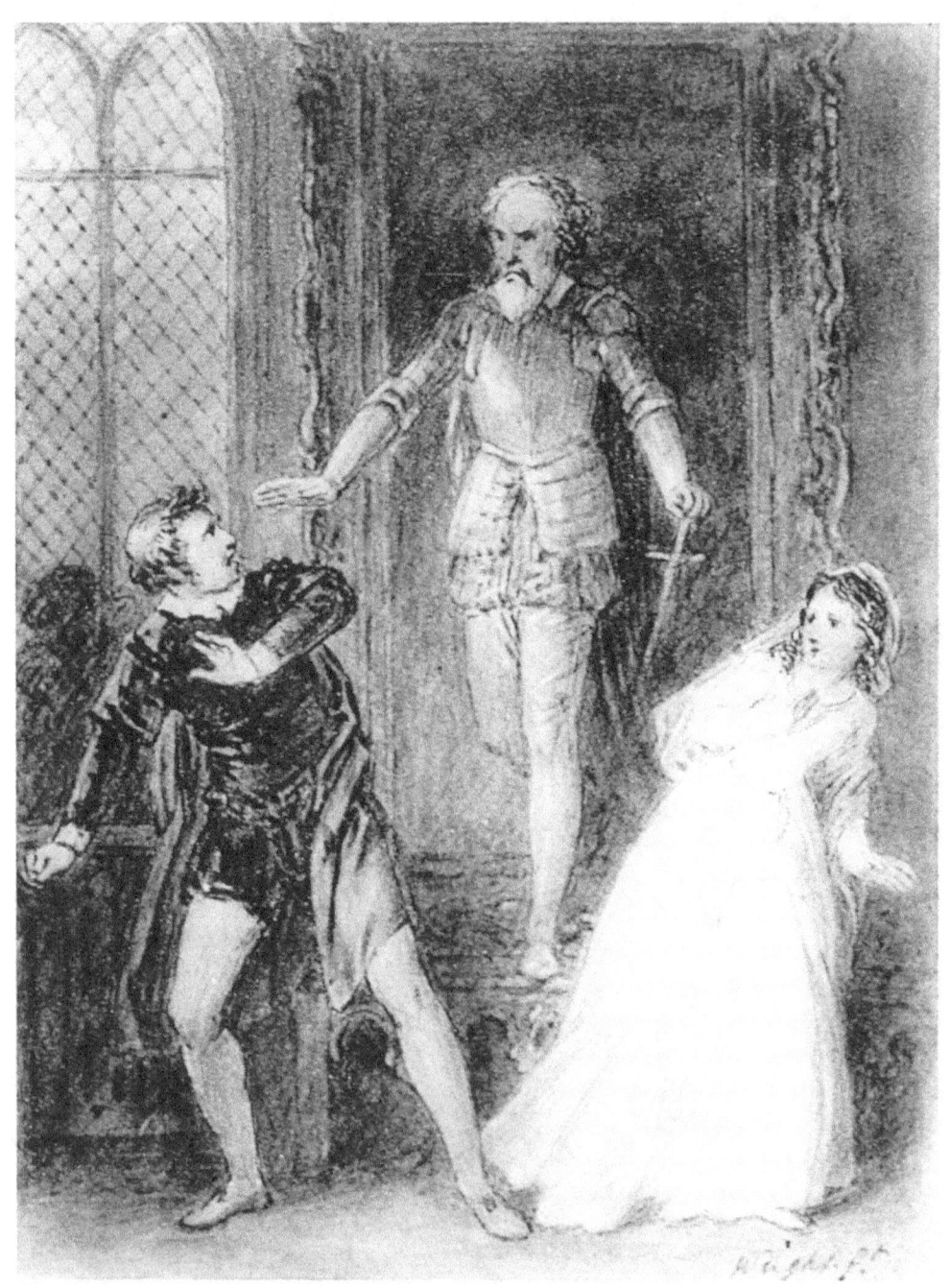

59. SCENE FROM *The Castle of Otranto*

of the seven copies[40] that he printed at his Press, "consists in its being written extempore and without any plan," like unconscious writing or drawing. His Postscript to the *Tales* added that they "deserve at most to be considered as an attempt to vary the stale and beaten class of stories and novels, which, though works of invention, are almost always devoid of imagination." Although the twenty-fifth century may find the *Tales* commonplace, they are too extravagant for us. It is a struggle to accept a pistachio nut drawn by an elephant and a ladybird, but a princess who speaks French in perfection and never was born is too much.

What did he think of his own writings? As you may have by now come to expect, he was of two minds about them. He insisted that they were "trifles" and that he was "an insignificant author," yet he arranged with Mary Berry and Mrs. Damer for his books and verses and essays and political pieces, together with a selection of his letters, to be published after his death. They appeared in 1798, five thick quarto volumes, *The Works of Horatio Walpole, Earl of Orford*. The excuse that he gave for ordering this posthumous publication was his fear that someone would bring out an edition of his writings after his death and add "some babes . . . that were no babes of mine."[41] He felt certain—as certain as he could be about anything—that his *Memoirs* and letters would live, yet he naturally wanted his other works to live also. The avowals of hasty composition and protestations of triviality in their prefaces were an attempt to take the wind out of his critics' sails, but when he ran down his work he was also being sincere: he was a perfectionist and he knew that it could be better.

Still, he was pleased on the whole with the public's reception of his writings. New editions of them were frequently called for; *The Castle of Otranto* had many imitators. Younger writers and antiquaries made pilgrimages to Strawberry Hill. His nephew sold the Houghton pictures

---

[40] This copy is now in the British Museum. Walpole's notes in it were printed by A. W. Evans in the Elkin Mathews edition of the *Tales* (1926). A seventh, unpublished, tale is at Farmington, and an eighth is perhaps hinted at by Mason in his letter to Harcourt of 20 Nov. 1788 (Yale Walpole, 29. 333–34).
[41] Walpole to Nicol, 30 Aug. 1792.

to Catherine the Great for her new gallery at The Hermitage, and that was like the death of a beloved relation, but his catalogues and the *Anecdotes of Painting* had made Englishmen more aware of pictures in general and their own school in particular. He knew that he had not been without influence as a writer in his generation.

He secured the contemporary fame that he craved, but we, looking back, see that if he had not written his *Memoirs* and letters, his readers today would be limited to historians of the arts in England and of the novel. We also know that before he was twenty he had begun to write for the audience that will always be his.

VI

THE LETTERS

WALPOLE'S first correspondent was his mother, as might be expected. His second letter to her, which was written when he was seven, asked for *The Earl of Essex* and *Jane Shore* and foreshadows his interest in historic personages and tragedy. Two letters from Eton just before his sixteenth birthday deal with a more immediate concern:

"My Dearest dear Mama,

I can gladly let you know now that this last Dose has succeeded as well as the first and worked the same; it is impossible it could do ill as your dear hands mixt'd it, which made me take it with the greatest pleasure. . . ."[1]

The reply, which must have been sent post, is missing, but its purport is clear from Horace's answer: "I was in hope I had finished my Physick, but since my Dear Mama desires it, to be sure I will take it again."[2]

Only two years later he had found his style and his forte. "Why mayn't we hold a classical correspondence?" he wrote from Cambridge to West at Oxford. "Let us extend the Roman Empire, and cultivate two barbarous towns o'errun with rusticity and mathematics."[3] He went on in that style and spirit for sixty-two years, until he reached his final months and wrote to Lady Ossory in mock despair that he was unable to tell an antiquarian friend of hers what kind of shoes King Stephen

---

[1] Walpole to Lady Walpole, 28 Sept. 1733.
[2] Ibid., 30 Sept. 1733.
[3] Walpole to West, 9 Nov. 1735.

wore. "Having outlived my vocation," he said, "I can furnish nothing but its ashes."[4] By "vocation" he meant imparting his knowledge of the past to his contemporaries and of the present to posterity. He knew that he did this most effectively in his private correspondence.

It is expected that the Yale edition of it will eventually have about four thousand letters from him. A quarter of these are notes or business letters; the remaining three thousand belong to what we may call his "grand design." My guess is that these three thousand represent about 40 per cent of the total number of such letters that he wrote, or about one every three days during his active writing life.[5]

He realized very early what his career was to be: in his nineteenth year he asked Montagu to keep his letters;[6] four years later at Florence he and Mann used to talk about holding a "circumstantial" correspondence filled with news. "Gazetteer" is the word that he used all his life to describe himself. "I will be like any gazette," he wrote to Conway, "and scrape together all the births, deaths, and marriages in the parish."[7] The difference between him and the public gazettes and newspapers would be that whereas they published "one thousand new lies" every day, his private intelligence would be truthful. He would send no reports until he had "heard their echo"; he would not write what he "might contradict next post." When he made a mistake he corrected it as soon as possible. The trait that runs through all his writing, the wish to inform, is apparent from the first, together with his concern for hav-

---

[4] Walpole to Lady Ossory, 20 Nov. 1796.

[5] All his letter-books have disappeared, and the only gauge we have is his list of letters written from Paris. The list is printed in the Yale Walpole, 7. 376–96. Of the 283 letters 97 have been recovered. He also kept a list of the letters he sent to France, 900-odd in number, of which all but 60-odd were to Mme du Deffand and are missing. If we eliminate his letters on business and household affairs we have about 40 per cent of the Paris list. In England he doubtless wrote many more business letters and little notes to say that he would or would not come to dinner, but the number of his grand-design letters was probably the same. The chief losses of his letters are, I think, those that he wrote to Lady Mary Churchill, Mrs. Damer, Lord and Lady Hertford, and the Duke and Duchess of Richmond.

[6] Walpole to Montagu, 2 May 1736.

[7] Walpole to Conway, 23 June 1752.

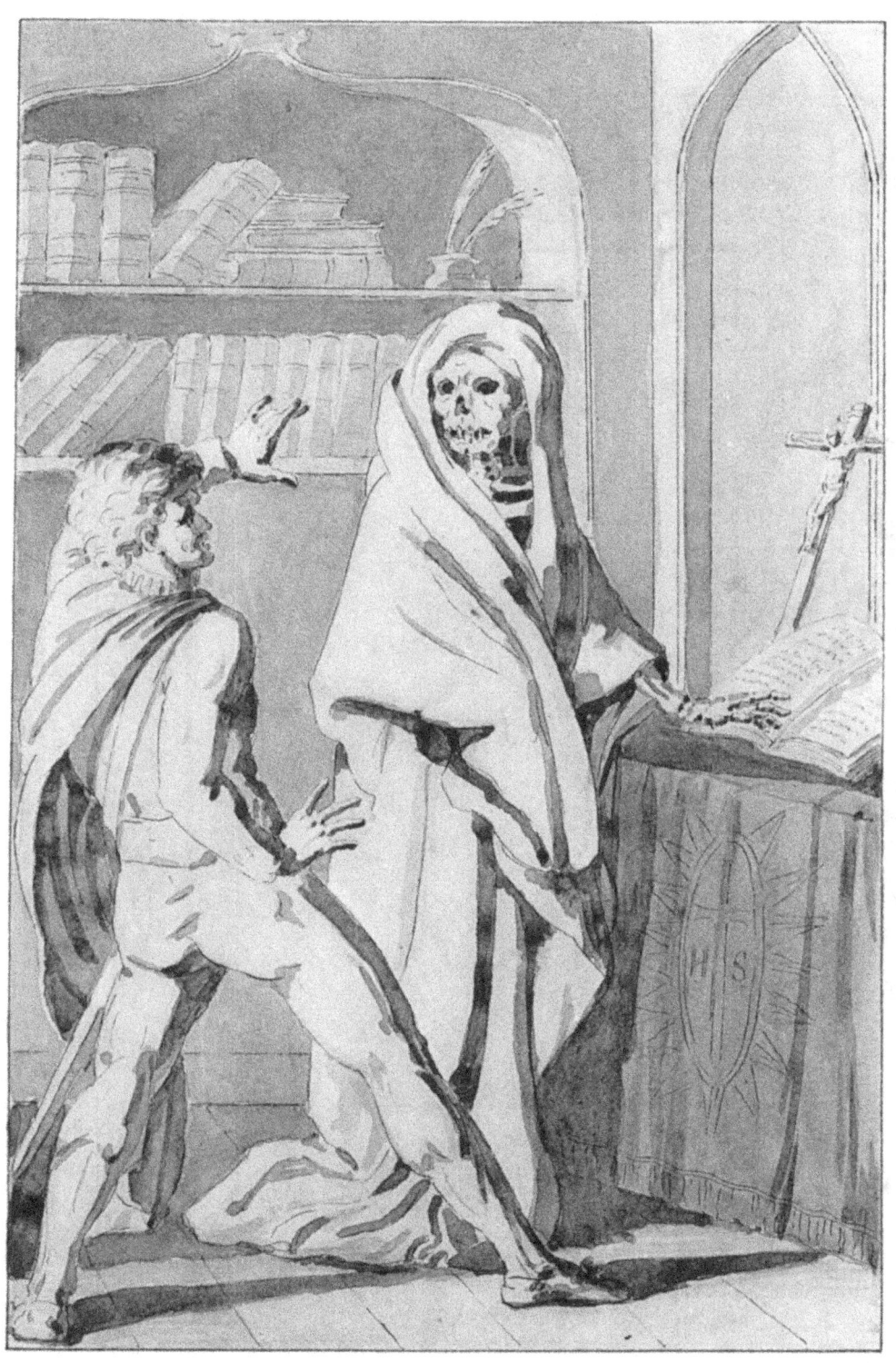

60. SCENE FROM *The Castle of Otranto*

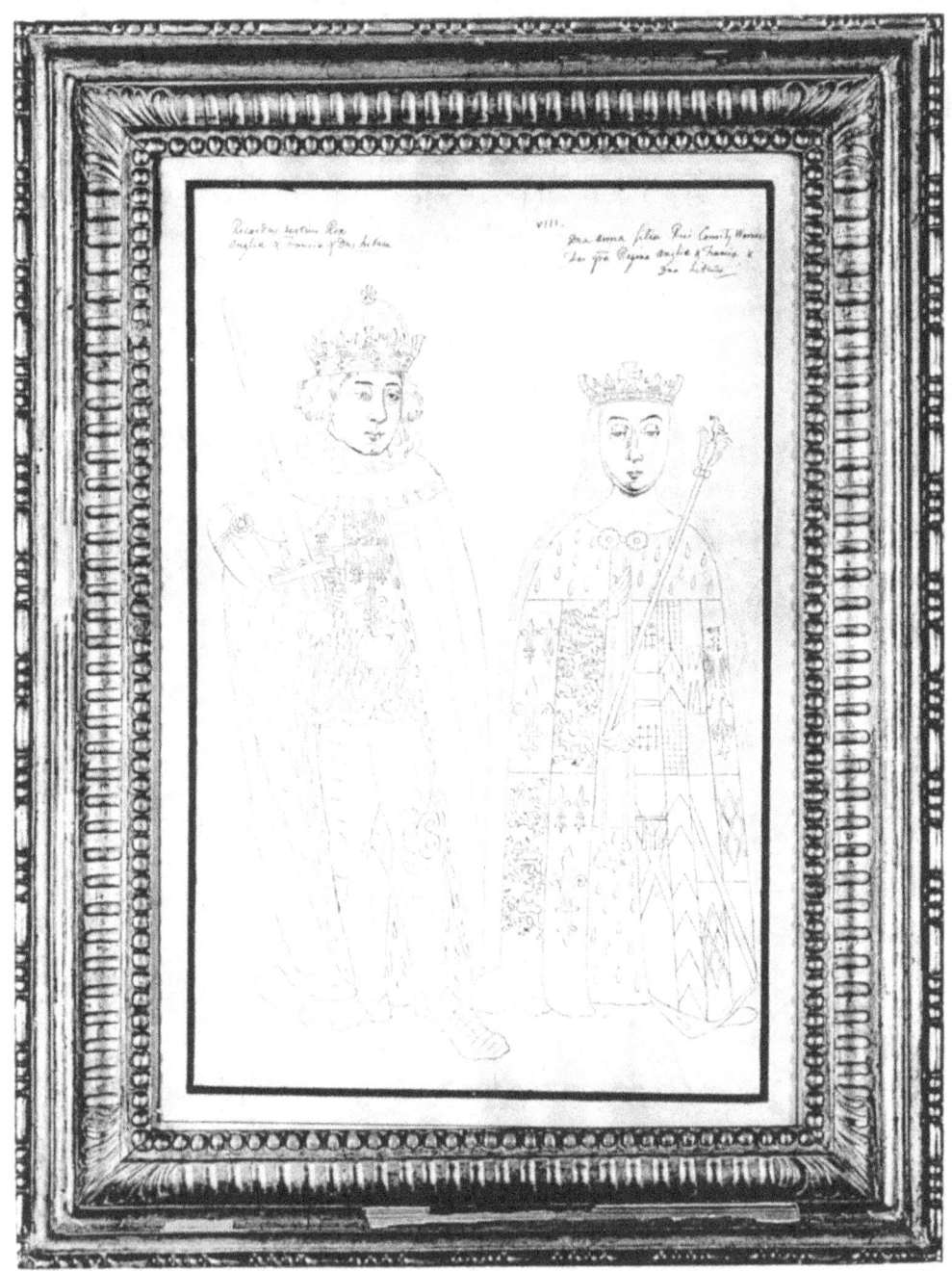

61. RICHARD III AND QUEEN ELEANOR, *by George Vertue*

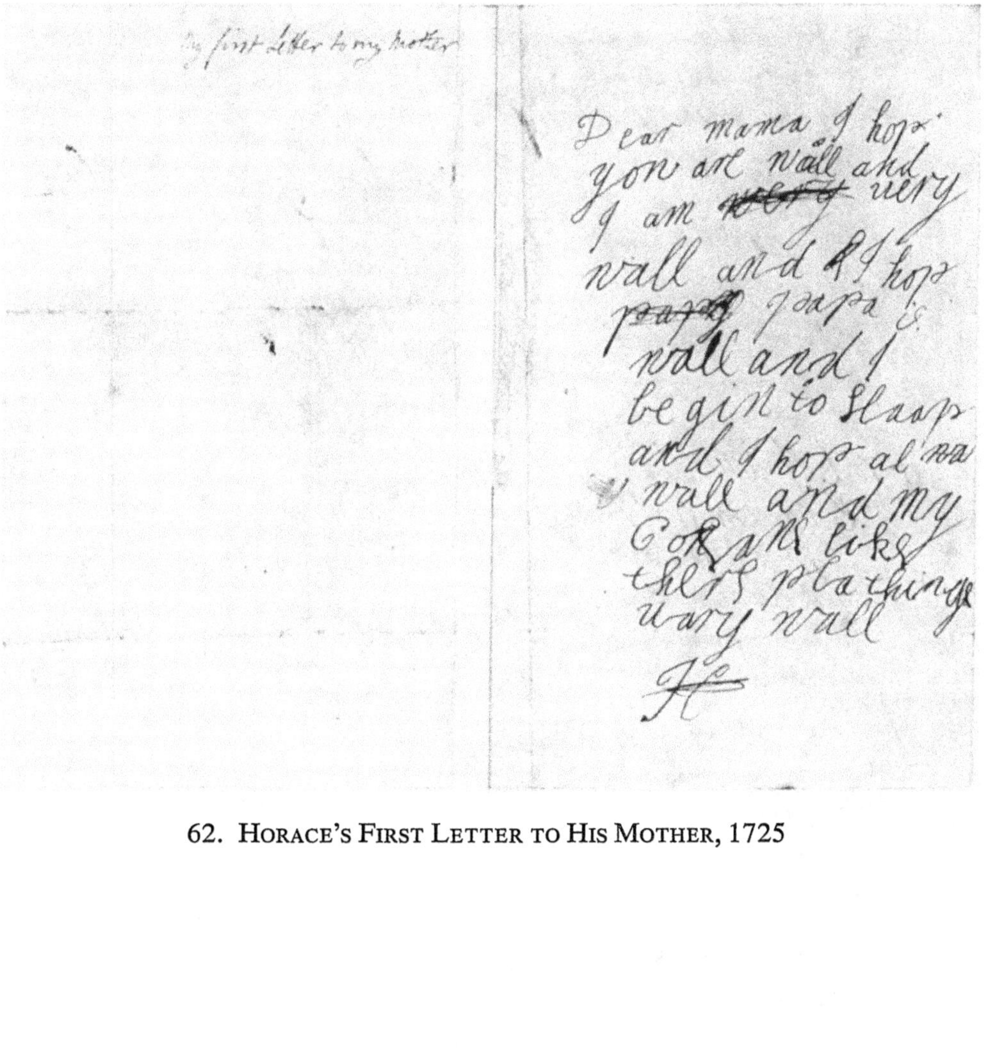

My first Letter to my Mother

Dear mama I hop
you are wall and
I am ~~very~~ very
wall and I I hop
~~papa~~ papa is
wall and I
begin to slaap
and I hop al na
wall and my
Cors all like
ther plaching
wary wall

H

62. HORACE'S FIRST LETTER TO HIS MOTHER, 1725

63. MEMORANDA FOR A LETTER

The Letters

ing his news accurate. But mere facts were not enough; his letters must also be entertaining. He sent Montagu a long story of an evening at Vauxhall with Lady Caroline Petersham to show him "the manners of the age, which are always as entertaining to a person fifty miles off as to one born an hundred and fifty years after the time."[8] He would be informative, trustworthy, and amusing.

He succeeded by being perfectly natural: he laid aside the "historical buskins." He said, "I have no patience with people that don't write just as they would talk";[9] and if his letters could not write themselves, he left them unwritten. I think that when he began the letter to Lady Ossory telling her of "Capability" Brown's death—"Your dryads must go into black gloves, Madam: their father-in-law, Lady Nature's second husband, is dead,"[10]—it was not the product of polish and revision, although I don't doubt that he thought about how he would report Brown's death to her before putting pen to paper. He stored up news for this person and that, and if he repeated it he was careful to do so in different words.

We can see him settling at his desk to chat with Mann or Montagu or Mason, choosing a sharp quill, rereading his correspondent's last letter, scribbling the headings for his reply on the back of it or on a scrap of paper that he had hoarded. These preliminaries over, he started off in high spirits, crossing out the headings in his list when he used them and dashing the pounce, which still glistens today, over the wet page. His friends agreed that his letters were like his conversation,[11] but his pen could not have kept up with his mind, no matter how fast he wrote, and his is not a hurried hand. It is legible and beautifully formed: he wanted his correspondents to read what he had to say with ease as well as pleasure. There are occasional corrections and blots, but a correction here,

---

[8] Walpole to Montagu, 23 June 1750.

[9] Walpole to Lincoln, 5 Sept. 1744.

[10] Walpole to Lady Ossory, 8 Feb. 1783.

[11] Bentley told Cole that Walpole "wrote with the greatest ease imaginable, with company in the room and even talking to other people at the time." Nichols, *Illustrations of the Literary History of the Eighteenth Century* (1858), VIII, 573.

a blot there, is a sign of intimacy—and he lacked the patience to rewrite his letters, which often run to a thousand words.

He read published letters, from Cicero and Pliny to Chesterfield and Dr. Johnson, with a rival's eye. "St Paul," he said, "is my model for letter-writing, who being a man of fashion, and very unaffected, never studies for what he shall say, but in one paragraph takes care of Timothy's soul, and in the next of his own cloak."[12] He pointed out repeatedly that the best letters were written by women. Lady Mary Wortley Montagu's were second only to Mme de Sévigné's.[13] Women's superiority in the art he attributed to their greater delicacy in sentiment and to a man's being "too jealous of the reputation of good sense, to condescend to hazard a thousand trifles and negligences, which give grace, ease, and familiarity to correspondence."[14] He scolded his friends who praised his letters and handed them about, even while he was secretly pleased that they were being preserved. "Don't commend me: you don't know what hurt it will do me,"[15] he told Montagu, and fifty years later he begged Lady Ossory not to praise his "idle notes." How could he be as nonsensical as he wanted to be and as he would be if he were talking tête-à-tête, how could he write "the first foolish thing that comes into one's head," when he knew that what he was writing was going to be read aloud to or by strangers? Letters, he said, ought to be "nothing but extempore conversations upon paper,"[16] and should on no account be printed so long as their contents might injure living persons.

His outward casualness concealed his seriousness. "Nothing," he wrote, "gives so just an idea of an age as genuine letters; nay, history waits for its last seal from them,"[17] and again, "familiar letters written by eye-witnesses, and that, without design, disclose circumstances that let us more intimately into important events, are genuine history;

---

[12] Walpole to Lady Ossory, 8 Oct. 1777.
[13] Walpole to Mann, 14 Oct. 1751.
[14] Walpole to Strafford, 11 Dec. 1783.
[15] Walpole to Montagu, 12 June 1746.
[16] Walpole to Lady Ossory, 25 Dec. 1781.
[17] Walpole to Sir David Dalrymple, 30 Nov. 1761.

The Letters

and as far as they go, more satisfactory than formal premeditated narratives."[18] Private letters may perform the miracle that occurs in *The Castle of Otranto* when the portrait sighs, heaves its breast, and steps from its frame; letters written by people living in the midst of affairs can be posterity's ultimate guides if they are accurate; it will help if they are also entertaining. The writers must trust and enjoy their correspondents. Walpole sensed this before he was twenty. The people to whom he sent his early letters with us in the back of his mind were Gray, West, Conway, and Montagu, all established friends eager for news and nonsense; his later chief correspondents were likewise people to whom he could write freely about the matters that interested him most: politics, the news of society, literature, the arts, and antiquarianism. His correspondents were his coadjutors in his grand design to inform and amuse posterity. When one of them died or a friendship cooled, he took up with a successor to whom he could write with equal ease on the same general subject. Occasionally one of them wandered into a second group, as when Gray strayed from literature into antiquarianism and Mason into politics, but, in general, they remained in the category where they started. With no two of them does he appear quite the same.

It would be going too far, I think, to say that he chose his interlocutors with calculated deliberation. I don't believe that when he gave up Montagu he said to himself, "Where shall I send my news and nonsense now?" I think, rather, that, wanting to write that sort of letter to someone, he drifted into sending it to Lady Ossory. Fond as he was of her, it was not until she retired to the country for good that she became one of his chief correspondents.

When she went to Florence with her first husband, the Duke of Grafton, he announced her to Mann as a passion of his and "one of our first great ladies."[19] Unfortunately, she was inclined to gallantry and gambling. The Duke, who liked gallantry, but not gambling, promptly divorced her when she had a child by Lord Ossory. Although Ossory as

---

[18] Walpole to Fenn, 29 June 1784.
[19] Walpole to Mann, 14 May 1761.

promptly married her, she was buried for the rest of her life in Bedford-shire and acquired for Walpole the added attraction of being one of the afflicted. Walpole did what he could to make her think that she was still part of the great world. She read his letters to her country neighbors, which he begged her not to do: the nonsense in them, he said, would prove that he took no care of his reputation and that she had not the best taste in the world to enjoy them.[20] From his forty-fifth year to his eightieth he sent her in four hundred and fifty letters his news and the news of the world: his playing pharaoh all night with Mme de Mirepoix or loo with Mme du Deffand, accounts of how he and Lady Browne were robbed only twenty yards from the Duchess of Montrose's gate by a highwayman, the triumphs of Benjamin Franklin, the discovery of Uranus, the betrothal of an heiress, or the suicide of a friend ruined at Brooks's. It is the correspondence in which Walpole is most consciously practicing the art of letter-writing.

The transition from Gray to Mason was even easier than from Montagu to Lady Ossory. When Mason began his life of Gray he applied to Walpole for help. Walpole gave it eagerly. Apart from wanting to do all he could for Gray's biographer he believed, along with most of his contemporaries, that Mason was a great poet. Before long he was calling Mason his "confessor in literature."[21] Then Mason assumed an even more important role, that of political satirist. Walpole saw the American Revolution as the beginning of the end of the British Empire and was convinced that George III and his ministers were determined to reduce the liberties of Englishmen at home as well as abroad, but Mason might yet save England if only he would lash the miscreants hard enough. "Brand the guilty," Walpole exhorted, "and reward the good."[22]

Seldom can contemporary criticism have been more wrong than the eighteenth-century's appraisal of William Mason. His satires are now forgotten; his life of Gray is remembered only because Boswell said he imitated it, because of Walpole's contributions to it, and because it in-

---

[20] Walpole to Lady Ossory, 23 July 1775.
[21] Walpole to Mason, 7 April 1774.
[22] Ibid., 28 Aug. 1778.

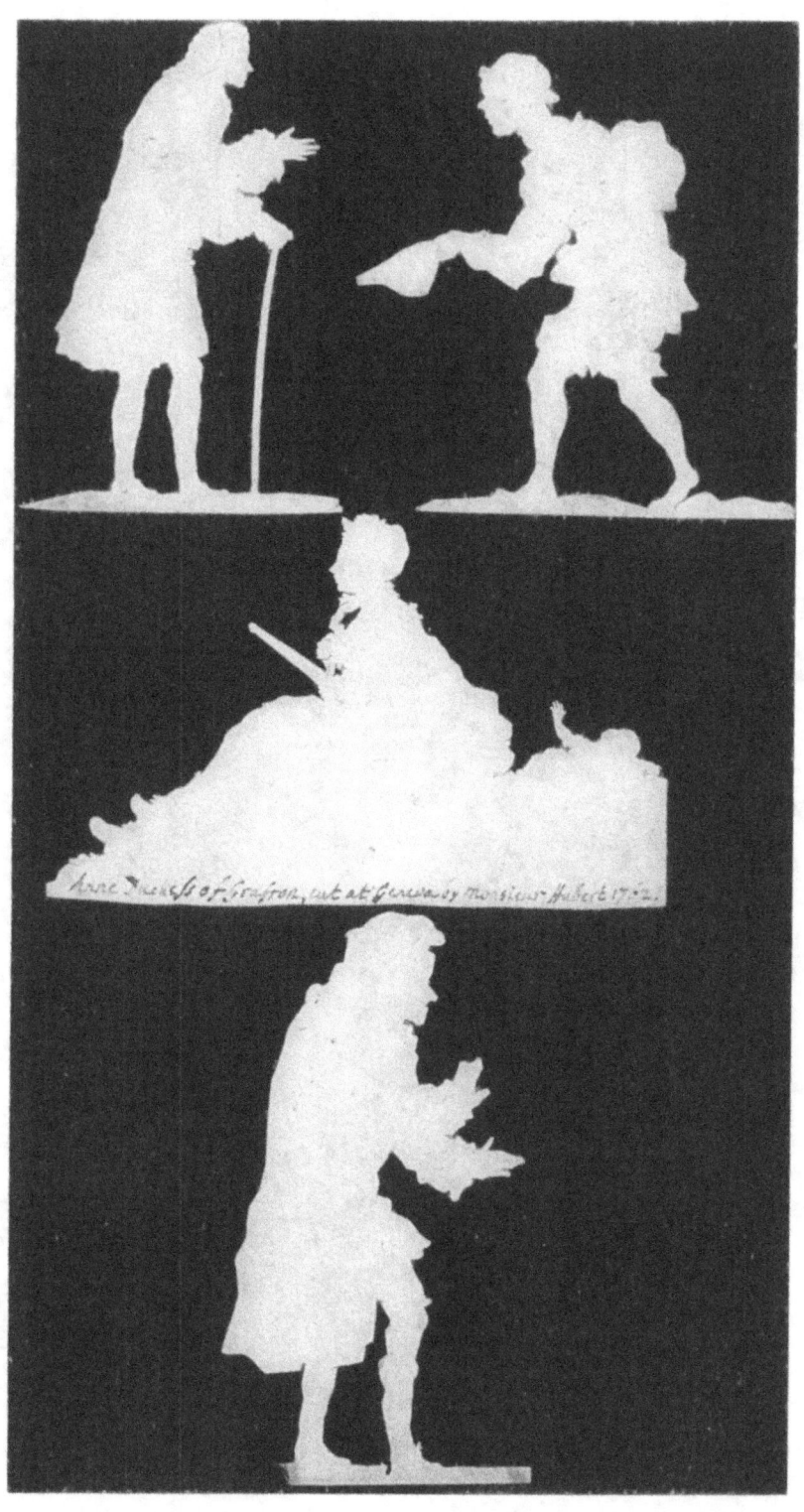

64. ANNE, DUCHESS OF GRAFTON, AFTERWARDS COUNTESS OF UPPER OSSORY

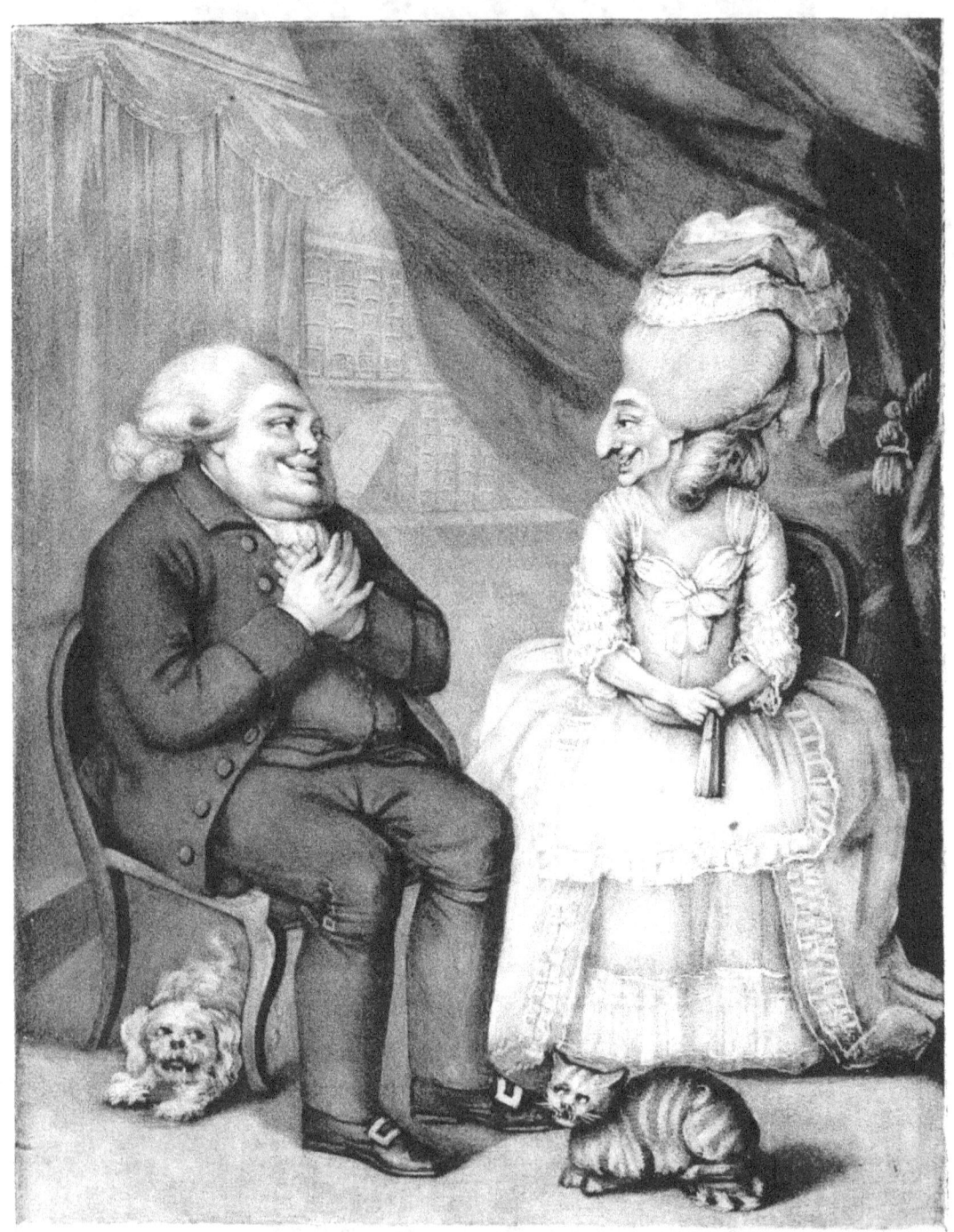

ABELARD AND ELOISA.

Printed for & Sold by CARINGTON BOWLES, at his Map & Print Warehouse, N.º 69 in S.ᵗ Paulis Church Yard, LONDON. Published as the Act directs, 20 Apr 1778.

65. WILLIAM MASON AND MRS. MONTAGU, 1778

cluded many of Gray's letters (which Mason mutilated in editing). He is the least agreeable of Walpole's major correspondents. When it became clear that he would never be a bishop and that he could amass in church preferments only the modern equivalent of about £12,000 a year, he grew even more rancorous and bitter. It was hateful to him to have to "go morning and afternoon to see the ancient maiden gentlewomen and decayed tradesmen . . . mumble their matins and their vespers"[23] in York Minster. Although he was flattered by Walpole's correspondence at first, he soon grew so bored with it that he answered briefly only every other letter. He ridiculed Walpole to Lord Harcourt, their common friend, and hoped to avoid a visit to Strawberry Hill: its owner was "at times so spitfire and at times so frighted."[24] Walpole was patient and humble for years, gulping down his anger at Mason's silences,[25] but when Mason went over to the Court party Walpole could endure him no longer. Mason in his Yorkshire solitude was reluctant to admit it, but he missed Walpole's news. A year before both of them died he made an overture of friendliness, which was warmly received.

When Walpole's correspondence with Mason became more and more political, his letters that were primarily on literature, past and present, went to Robertson, the historian, Pinkerton, Hannah More, and others. He singled out Robert Jephson, the young Irish playwright who turned *The Castle of Otranto* into a play.[26] Walpole said that Jephson was "the only man capable of restoring and improving our stage" and tried to instruct him in the drama as he tried to instruct Bentley in drawing, Mason in satire, Robertson and Pinkerton in history, and his Conway cousins and the Duke of Richmond in politics. What he urged Jephson to do was to choose a subject and to handle it in "*a very new and peculiar style* [italics Walpole's]. By fixing on some region of whose lan-

---

[23] Mason to Walpole, 3 March 1775.

[24] Mason to Harcourt, 1 June 1780 (Yale Walpole, 28. xxviii).

[25] Walpole to Mason, 15 May 1778.

[26] *The Count of Narbonne,* a play, which Miss Seward, the Swan of Lichfield, considered "our modern Macbeth." Anna Seward, *Letters* (Edinburgh, 1811), IV, 334.

guage we have little or no idea," he said, "as of the Peruvians in the story of Atabalipa, you might frame a new diction"—as Shakespeare had "formed a style for Caliban that could suit no other kind of being."[27] He seems to have had in mind something like his own *Hieroglyphic Tales*.

Thousands of references to books and authors from the Psalms of David to Erasmus Darwin are scattered throughout his works and correspondence.[28] To any of his friends he might toss off a comment on Virgil or Racine or launch into a panegyric on Shakespeare. Although much of this was what he called "foolery," one can't always be certain when he was being serious and when not. We know that he thought Otway and Southerne were second only to Shakespeare among English tragic poets, but did he really think that Aristophanes was "a blackguard," and Dante "a Methodist parson in Bedlam"? Good letters are full of indiscreet and offhand remarks; they cannot be written by one who never writes anything that he would not be willing to see on the front page of the *New York Times*. When they are printed, bursts of spleen or silliness or flattery instead of floating away in conversation acquire permanence, and these peccadilloes of private correspondence may become the subject of a solemn monograph two hundred years later in South Dakota. Walpole, who wrote so much over so many years in varying moods and with little reserve, has suffered from his openness, as he foresaw that he would. Readers pounce upon a remark that he dashed off in a fit of ill-nature or frivolity, and, removing it for study, confer upon it the weight of an opinion by Lord Mansfield. We are amused when he ridicules a person we never heard of, but if we think highly of his target we don't like it at all. When we read in his verses on Lord Sandys, a bitter opponent of his father's, that

no worth
Call'd from his mud the sluggish reptile forth,

---

[27] Walpole to Jephson [Feb. 1775].

[28] A large collection of them was made some years ago by Dr. Clyde S. Kilby of Wheaton College, who very kindly gave them to me. Recent discoveries have made it even more extensive.

we don't mind, because Walpole was standing by his father, and who was Sandys anyway? But when he calls Dr. Johnson "a saucy Caliban,"[29] a thousand swords leap from their scabbards.

Whereas few received his "gazettes," his letters on antiquities went to dozens of people. The earliest of them were sent to Conyers Middleton; the last went to young and ardent enthusiasts who showed promise of rescuing the study of ancient manners from the dry-as-dust. In the years between were the strangers (including Chatterton) who wrote to tell him how much they enjoyed the *Catalogue of the Royal and Noble Authors, Anecdotes of Painting in England,* and *Historic Doubts,* and who offered comment and information. He was pleased and flattered by this approval of his work, and he answered his correspondents fully and with extreme courtesy, although, as we have seen, he had no intention of using "the lights" that they volunteered. "Every letter I receive from you is a new obligation," he wrote to one of them, "but sure my *Catalogue* was not worthy of giving you so much trouble."[30] Famous names and names now forgotten float in and out of these antiquarian correspondences, together with the niceties of medieval dress, the details of Gothic ornament, anecdotes of kings and their queens and mistresses, and obscure genealogies. "I do not see why," he wrote, "books of antiquities should not be made as amusing as writings on any other subject."[31] Cole was his major antiquarian correspondent, but Walpole had the time and inclination to write in his highest style to Sir David Dalrymple and Lord Buchan, even though the latter was asphyxiatingly dull. "Lord Ossory asks very reasonably why I correspond with Lord Buchan," Walpole wrote to Lady Ossory; it was, he said, "because I cannot help it now and then: I am his Tom Hearne, and he *will* extract from me whatever in the course of my antiquarian dips I have picked up about Scottish kings and queens, for whom in truth I never cared a straw."[32] We see antiquaries all over Britain turning to the fashionable and ingenious Mr. Walpole for further

[29] Walpole to Mason, 9 Feb. 1781.
[30] Walpole to Henry Zouch, 21 Oct. 1758.
[31] Ibid., 20 March 1762.
[32] Walpole to Lady Ossory, 10 Nov. 1782.

enlightenment about early English architecture, painting, genealogy, and manners.

Leslie Stephen said, "The history of England throughout a very large segment of the eighteenth century is simply a synonym for the works of Horace Walpole."[33] No statement by posterity would have pleased Walpole more: posterity had accepted his life work and his view of history. His view was that whereas historians should get their facts right, mere chronicles are not enough, and that "without some romance" history "is nothing but a register of crimes and calamities."[34] Visions were evoked by remembering that the people of former ages were human beings. Whom they married and begot, what years they flourished, what wars they fought, or when they died was of less interest to him than what they thought, what they wore and how they wore it, what they ate and how they ate it, the value of their money, their diversions, the laws that they made and flouted, their arts and literature: what today is called "social history," which he illustrated with such details as that women wore looking-glasses from their girdles in the reign of Edward I, that Mary Queen of Scots put ointment on one of her feet the night before her execution, and that Scaliger and Cardan had a dispute whether parrots were ugly or not. When you know the details of everyday life and "the nonsense uttered by the learned men of an age" you become more at home in it. He would have taken Leslie Stephen's tribute as proof that like-minded men of the future had welcomed an authentic account of the eighteenth century laced with instances of its follies and virtues, and the pride, eccentricity, ambition, malice, and good nature of its leading characters.

The past offered a haven to him from the irritations and disappointments of the present. He might picture himself of a party in Gramont's time, strolling through the gardens at Hampton Court on a summer night, but the eighteenth century dragged him back, and the vision of himself in the past faded away. Romancing about the future was still

---

[33] *Hours in a Library* (1909), I, 322.
[34] Walpole to Mary Berry, 10 July 1790.

Strawberry hill
June 25. 1778.

I am quite astonished, Madam, at not hearing of Mr
Conway's being returned! what is He doing? Is he revolting &
setting up for himself like our Nabobs in India? or is he for-
-ming Jersey, Guernsey, Alderney & Sark into the United provinces
in the compass of a silver penny? I shoud not wonder if this was
to be the fate of our distracted empire, which we seem to have
made so large, only that It might afford to split into seperate
kingdoms. I told Mr C. I shoud not write any more, coreluding
he woud not stay a twinkling; & yr Ladyship's last encouraged
my expecting him. In truth I had nothing to tell him if I
had written.

I am impatient too to know how poor Lord William does, and
if you have better hopes of him. I long to hear that my dear
Mrs Damer is well again. I hope it was nothing at all serious.

I have been in town but one single night this age, as I coud
not bear to throw away this phœnix June. It has rained a
good deal this morning, but only made it more delightfull.
The flowers are all Arabian — I have found but one inconvenience

66. WALPOLE TO LADY AILESBURY, 25 June 1778

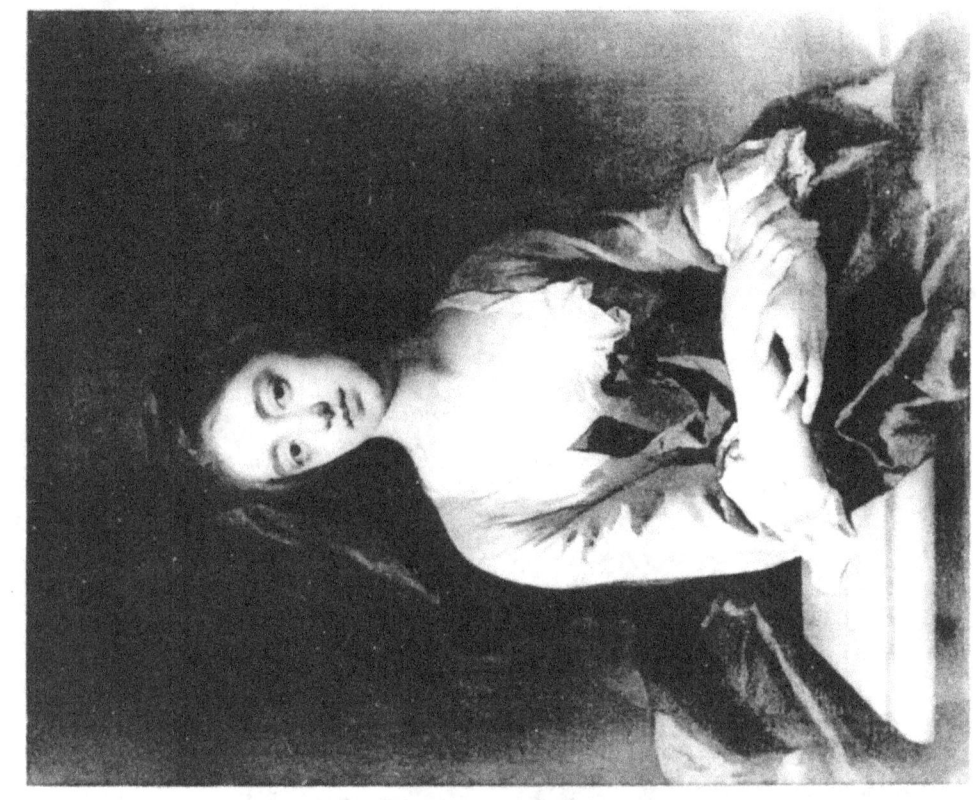

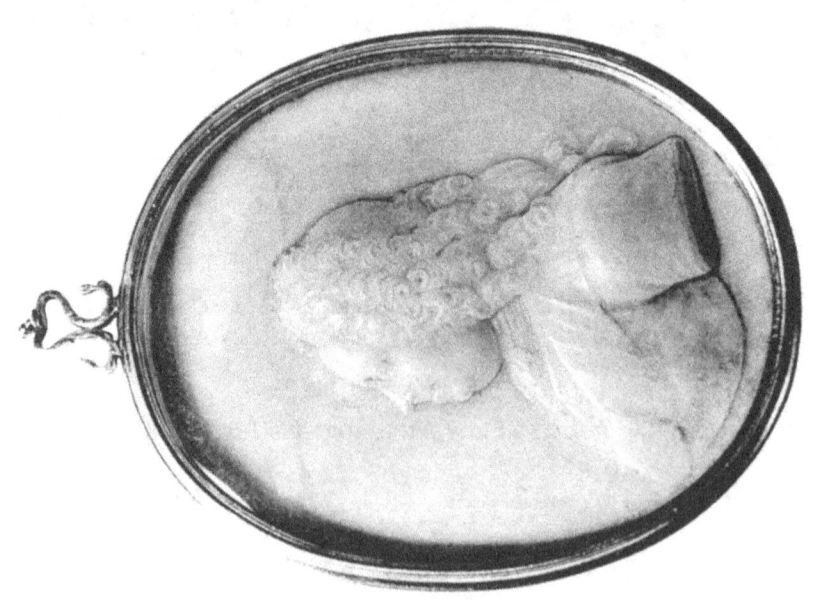

67. Sir Robert and Lady Walpole

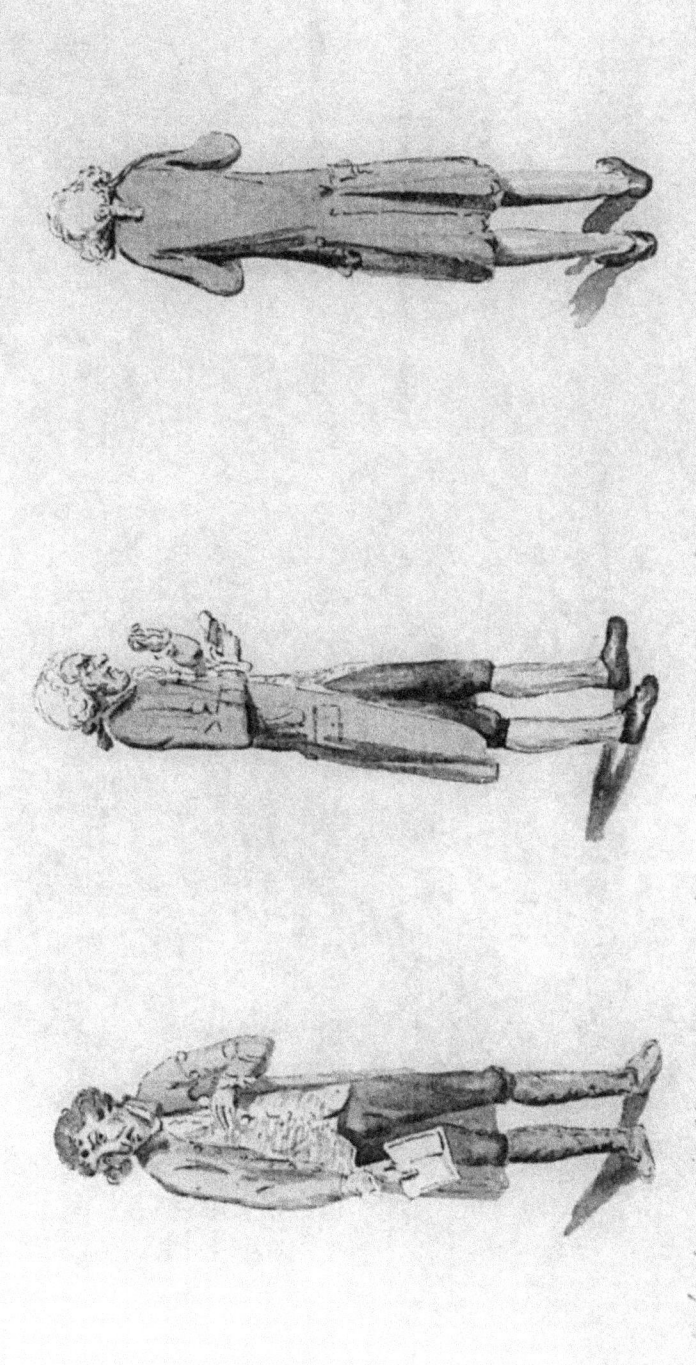

after breakfast, in his study. — Before Dinner, when Guest, in the Cabinet. — after Dinner, in the Gallery.

68. WALPOLE, *by John Carter, 1788*

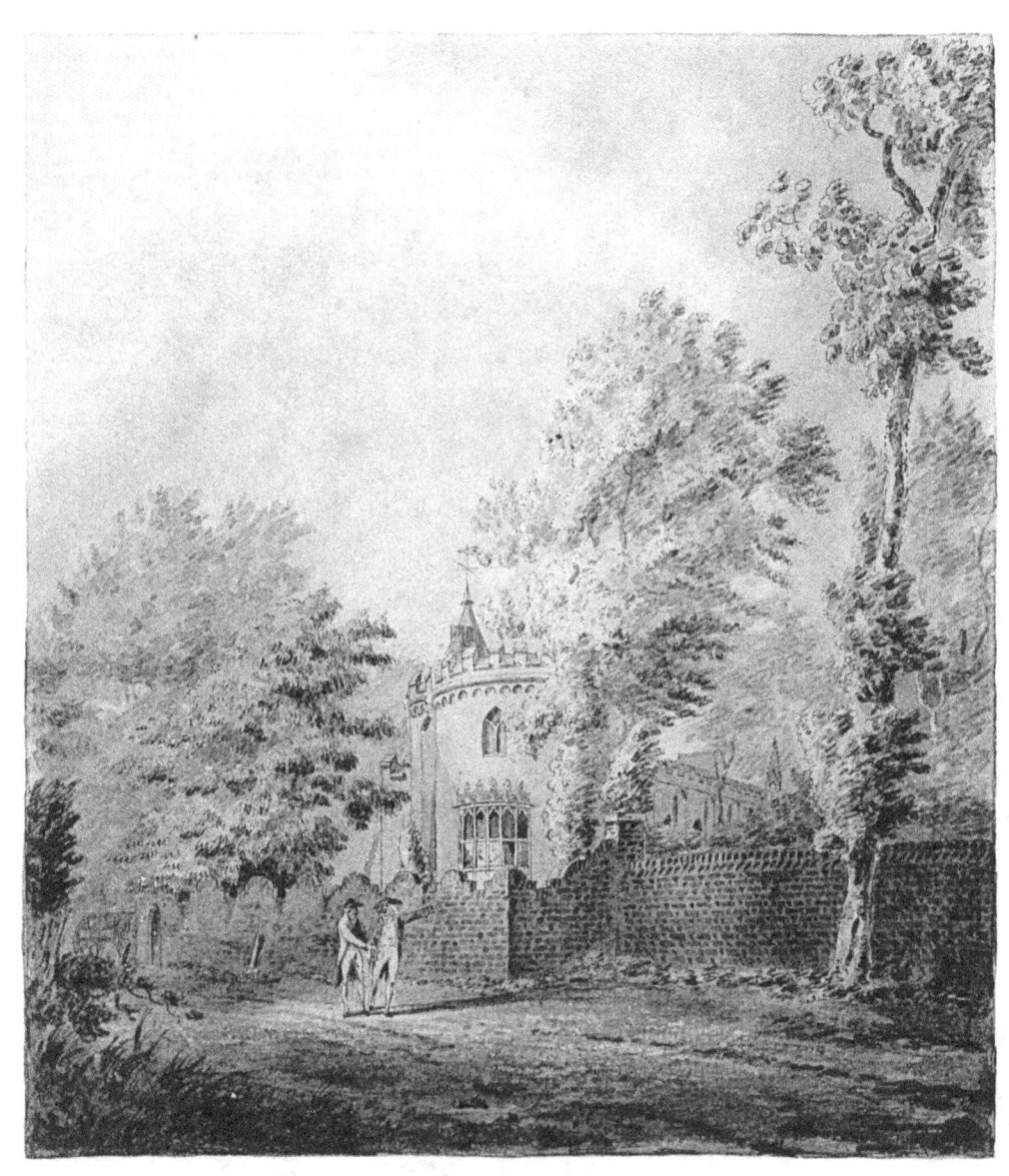

69. STRAWBERRY HILL FROM THE WEST, *by J. C. Barrow,* 1789

more intoxicating because even though he could not picture us he could dream of being our guide to his own time. Our acceptance of his record would assure him of the only immortality that he believed in, the remembrance of future ages.

"All we can do," he wrote Mason, "is to appeal to that undutiful urchin, posterity."[35] "Great posterity," he called us, "giant posterity," "pert posterity." We would be his judges. He feared us; he courted us; he made us into beings of superhuman knowledge and placed us in the world of fabulous discoveries that we should make, especially in America. Shortly after Concord and Lexington he said to Mason, "I love to skip into futurity and imagine what will be done on the giant scale of a new hemisphere."[36] A year earlier he wrote to Mann, "The next Augustan age will dawn on the other side of the Atlantic. There will, perhaps, be a Thucydides at Boston, a Xenophon at New York, and, in time, a Virgil at Mexico, and a Newton at Peru. At last, some curious traveler from Lima will visit England and give a description of the ruins of St. Paul's, like the editions of Balbec and Palmyra, but am I not prophesying, contrary to my consummate prudence, and casting horoscopes of empires like Rousseau? Yes; well I will go and dream of my visions,"[37] which, for all we know, included one in which twentieth-century Americans would meet in their National Gallery to listen to lectures upon him.

His ever-growing piles of journals, returned and annotated letters, notebooks, and the marginalia throughout his library would carry him safely to us, yet one who writes for posterity runs the risk of being ridiculous, and being ridiculous was what he feared more than anything else. He must make light of what he was doing, even though he was deadly serious about it. He believed that nobody was in a better position to inform us of the manners, fashions, politics, and characters of his age, and he said so; but at the same time he tried to ward off possible criticism, as in the prefaces and postscripts to his works. Would we think his account

---

[35] Walpole to Mason, 3 April 1775.
[36] Ibid., 27 Nov. 1775.
[37] Walpole to Mann, 24 Nov. 1774.

trivial, prejudiced, and inaccurate? "It is cruel to a person who collects the follies of the age for the information of posterity," he wrote, "to have one's veracity doubted; it is the truth of them that makes them worth notice."[38] Suppose, too, we should find him dull as well as uninformative? The epigraph in his last notebook is a passage from Cibber's *Apology:* "Such remaining scraps—as may not perhaps be worth the reader's notice: but if they are such as tempt me to write them, why may not I hope that in this wide world there may be many an idle soul no wiser than myself, who may be equally tempted to read them?"[39] Even his note-books, you see, were to have readers who, he hoped and expected, would find them informative and entertaining.

Gray once said to him that any fool might write a most valuable book if he would only tell us what he heard and saw with veracity.[40] Walpole did this for the eighteenth century in his letters, and he impressed his own personality upon what he wrote. No one confuses his style with another's. Pastiches of Dr. Johnson, Gibbon, and Sterne can be written by the winners of week-end competitions in English weeklies, but Walpole's style eludes all attempts to reproduce it, as Macaulay was the first to point out.

The correspondence with Mann is the one in which Walpole is most deliberately being the historian of his time. Since the two men never met after Walpole left Florence, "the little circumstances of each other's society . . . the soul of letters" were soon lost to them. Walpole wrote Mann two years after he got home that they were "forced to deal only in great events, like historians."[41] Years later he pointed out to him that "distance and absence deprive us of the little incidents of common correspondence. I am forced to write to you of such events only as one would write to posterity."[42] That is, Walpole's letters to Mann were written as much to us as

---

38 Walpole to Bentley, 17 July 1755.
39 MS at Farmington. It was begun in 1786.
40 Gray to Walpole, 25 Feb. 1768.
41 Walpole to Mann, 22 July 1744.
42 Ibid., 9 March 1779.

The Letters

to Mann. As early as 1749 he began getting them back; soon afterwards he started transcribing them into six folio blank books. He cut out a few passages, such as references to his quarrel with Gray, but in a few years he let Kirgate copy the rest, merely adding the number of each letter and a few footnotes.[43] He made a title page for the first of the volumes and added an epigraph taken from a letter of Pliny to Tacitus that wondered whether posterity would have any concern about them,[44] but in an advertisement to the whole he showed little doubt. "Knowing how much pleasure," he wrote, "not only himself, but many other persons have often found in a series of private and familiar letters, he thought it worth his while to preserve these, as they contain something of the customs, fashions, politics, diversions, and private history of several years; which, if worthy of any existence, can be properly transmitted to posterity only in this manner."

He did not add that manners, events, diversions, and so on must be transmitted by someone who can make the transmission easy, but as he reread his letters with us in mind he trusted to our being fundamentally the same as himself, however different our everyday lives might be. We would understand him as he understood Gramont and Mme de Sévigné, which is the way it has turned out. What surprised Henry Adams most in Walpole was "that he is so extremely like ourselves. . . . I perpetually catch myself," Adams says, "thinking of it all as of something I have myself known, until I trip over a sword, or discover there were

---

[43] These six volumes are at Farmington; the originals were presumably destroyed after his death. See the Yale Walpole, 17. xlii–xlviii for the history of these letters.

[44] *Posteris an aliqua cura, nescio!* (Pliny, *Epist.* ix.14). Walpole omitted *"nostri"* before *"nescio."* The whole letter, the translation of which has been kindly supplied to me by Professor C. W. Mendell, expresses Walpole's attitude towards his correspondents: "You never flatter yourself and I never write anything more sincerely than what I write about you. *Whether there will be any concern about us on the part of posterity I do not know* but surely we deserve some such interest. I do not say because of our genius (that would be arrogance), but because of our persistent purpose, our constant effort and our respect for posterity. Let us only persist in our chosen course which has raised few men to glory and fame but has lifted many from obscurity and silence. Farewell."

no railways then."[45] Nearly a hundred years after Adams wrote this we have the same feeling of intimacy. It may come to us at any time, but most often when Walpole shows himself in a comical situation, such as the one he described to Lord Strafford:

"As your Lordship, I know, is so good as to interest yourself in the calamities of your friends, I will, as shortly as I can, describe and grieve your heart with a catastrophe that has happened to two of them. My Lady Ailesbury, Mr. Conway, and Miss Rich passed two days last week at Strawberry Hill. We were returning from Mrs. Clive's through the long field, and had got over the high stile that comes into the road; that is, three of us. It had rained, and the stile was wet. I could not let Miss Rich straddle across so damp a palfrey, but took her in my arms to lift her over. At that instant I saw a coach and six come thundering down the hill from my house; and hurrying to set down my charge, and stepping backwards, I missed the first step, came down headlong with the nymph in my arms; but turning quite round as we rushed to the ground, the first thing that touched the earth was Miss Rich's head. You must guess in how improper a situation we fell; and you must not tell my lady Strafford before anybody that every petticoat, etc. in the world were canted—high enough indeed! The coach came on, and never stopped. The apprehension that it would run over my Chloe made me lie where I was, holding out my arm to keep off the horses, which narrowly missed trampling us to death. The ladies, who were Lady Holdernesse, Miss Pelham, and your sister Lady Mary Coke, stared with astonishment at the theatre which they thought I had chosen to celebrate our loves; the footmen laughed; and you may imagine the astonishment of Mr. Conway and Lady Ailesbury, who did not see the fall, but turned and saw our attitude. It was these spectators that amazed Miss Pelham, who described the adventure to Mrs. Pitt, and said, 'What was most amazing, there were Mr. Conway and Lady Ailesbury looking on!' "[46]

---

[45] *The Selected Letters of Henry Adams,* ed. Newton Arvin (New York, 1951), p. 55.

[46] Walpole to Lord Strafford, 6 June 1756.

The Letters

We who read Walpole's letters on the printed page and know that they are of their kind "classics" can hardly imagine what it was like to break the seal on one of the originals and read it for the first time. To have the latest news written especially for us with so much freshness, wit, wisdom, sympathy, cynicism, and sentiment by a man of the world who wanted it to be a better place, this must have made us feel that we were very fortunate to have such a friend. We do not have his correspondents' personal intimacy with him, but we can survey, as they could not, the whole panorama that he spread out for us. Saintsbury said that Walpole's letters are like a very long novel, vast, various, unfailing in interest, and with a "not too obviously intelligible life-panorama."[47] Virginia Woolf concluded that "somehow he was not only the wittiest of men, but the most observant and not the least kindly. And among the writers of English prose he wears forever and with a peculiar grace a coronet of his own earning."[48] She, like everyone else who has read and reread Walpole, speculated upon the "not too obviously intelligible life-panorama."

In my first lecture I quoted her remark about the "connecting word" that may be found in every man's biography and that gives his life coherence, whether it be love, money, sport, or whatever. I hoped that the connecting word that illuminates Walpole's life would emerge during our talks, and I trust that by now it has. I think that this word in his life is "fame," "the condition of being much read and talked about"; fame while he lived and fame in the future; but having found the connecting word we must add that it leaves a good deal unexplained.

Why was Horace Walpole as he was? The ready answer, "heredity and environment," does not solve the enigma. Although the Walpoles were an army of squires from the middle of the thirteenth century, none of them was outstanding before Sir Robert. On Lady Walpole's side there was little eminence. Walpole claimed Dryden as a maternal great-uncle, but Dryden turns out to have been only a first cousin twice removed. Horace had Sir Robert's powers of persuasion, shrewdness, ambition,

---

[47] George Saintsbury, *The Peace of the Augustans* (1916), pp. 230–31.
[48] Virginia Woolf, *Granite and Rainbow*, p. 186.

117

Horace Walpole

gift of friendship, and passion for collecting. Lady Walpole reinforced her son's love of the arts and heightened his taste for the ridiculous. Both contributed to his inner uncertainties; his mother by her possessiveness and hatred of his father; Sir Robert by his initial aloofness, by the rejection of Horace's mother, and by his power. From childhood Horace was pulled back and forth between love and hatred, fear and confidence, desire for money and contempt for it, pride and humility, idealism and disillusionment, his flair for friendship and his dislike of people at too close quarters. He had to find the middle way between these conflicts if he was going to have fame in his own right apart from his father's. Very early he saw that he could get it by writing the history of his time in his own informal manner. Although he was occasionally blown off course by his inner turbulence, he stuck to his project through thick and thin. Letter-writing was how he would get what he wanted. It also enabled him to express his affection for his friends at a distance.

His reporting of events has been subjected to microscopic study and has been confirmed at every turn. We now know that he is the fullest and most dependable guide to his time. His other goal, to win a following among the sort of people that he liked while he lived, has also been reached. It is not a large following by Johnsonian standards and probably never will be: one cannot picture Walpole Societies in Oslo and Spokane, meeting on his birthday and drinking to his immortal memory in "iced" water. Many of the people who read him for pleasure are those who love *Iolanthe* in spite of not knowing who Captain Shaw was, and Max Beerbohm's Johnsonian Clergyman without trying to identify him. For this small group, reading Walpole is like being a traveler in a country that you know well and any part of which you can revisit whenever you want to. You go back to an episode or to a remark that struck you long ago. There it still is, yet it is not quite the same; if it belongs to Walpole's early life the light has somehow faded from it; if to a time nearer your present age, it has become more luminous. And when you are looking up a particular passage—revisiting that bit of the familiar country—you may come across a stretch that you do not remember, an anecdote, a turn of phrase, a glimpse of contemporary manners that has

The Letters

all the freshness of a discovery and that makes you realize that you will never learn and absorb all that there is to know in this country of inexhaustible instruction and entertainment.

The understanding of his time will become more difficult as eighteenth-century customs, manners, and tacit assumptions recede farther and farther into the past. We whose memories go back fifty years are the last generation that can sense what the eighteenth century was like. This is because, for one thing, we were born in a horse-drawn world when it took a long time by present reckoning to go a short distance. We can recall its sights, sounds, and smells. We were also born into a class-conscious world, in which domestic servants were readily available at twenty dollars a month, a world virtually free of taxes, a world in which people cultivated good manners and did not fear leisure or the future. Like the eighteenth century it was a world in which new discoveries were constantly being made and one in which the first flush of the Millennium was plainly visible. Those born after 1930 cannot know what it was like to live in such a world any more than we can know what it was like to live in Periclean Athens.

On the other hand, understanding Walpole's character and personality has become easier owing to our increased awareness of what goes on beneath the surface of consciousness. The insights revealed may be disturbing and the language in which they are described repellent, but there they are. That Horace Walpole was as he was in part because of the conflicts established in him by an unstable, possessive mother and a powerful, remote father is too obvious to be labored today. Nor do we longer question the influence of the mind and spirit upon the body and how this is expressed through illness. We are not surprised that Walpole was frequently ill. We see him buoyed up by hope, cast down by doubt, striking out in fear, longing for approval, rejecting intimacy; now under the domination of one emotion and then of its opposite; escaping into the past and the future. In one letter he is dressing Lady Suffolk's hair for the coronation of George III;[49] in another, working to alleviate the

---

[49] Walpole to Montagu, 24 Sept. 1761.

119

condition of chimney sweeps.[50] Instead of being baffled by these inconsistencies of character and behavior we can reconcile them and accept him as a man of extraordinary talents and opportunities who carried out as ambitious a design as one can imagine in spite of his unresolved inner conflicts.

That he sensed the injuries he received as a child I do not doubt (he was not one of those who believe that there is nothing wrong with boys that cannot be cured by cold baths and football), but he did not waste time in bewailing them. Consecrated to the task he had set himself, he hurried along his high plateau alone. It had no peaks of ecstasy and few chasms of anguish. When his mother died he knew protracted grief, which carried to the lengths that he carried it we are told is a sign of guilt and a desire for atonement; he also felt guilt in his quarrel with Gray; what he regarded as Conway's failure of friendship was a third traumatic experience; but when these crises subsided they left him pretty much as he was before: there had been no purgation of his soul. The *Memoirs, Mysterious Mother,* and *Hieroglyphic Tales* show the storms that continued to rage within, but common sense and "character" kept him from being overwhelmed by them.

In his old age he did not wish that he had lived his life differently. He did not think that things had been better in his youth. Nor did he believe that the future was hopeless because America was lost, France was given over to horror, and young men of fashion had become careless in their dress. He avoided one of the familiar penalties of a well-spent youth, senile salaciousness: the author of the verses to Lord Lincoln was shocked by Payne Knight's scholarly *Worship of Priapus.* He was not just a self-centered old bachelor with aesthetic tastes. His interest in life never let up, nor his longing to have the world a better place in which to live, nor the compulsion to record his time for us. His enjoyment of this work was lessened by the fear of not reaching his own excessively high standards, of not being pointed out by the finger of those passing by; there was always more to be done, and it could always be done better.

---

[50] Walpole to Conway, 28 Nov. 1784, and to Lort, 5 July 1789.

The Letters

His modesty induced waves of loneliness, but one feels that the talk about death, which he began early, was partly romantic titillation, as was also what he called his melancholy. When Mrs. Damer's husband went to the Bedford Arms in Covent Garden with four prostitutes and a blind fiddler and shot himself, Walpole wrote to Lady Ossory, "You are not alone as I am, given up to melancholy ideas, with the rain beating on the skylight and gusts of wind."[51] What were these melancholy ideas? No doubt that he was in his sixtieth year, subject to periodic attacks of a very painful illness; perhaps, too, he was dimly aware that in the unwavering pursuit of his grand design he had cheated the richest part of himself; and there was the recurring fear that all this labor might be rejected in the end. Such thoughts would make him feel alone, but one who has never shared his life, day in and day out, year in and year out, with a beloved companion whom he has lost cannot know what loneliness may be. While the rain beat on the skylight and the wind guttered the candles on his desk he could be sorry for himself, but he was never near despair. Although the frequent suicides of the time fascinated and depressed him, there is no hint of his following suit. During most of his waking hours he could repeat what he once wrote to Mann, "My mind is of no gloomy turn, and I have a thousand ways of amusing myself."[52]

He solicited our forgiveness of his faults by calling them to our attention—self-love, emulation, the will to dominate, touchiness, his "warmth" and "wildness"—yet we get the impression that he was rather proud of these weaknesses, as he was of what he called his "shyness," and that by naming them he sought to make them less objectionable. On the other hand, he let us discover his virtues by ourselves, and what do we find? Patience with Montagu, Selwyn, Mme du Deffand, Lady Mary Coke; humility with Mason; contrition with Gray; forgiveness for Conway; charity for Lady Ossory; devotion to his family; loyalty and affection for all his friends. What Pope called "the strong benevolence of soul" is everywhere evident in Walpole's writings. He did not himself reform

---

[51] Walpole to Lady Ossory, 16 Aug. 1776.
[52] Walpole to Mann, 29 Sept. 1757.

121

hospitals and schools and prisons, but his passionate desire to improve the lot of man made him a supporter of those who did. His "Epistle from Florence to Thomas Ashton" in 1740 sums up Ashton's duty as tutor to Lord Plymouth and the duty of all right-thinking men:

> *Yours is the task—and glorious is the plan,*
> *To build the Free, the Sensible, Good Man.*

When Walpole died fifty-seven years later he was still subscribing to this formula. Liberty, wisdom, and altruism would bring in the New Day.

He had self-knowledge and self-control. From his earliest years he accepted his limitations and abilities, and he spent his life in doing what he knew he could do. One part of his success can be measured by the tens of thousands of footnotes that verify the integrity of his life work. There is also the long shadow cast by Strawberry Hill and *The Castle of Otranto*. Like all original artists, Horace Walpole gave form and meaning to his time and imposed his mind and work upon the future. When the balance has been struck between his virtues and his faults we must respect him as a man who despite his shortcomings made the most of the great gifts that were his.

As we take leave of him now let us think of him on a certain night at Strawberry. Chute was ill there with the gout. Walpole sat by his bedside writing to Mann. His letter ends, "Well, we bid you good night; we have nothing more to tell you; he is going to sleep, and I and my dogs are retiring to the library."[53]

---

[53] Ibid., 21 Oct. 1764.

GPSR Authorized Representative: Easy Access System Europe - Mustamäe tee
50, 10621 Tallinn, Estonia, gpsr.requests@easproject.com

www.ingramcontent.com/pod-product-compliance
Lightning Source LLC
Chambersburg PA
CBHW080957170526
45158CB00010B/2825